THE IRISH ECONOMY IN TRANSITION:

SUCCESSES, PROBLEMS, AND PROSPECTS

CONTEMPORARY STUDIES IN ECONOMIC AND FINANCIAL ANALYSIS

Series Editors: Robert J. Thornton and J. Richard Aronson

CONTEMPORARY STUDIES IN ECONOMIC AND FINANCIAL
ANALYSIS   VOLUME 85

THE IRISH ECONOMY IN TRANSITION:

SUCCESSES, PROBLEMS, AND PROSPECTS

EDITED BY

VINCENT G. MUNLEY
Department of Economics, Lehigh University, USA

ROBERT J. THORNTON
Department of Economics, Lehigh University, USA

J. RICHARD ARONSON
Department of Economics, Lehigh University, USA

2002

JAI
An Imprint of Elsevier Science

Amsterdam – Boston – London – New York – Oxford – Paris
San Diego – San Francisco – Singapore – Sydney – Tokyo

ELSEVIER SCIENCE Ltd
The Boulevard, Langford Lane
Kidlington, Oxford OX5 1GB, UK

First edition 2002

Library of Congress Cataloging in Publication Data

The Irish economy in transition: successes, problems, and prospects/edited by Vincent G. Munley, Robert J. Thornton, J. Richard Aronson.
　　p. cm.
　Papers presented at a conference at Lehigh University, March 2001.
　ISBN 0-7623-0979-2
　　1. Ireland – Economic conditions – 1949 – Congresses. 2. Ireland – Economic policy – Congresses. I. Munley, Vincent. II. Thornton, Robert J. III. Aronson, J. Richard (Jay Richard), 1937–

　HC260.5.17374 2002
　330.9417–dc21   2002035238

British Library Cataloguing in Publication Data
A catalogue record from the British Library has been applied for.

ISBN: 0-7623-0979-2
ISSN: 01569-3759 (Series)

⊗The paper used in this publication meets the requirements of ANSI/NISO Z39.48-1992 (Permanence of Paper).
Printed in The Netherlands.

CONTENTS

v

LIST OF CONTRIBUTORS

Mark Cassidy	Central Bank of Ireland, College Green, Dublin, Ireland
Joe Durkan	Department of Economics, University College, Dublin, Ireland
Connell Fanning	University College Cork, Department of Economics, Cork, Ireland
Eithne Fitzgerald	Department of Social Studies, Trinity College, Dublin, Ireland
John Fitz Gerald	ESRI, Dublin, Ireland
Michael J. Keane	National University of Ireland, Department of Economics, Galway, Ireland
Moore McDowell	Department of Economics, University College Dublin, Ireland
John McHale	Queen's University, The Queen's School of Business, Ontario, Canada
Michael P. Mortell	Department of Applied Mathematics, University College Cork, Cork, Ireland
Vincent G. Munley	Department of Economics, Lehigh University, Bethlehem, USA
Ciaran Murphy	Business Information Systems, University College Cork, Cork, Ireland
Rodney Thom	Department of Economics, University College Dublin, Ireland

Robert J. Thornton   Department of Economics & Martindale
                                                Center for the Study of Private Enterprise,
                                                Lehigh University, Bethlehem, USA

ACKNOWLEDGMENTS

The articles in this volume resulted from the conference entitled "Ireland – Open for Business: Successes, Problems, and Prospects," held at Lehigh University, March 7–9, 2001. The conference was sponsored by the Martindale Center for the Study of Private Enterprise at Lehigh University. We wish to thank Crystal Signatures of Bethlehem, PA, and Waterford Wedgewood PLC of Waterford, Ireland, for helping to underwrite the event.

There are a number of individuals who deserve special acknowledgement for the success of the conference. Geraldo Vasconcellos provided organizational leadership in designing the conference sessions, and Rosemary Krauss and Amy Scott saw to all the logistical details of running a complicated set of meetings. Rene Hollinger also deserves special thanks for helping prepare the final manuscript.

We also wish to recognize Malcolm Rees, University of Buckingham, U.K., and Howard Whitcomb, Lehigh University, who served as general discussants for many of the papers presented at the conference. Their remarks not only stimulated a lively discussion but also helped the authors in revising their manuscripts for publication.

$\bigcup_{\iota} \bigwedge$

1. THE IRISH ECONOMY IN TRANSITION

Vincent G. Munley and Robert J. Thornton

The term "Celtic Tiger" is widely recognized as symbolizing the spectacular performance of the Irish economy throughout the 1990s. During this decade of consistently high growth in gross domestic product – by far the highest within the European community – the unemployment rate in the Republic of Ireland fell from nearly 20% to the current level of about 5%. A pattern of emigration, especially among young people, that had persisted since the great famine of the late 1840s reversed itself; and Ireland is now experiencing net immigration. At the turn of the millennium, Ireland has assumed a new position in the order of world commerce – no longer a weak sister in the economic shadow of the United Kingdom, but rather a vibrant member of the European community.

Several factors have contributed to this success story. Changes in public policy have been important. In the 1960s the Irish government made access to second level education universal, which created a highly educated and productive workforce. In the 1980s the government reversed a pattern of lax domestic fiscal policy. A key result of putting national fiscal affairs in order was the ability to offer an extremely low corporate income tax rate as a further incentive for foreign direct investment. The reputation, and reality, of a welcoming environment of friendly people no doubt helped as well. But the salient explanation for Ireland's prosperity is without question its entrance in 1973 to the European Union. This made Ireland – an English speaking country on the western fringe of the EU – an inviting gateway to the European market for North American-based multi-national firms. It also allowed Ireland to become the beneficiary of a European Union

The Irish Economy in Transition: Successes, Problems, and Prospects, Volume 85, pages 1–4.

policy that provides financial assistance to its less-well-off members. Direct grants in the form of Structural Funds from the EU have infused capital into the Irish economy for sorely needed infrastructure investments. Over recent years the aggregate level of this funding has totalled tens of billions of U.S. dollars.

Such was the situation in March of 2001 when Lehigh University's Martindale Center for the Study of Private Enterprise hosted a conference entitled: "Ireland – Open for Business: Successes, Problems, and Prospects." The chapters of this volume contain the papers presented at this conference. The main intent of this volume is not to offer another analysis of how or why the phenomenon of the Celtic Tiger occurred. There are other, quite well done and insightful, analyses that deal with the governmental policies and macroeconomic events that influenced Ireland's growth through the decade of the 1990s.[1] Rather, the papers in the volume focus on several key issues that have emerged, or in some cases persisted, through this time of prosperity – e.g. infrastructure needs, unbalanced regional growth, and privatization of state enterprises.

The year following the Lehigh conference witnessed events that shook the world. As a small, open economy, Ireland was particularly exposed to the aftermath of these events. And, while Ireland's long term outlook continues to be optimistic, in the short term the Irish government faces challenges as it seeks to implement policies that will allow economic growth to continue. Because of this, the focus of the papers in this volume may very well be of more importance now than they were at the time they were prepared. They offer insights about issues at the forefront of the Irish policy agenda and should prove most helpful to the various members of the public policy arena who are charged with making decisions about these issues.

The papers in this volume may prove particularly interesting to yet another audience, broader than those interested in the continued economic progress of Ireland. As the European Union prepares to expand its membership in a substantial way, the nations of central and eastern Europe intent on joining this union – most especially the smaller of these nations – will look to the Irish experience as a model. Because these papers focus on the challenges that accompany the economic growth and prosperity that is attainable within the EU framework, policy makers in these countries have much to glean from the analysis that is presented here. Brief synopses of each of the papers follow.

In Chapter 2, Mark Cassidy provides an overview of Ireland's economic performance since 1987, comparing it to that of the nation's first 65 years after independence in 1922. He notes that Ireland's pace of economic growth "has exceeded even the most optimistic expectations." Irish growth has also reversed the long-running trend of emigration and built a new national self-confidence. Cassidy also discusses the future prospects for the economy.

Joe Durkan analyzes foreign domestic investment (FDI) in Ireland in Chapter 3, focusing in particular on the pharmaceutical and electronics industries. Both industries have been key ones in Ireland's recent development success. The latter sector (broadly defined to include computers, electrical and instrument engineering, and software) experienced a doubling of employment over the period 1993–2000 and now employs about 6% of all workers in the Republic of Ireland.

In Chapter 4, "Nurturing Indigenous Entrepreneurship in Ireland," Connell Fanning and Ciaran Murphy note that Ireland has become the largest exporter of software in the world, a remarkable success story for a nation of 3.7 million people. In this chapter they evaluate the role played by the FDI software companies, venture capitalists, and the government in nurturing entrepreneurship in the indigenous software sector.

In Chapter 5, Rodney Thom notes that the euro has radically changed the rules governing macroeconomic policy in the participating EU countries. The resulting "complete loss of monetary independence and the limitations on fiscal policy" promise to present more significant challenges for Ireland than for other countries, according to Thom. In the chapter he discusses the ways in which Ireland can face up to these challenges.

John McHale next discusses a serious dilemma faced by Ireland in "Fiscal Policy and the Public Finances: Creative Approaches to Pension Funding" (Chapter 6). Since the late 1980s the government has effected national agreements between unions and employers that have achieved wage restraint in return for tax cuts (the "social partnership"). Although this policy worked well in times of low inflation and high unemployment, with inflation on the rise the government faces the choice of either implementing cyclically inappropriate tax cuts or else risking the collapse of the social partnership. The solution suggested by McHale is to adjust the social partnership framework to allow for deferred compensation. This would take the form of contributions to worker retirement accounts.

Moore McDowell turns the focus to privatization in Chapter 7. He notes that privatization is a much more recent development in Ireland than in the other European Union states, a result of the longstanding and widely held acceptance of the involvement of the state in economic activity in Ireland. McDowell observes that the privatization process has not been smooth, one of the reasons being a lack of clarity as to just why it was being implemented.

In "Has Ireland Outgrown Its Clothes?," John Fitz Gerald directs attention in Chapter 8 to Ireland's infrastructure, which he says was adequate for a relatively poor economy two decades ago, but "wholly inadequate to deal with the needs of the present." Fitz Gerald also analyzes the environmental constraints which rapid economic growth has brought about, in particular the pollution of waterways and the growth in greenhouse gas emissions.

Michael Keane focuses on the problem of unbalanced regional development in Ireland in Chapter 9. Noting that it is often the case that countries enjoying a high national growth rate will also see a widening of regional disparities, Keane finds that these disparities within Ireland have become substantial, with the Border, Midlands, and West regions (the BMW area) lagging behind. He also addresses some of the policy and planning challenges that the problem presents.

In Chapter 10, "Ireland's Social Safety Net," Eithne Fitzgerald provides an in-depth examination of Ireland's system of providing income maintenance and health services. With Ireland's welfare system long having been among the least generous of countries in the European Union, she contends that Ireland can now use some of its newly-found wealth to fashion higher standards of social protection.

The volume concludes with Michael Mortell's "The Celtic Tiger: A View from the Trenches of Academia" (Chapter 11). As a former president of University College Cork, Mortell provides an insider's perspective on both the importance of higher education to Ireland's economic success and the difficulties faced in persuading government ministers to properly fund the growing university sector for the benefit of the nation. Mortell's paper served as the keynote address for the conference and the capstone to this volume.

The papers that follow comprise a highly readable and very timely overview of Ireland's recent economic story. As a collection they provide a wealth of information that should prove interesting to readers – from business men and women interested in investment opportunities in Ireland to casual observers who simply wish to gain a better understanding about how such good things have happened in such a short time on this island at the western edge of Europe.

NOTE

1. See for example, Nolan, B., O'Connell, P., and Whelan, C., Bust to Boom? The Irish Experience of Growth and Inequality. Dublin, Institute of Public Administration, 2000; and Barry, F., Understanding Ireland's Economic Growth. Basingstoke, Macmillan Press Ltd. Administration, 1999.

2. THE IRISH ECONOMY: RECENT EXPERIENCE AND PROSPECTS

Mark Cassidy*

1. INTRODUCTION

Over the past fifteen years the Irish economy has undergone a remarkable transformation. In 1986, Ireland was one of the poorest countries in the European Union with a GDP per capita below 64% of the average, unemployment in excess of 18%, high real interest rates, heavy emigration and a national debt of around 120% of GNP. Since then the economy has enjoyed its most vigorous and sustained period of economic growth since independence was achieved in 1922. Its strength over the past fifteen years has manifested itself in a rapid increase in employment, a significant reduction in the unemployment rate, an increase in living standards and a marked improvement in both the public finances and national morale.

To a significant extent Ireland's rapid growth relative to the rest of the EU has been an example of economic convergence as output, living standards and productivity have been catching up with the EU average. The convergence process has been driven by above average rates of increase in both the labour supply and total factor productivity and has been facilitated by a number of "enabling" factors. National productivity has been boosted by high-tech foreign direct investment inflows from the U.S., sectoral shifts in industry, investment

* The views expressed in this article are not necessarily those held by the Central Bank of Ireland and are the personal responsibility of the author.

The Irish Economy in Transition: Successes, Problems, and Prospects, Volume 85, pages 5–32.
Copyright © 2002 by Elsevier Science Ltd.
All rights of reproduction in any form reserved.
ISBN: 0-7623-0979-2

in human capital and infrastructural improvements. The international cost-competitiveness of the labour force as well as favourable demographic factors, net inward migration and increased participation rates, particularly among females, have simultaneously boosted employment and enabled the growth process to develop momentum. Economic expansion has been facilitated by macroeconomic stability, completion of the European single market, favourable exchange rate and international economic developments, an increase in structural funds received from the EU, regulatory reform and fiscal stabilization.

At a policy level, an overview of Ireland's recent economic performance shows the importance of a long term, consistent strategy for economic development. As will be argued in Section 3, it was the absence of such a long term perspective which prevented the Irish economy from realizing its full economic potential during the first forty years of independence. Similarly, many of the foundations for the recent success of the economy can be traced back to the adoption in the 1950s and 1960s of an outward-looking development strategy appropriate for a small open economy like Ireland. In particular, a long-term strategy – which has been consistent, pro-active and selective – of attracting foreign direct investment has facilitated the transition from a relatively poor, closed economy, dependent upon agriculture, traditional manufacturing industry and trade relations with the U.K., into a dynamic centre for high-tech industry which is fully integrated into the international economy and which appears to possess the capacity to develop into one of the richest countries in Europe.

Future prospects for economic development depend upon the economy's ability to maintain macroeconomic stability and further enhance its productive capability. The former objective has been complicated by the constraints imposed by membership of EMU on macro-stabilization policies. Supply-side requirements include public investment to ease infrastructural bottlenecks and policies to enhance the productivity and sustainability of indigenous enterprises, improve labour market flexibility and increase standards of competition, particularly in non-traded sectors. If the economy can enhance and produce close to its productive potential, the opportunity will present itself to address the distributional and "quality of life" concerns which have emerged as a by-product of the recent rapid period of growth.

The objective of this chapter is to provide a brief overview of Ireland's recent economic performance. Section 2 outlines the extent of the economy's recovery since 1987. This recent performance compares favourably with that of the first sixty-five years of the economy's existence which was disappointing in terms of growth and employment creation. In order to demonstrate this, a brief outline of Ireland's economic development between independence in 1922 and the beginning of the current period of growth in 1987 is presented in Section 3. Section 4 examines some of the factors which have contributed to the economy's success during the past fifteen years while the future prospects for the economy are discussed in Section 5.

2. RECENT ECONOMIC PERFORMANCE

A notable feature of the Irish economy's performance since 1987 has been the fact that there has been such a marked improvement across such a broad range of economic spheres. Record growth has been accompanied by a dramatic reduction in the unemployment rate. During the same period, the national finances have been transformed from a crisis situation into among the most healthy in the EU. All this has been achieved in an environment of price stability and a favourable balance of payments position. Meanwhile, an improvement in the economy's industrial structure has enabled it to move up the value-added chain of production and put itself in a position to further increase national productivity in the future.

Since 1987, real Gross Domestic Product has increased at an average annual rate of around $6^{1}/_{2}\%$. Most of this growth has been concentrated in the past seven years which have witnessed a rate of growth of around 9% per annum, far in excess of any other OECD economy (Fig. 1). As is now generally accepted, GDP is an inappropriate measure of both the output and living standards of the Irish economy because it includes the repatriated profits of foreign multinationals operating in Ireland. A superior measure of economic performance is Gross National Product which adjusts for net factor incomes sent abroad.[1] However, as Fig. 1 shows, the pace of growth of GNP has also been impressive and significantly above that of any other OECD country. Between 1994 and 2000, GNP increased by an average annual rate of about 8% and living standards, as measured by GNP per capita, are now approaching the EU average.[2]

The rapid expansion of GNP reflects a combination of rising employment and rising output per worker (labour productivity). Table 1 suggests that the current period of growth is part of a longer term convergence process dating back to the early 1970s. Since then national income has been increasing at a faster rate than the EU average, driven by above-average labour productivity. However, the poor employment performance of the Irish economy before 1994 prevented a more rapid convergence. Since 1994 productivity growth has remained strong compared to the rest of Europe but it has been the remarkable growth in employment which has underpinned the recent transformation of the economy. This contrasts with the experience of the majority of EU countries

Table 1.   Percentage Changes in Output, Employment and Labour
Productivity.

		1961–1970	1971–1980	1981–1990	1991–1993	1994–2000
GDP	Ireland	4.2%	4.7%	3.6%	2.6%	8.9%
	EU-15	4.9%	3%	2.4%	0.8%	2.5%
Employment	Ireland	0%	0.9%	−0.2%	0.5%	4.6%
	EU-15	0.3%	0.4%	0.5%	−0.9%	1.2%
Output						
per worker	Ireland	4.2%	3.8%	3.8%	2.1%	4.3%
	EU-15	4.6%	2.6%	1.9%	+1.8%	1.3%

Source: Eurostat.

which have experienced, on average, a negative contribution from labour inputs
to per capita growth over the past decade.[3] Since 1994, total employment in
Ireland has increased by over 40% and unemployment has fallen from 15.7%
in 1993 to 4.3% in 2000. For an economy which has traditionally struggled to
find employment for its population, the attainment of full employment is
probably the greatest achievement of the past fifteen years.

The past fifteen years have also witnessed a significant change in the
economy's industrial structure. Growth has been primarily driven by a small
number of high-tech, foreign-dominated sectors including pharmaceuticals,
chemicals, electronics (including computer software) and electrical and instrument engineering. Indeed, the Irish economy has recently overtaken the United
States as the world's largest exporter of computer software. Although this is a
somewhat misleading statistic as it does not account for computer software
produced in the U.S. for the U.S. market, it does reflect the transition in the
Irish economy away from agriculture and traditional industries such as food
and drink and clothing and footwear. In 1998, high-tech sectors accounted for
almost 70% of manufacturing output of which over 90% was produced by
foreign-owned companies. The role of foreign, particularly U.S., multinationals
will be discussed in more detail in Section 4.

Economic expansion has been facilitated by macroeconomic stability including
reform of the public finances and price stability. The 1970s were a period of
unprecedented fiscal expansion with an average annual increase in real government expenditure of $6^{1}/_{4}\%$. This was partly in response to deteriorating
international conditions and rising domestic unemployment. But although the
economy's growth performance in the 1970s was good, the price for fiscal irre-
sponsibility was paid in the 1980s when the national debt rose above 120% of
GNP and the real overdraft interest rate increased to 17%. Since 1987, however,
there has been a rapid transformation in the public finances. Expenditure as a

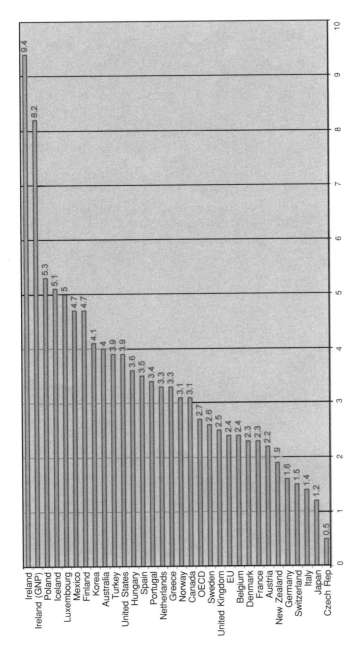

Fig. 1.   GDP Growth: Average Annual Real Percentage Change, 1995–2000.

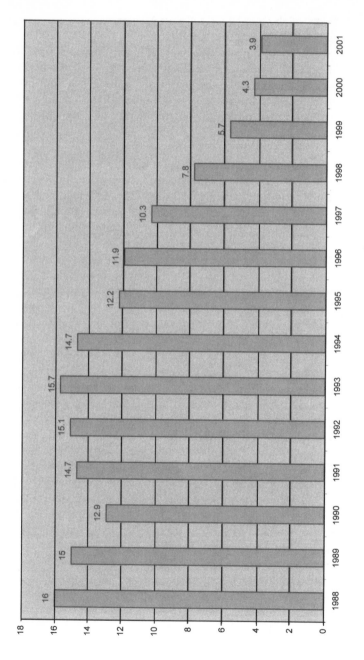

Fig. 2. Unemployment Rate, 1988–2001.

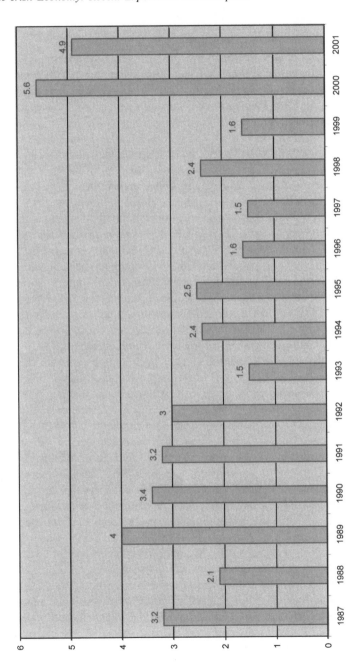

Fig. 3. Inflation, 1987–2001.

percentage of national income has been reduced significantly and is now closer to the low levels of government intervention in the U.S. than to the EU average. In recent years, the success of the economy has been reflected in rising tax revenues which have enabled the government to reduce income tax rates and encourage wage restraint. As a result, a surplus has been recorded in the general government balance since 1997 while the ratio of debt to GDP fell to around 40% last year and continues to decline.

3. THE ECONOMY SINCE INDEPENDENCE

The Irish Economy at Independence

The Irish economy, at independence, was still essentially a rural economy, primarily based around its agriculture sector. As a region of the U.K., Ireland had not developed a strong industrial base during the nineteenth century.[4] By 1922, two-thirds of the Irish population still lived in rural areas while over half the labour force were employed in agriculture. National income, as measured by GDP per capita, was only around 60% of that in the U.K.[5] However, at the beginning of the twentieth century the U.K. was the richest and most powerful country in Europe and comparison with other European economies suggests that Irish living standards were roughly similar to the average for the rest of Western Europe. Moreover, at independence the economy had satisfactory rail and communications networks, a well developed banking system, and a high level of literacy.

From Free Trade to Protectionism

The Irish Free State came into existence through the Treaty of Independence of December 1921 which granted independence to 26 of the 32 counties of Ireland. Supporters of the Cumann na nGaedheal (later Fine Gael) government accepted the Treaty of Independence, at least as a stepping stone towards full independence. The Treaty precipitated a bitter and violent civil war between supporters of the government and those who rejected the treaty which lasted until August 1923. The anti-treaty party, under the leadership of Eamon de Valera, eventually entered parliament in 1927 under the name Fianna Fáil and were elected to power in 1932.

Cumann na nGaedheal were the party of government between 1922 and 1932. Much of their support derived from the middle and upper classes, including large farmers, professionals and businessmen, who favoured low tariffs, low taxes, minimal government intervention and maintaining favourable trade

relations with the U.K. Civil servants and economic advisors of this first government, many of whom were inherited from the British regime, were also naturally
conservative and disposed towards resuming normalcy in relations between the
U.K. and Ireland. During this period the already dominant agricultural sector
was promoted at the expense of attempts to develop an industrial base. Free
trade and a tight fiscal stance were judged necessary to support Irish agricultural exports. In addition, the currency link with sterling was maintained through
the Currency Act of 1927, a deflationary link which removed the possibility of
independent monetary policy.

By 1931, the deterioration in global economic conditions had prompted many
European countries to introduce protectionist measures. When the U.K. departed
from its free trade position at the end of 1931 it became likely that the Irish
economy, even without a change of government, would embark upon a similar
path. The transition from free trade to protectionism became inevitable when
the nationalist Fianna Fáil party was elected to power in 1932. Fianna Fáil
favoured economic self-sufficiency and regarded the development of an
indigenous industrial sector and the need to halt emigration as much as cultural
and political issues as economic ones. A protectionist strategy was implemented
which was to be maintained until the late 1950s, even during periods when
Fianna Fáil were replaced in power by coalition governments.[6]

Between 1931 and 1936 the average tariff on imports increased from 9% to
45%. Other measures to promote an indigenous manufacturing sector included
the Control of Manufacturers Acts of 1932 and 1934 which required that, for
all new manufacturing companies, Irish nationals must hold at least 51% of the
nominal share capital. The Act required a license for foreign-owned companies
which could be granted subject to conditions relating to location, size and type
of output. Often the Act was used to direct foreign industries to designated
rural areas and reserve employment for male workers as part of the government's
industrial decentralization program. Non-tariff barriers, including quotas and
import licenses, were also used extensively following the Control of Imports
Act of 1934.

De Valera and Fianna Fáil remained in power until 1948 when they were
replaced by a coalition government led by J. A. Costello. By this time the policy
of industrial development pursued through protectionism was taken for granted.
In line with international trends, fiscal policy was introduced as a tool of macroeconomic policy after the Second World War. Investment and employment were
boosted by the government's expansionary public capital programme which
targeted infrastructural and social investment projects. Domestic demand recovered from the low level it had reached during the war and a false impression
was created that the drive for self-sufficiency was reaping rewards. Industrial

production, however, was still dependent upon traditional, low-technology sectors with minimal prospects for sustained development such as food, drink, tobacco and textiles. Output was primarily geared to accommodate domestic demand and over 92% of exports were destined for U.K. markets.

The 1950s were a period of stagnation. Rising domestic demand during the post-war period was partly accommodated by an increase in imports, particularly from the U.S.. The trade balance was initially paid for out of the external reserves which had been accumulated during the war. However, a sharp rise in import prices as a consequence of U.S. involvement in the Korean War and the 1949 devaluation of sterling meant a deterioration in the terms of trade. The government's response was a reversal of the expansionary fiscal policy of the late 1940s, including higher taxes and cutbacks on public spending. The 1952 budget was highly deflationary and capital expenditure was allowed to fall in real terms over the next four years before another deflationary budget in 1957 when the economy was already in recession. New and higher import levies were introduced which further increased the pressure on industry. Over this period, real income virtually stagnated, increasing by less than 0.5% per annum between 1952 and 1958. Emigration soared, reaching record levels for the twentieth century. By 1958 the volume of GDP was 2.5% below its 1955 level. In the post-war period Ireland also lagged behind other European economies in terms of public investment in education.

However, Kennedy et al. (1988) note that the 1950s also represented a period of transition as the economy took the first steps towards a more outward looking orientation. The Irish Export Board was established in 1951 and the Industrial Development Authority was given the role of attracting foreign direct investment to Ireland. Under the Finance Act of 1956, tax reliefs on new or increased exports were allowed, while grants were available, initially in underdeveloped areas and then throughout Ireland, to export-oriented industries. As Ruane and Görg (1997) note, Ireland began encouraging foreign direct investment to locate in Ireland at a time when most European countries were at best indifferent towards FDI.

By 1958 a consensus had begun to emerge that economic expansion could only be driven by an internationally competitive export sector. It was clear that the sheltered and inefficient manufacturing sector was incapable of creating enough new jobs to offset the decline in agricultural employment. This new outlook was articulated in a report by the Department of Finance called *Economic Development*, which favoured increased international integration and a switch from social to productive investment. This report in turn, formed the basis for the government's *First Programme of Economic Expansion* for the period 1959–1963.[7] In 1965, an important impetus to free trade came with the signing of the Anglo-Irish Free Trade Agreement which paved the way for eventual membership of the EEC in 1973. Domestic policies were facilitated by buoyant global economic conditions and an increase in international trade and capital flows. Ireland's more open outlook ensured that economic performance would in the future depend in large part upon the terms of trade, and favourable developments in this regard enabled the economy to share in this time of international prosperity and enjoy a period of unprecedented economic growth between 1958–1973. Economic progress was accompanied by cultural and social changes which reflected the new openness of the economy and the influence of television and other media channels.

Economic expansion during this period was driven by the export sector. Exporters began to develop new markets outside the U.K. such that the proportion of foreign sales going to the U.K. declined from 80% in 1958 to less than 60% in 1973. The period was also notable for a marked improvement in Ireland's terms of trade and rising real wages as a result of productivity increases. Investment grew strongly, reflecting inward direct investment and high levels of government investment. The high levels of emigration of the 1950s declined sharply such that by the early 1970s Ireland was experiencing new inward migration and the population began to rise from an all-time low of 2.8 million in 1961.

Ireland joined the EEC in 1973 with high hopes for continued economic prosperity. Free access to EEC markets provided those firms which could compete efficiently in international markets with improved export opportunities and also enhanced the attractiveness of the Irish economy as a location for inward direct investment. Agriculture in particular was expected to benefit through new markets, direct transfers and higher prices as a result of tariff protection under the European Common Agricultural Policy (CAP). However, the period between 1973 and 1986 was in fact characterised by volatile growth rates, rising unemployment, the resumption of emigration, high inflation and fiscal crisis. While international events played an important part in this, domestic policy, in particular deficit spending, also contributed to the gloom.

Ireland reacted to the terms of trade loss resulting from the first oil crisis of 1973 by increasing borrowing to finance current expenditure. Between 1973 and 1975 the current budget deficit increased from 0.4% of GNP to 6.9%. This attempt to cushion the deflationary consequences of higher oil prices was not unusual in the context of the reaction of other non-oil producing economies; and when oil prices fell back from the high levels of 1974, the government cut back on borrowing in the budgets of 1976 and 1977. Kennedy et al. (1988) argue that, if this policy had been continued in 1978–1979, the public finances would have been largely restored to order before the second oil crisis. Instead, however, a new Fianna Fáil government came to power in 1977 with a programme to reduce soaring unemployment through increased public spending and lower taxes. Although this pro-cyclical stimulus ensured that the economy grew strongly between 1977–1979, it was inappropriate given the economic circumstances and was to have long-lasting negative effects. By 1979, the balance of payments deficit was 13.5% of GNP and the exchequer borrowing requirement over 13% of GNP. Inflation between 1973 and 1982 averaged around 16%, lower only than Greece and Italy within the EEC.

By the time of the second oil crisis, other European governments no longer tried to offset the negative income and inflationary consequences of a sharp rise in oil prices through expansionary fiscal or monetary policy. However, the Irish government continued with an expansionary budgetary policy despite the worsening state of the public finances. Public sector wages in particular were allowed to rise sharply. The price paid for attempting to continue the prosperity of the 1960s throughout the 1970s, despite adverse international conditions, was stagnation during the 1980s. Deflationary budgets required to keep some order on the public finances stunted economic growth. Real GDP increased by only about 1.5% per annum between 1979 and 1986 and this figure was inflated by transfers received from the EEC and overstated increases in living standards because of the increase in net factor income outflows and increases in taxation.

By 1986 Ireland was one of the poorest countries in the EEC with per capita GDP below 64% of the average. The unemployment rate was over 18%, heavy emigration had resumed, taking away many of the best educated, and the public finances were in a mess. The current budget deficit equalled 8.5% of GNP and the overall national debt climbed above 120% of GNP while the foreign component of the debt was equal to 60% of GNP. As stated earlier, the real overdraft interest rate was 17%, which had a depressing impact on investment and consumer demand, and in 1986 GNP actually fell by 1.5%.

The national finances were effectively restored to order by a minority Fianna Fáil government which came to power in 1987. Public expenditure was cut back dramatically, and the process of social partnership, based on a shared consensus between government, employers and trade unions, ensured wage moderation and peaceful industrial operations to improve Ireland's international cost competitiveness. Favourable international economic conditions, a significant increase in structural funds received from the EU, favourable demographic conditions and a low-inflation environment assisted in the process of economic recovery. A longer term perspective, however, shows that many of the foundations for success had been laid in the late 1950s and 1960s, most notably the move towards free trade and increased international integration and increased public investment in education and human capital.

4. DETERMINANTS OF ECONOMIC GROWTH

Free Trade and European Integration

Economic isolationism was unable to provide a basis for sustained economic expansion for a small economy like Ireland. Industrial development until the 1950s was constrained by limited domestic demand which prevented indigenous industry from exploiting economies of scale and enhancing its productive efficiency. The under-developed nature of the economy ensured that the range of output was restricted to goods and services with low income elasticities of demand and little potential for strong sales growth. As a result, the structure of industry in the 1950s remained dominated by traditional sectors such as food, drink, tobacco and textiles and tended to be characterised by a lack of scale and low levels of technological sophistication. The lack of exposure to international competition also rendered industrial production inefficient while the failure to develop export markets beyond the U.K. meant that the economy failed to benefit from buoyant global demand conditions in the 1950s.

The opening up of the economy in the 1950s was undertaken through a dual strategy of promoting the export-orientation of the indigenous manufacturing sector and attracting foreign manufacturing companies to produce in Ireland for export markets. Two significant periods in the opening up of the Irish economy were the transition from protectionism to free trade which started with the Anglo Irish Free Trade Agreement of 1965 and culminated with membership of the EEC in 1973 and, secondly, the completion of the Single European Market over an eight-year period up to 1992. Membership in the EEC, later the European Union, created new export markets for Irish manufacturers, aided the agricultural sector through grants and subsidies under the CAP and entitled Ireland to significant structural and cohesion funds. More recently the Single European Act has removed technical and other barriers to the free movement of goods and services, labour and capital between member countries and paved the way for the introduction of a single currency, the final step of Economic and Monetary Union.

Industrial Policy and Foreign Direct Investment

European integration has, as was expected, accelerated the decline of many traditional manufacturing industries. The transition process has been eased by the receipt of structural funds from the EU and the economy's ability to attract foreign direct investment. Inward investment provided support for manufacturing employment which otherwise would have declined through the exposure to international competition of domestically-owned industry. Ruane and Görg (1997) attribute much of the subsequent success of industrial policy in attracting foreign investment to Ireland to its long term perspective as well as its proactive and selective nature. Generous corporate tax incentives were made available, initially in the form of a zero tax rate for exports and, since 1981, a low rate of 10% for all manufacturing companies and subsequently for certain internationally traded services. In addition, discretionary grants and subsidies enabled the IDA to select investment projects on a strategic basis. Since the 1970s, particular emphasis has been placed on attracting high-tech, innovative firms in knowledge-intensive, high-value-added industries (notably electronics, including software, pharmaceuticals, chemicals and electrical and instrument engineering). The U.S. was also correctly identified by the IDA as the most likely market source for such projects, and the personal involvement of IDA executives and government ministers has often played a role in attracting targeted projects.

The continuity of industrial policy since the late 1960s and the strategic approach of the IDA have been key elements in attracting multinational companies to Ireland. The success of this strategy is evident in the sectoral adjustment of the Irish manufacturing sector since the 1960s, in particular the decline in the share of traditional sectors. In 1998, the latest year for which data are available, high tech firms accounted for 46% of total manufacturing employment, 68% of gross manufacturing output and 78% of net output.[8] These high tech, export-oriented sectors have to a large extent driven Ireland's recent growth performance. The contribution of foreign investment is stark. Foreign companies accounted for 68% of employment, 91% of gross output and 93% of net output. There appears to be a clear productivity difference between indigenous and foreign manufacturing companies. Net output per employee in foreign-owned high tech companies is £250,000 compared with £41,600 in domestically-owned enterprises. However, it is important to note that measured productivity growth in foreign-owned sectors is artificially high because it includes returns to invisible factors of production carried out in the country of ownership, such as research and development and marketing activities, which are independent of domestic capital and labour productivity. For this reason it is perhaps more informative to compare the employment performance of foreign and indigenous companies. Overall, permanent full time employment in manufacturing and internationally traded/financial services increased by 75,662 (35.2%) over the ten-year period 1990–1999.[9] Employment in foreign-owned companies grew by 52,211 jobs (54.5%) over the period while employment in Irish-owned companies grew by 23,451 (19.7%).

Apart from the direct output and employment effects, foreign multinational firms have enhanced the international competitiveness of the domestic economy, aided in the importation and diffusion of technology and have had a positive influence on the scale, efficiency and technological sophistication of domestic enterprises. Multinational firms create additional demand for domestically produced intermediate goods which, assuming scale economies, reduces the average costs of domestic producers and facilitates their expansion. This backward linkage in turn leads to reduced costs of these intermediate products for domestic producers of final goods, the forward linkage. Results from the *Forfás Annual Survey of Irish Economy Expenditures* show a substantial increase in backward linkages, as measured by the proportion of raw materials used by foreign firms which are sourced in Ireland, between 1988 and 1998. O'Malley (1995) reports an increasing number of jobs created in indigenous companies associated with every 100 jobs in foreign manufacturing. Foreign direct investment can also facilitate the introduction of new technologies and managerial and working practices in the host country through spillover effects. The rate of growth of research and development expenditure of both indigenous and foreign companies since 1987 suggests that foreign firms are locating more of their high value-added processes in Ireland and also that Irish companies are benefiting from technological spillovers (Forfás, 1999). In addition, a recent study has found that R&D active foreign firms are more committed to the Irish economy and provide a better quality employment than non-R&D active firms (Kearns & Ruane,1998).

The results of Görg and Strobl (2000) indicate that multinational companies, through the creation of linkages with indigenous suppliers, have had a positive effect on the development of indigenous enterprises. In recent years many high-tech companies have also been investing directly in developing Irish technology companies to aid market development and ensure the availability of domestic sub-suppliers. Agglomeration economies have provided momentum for the establishment of increasing numbers of knowledge-intensive foreign multinationals. In addition, rising corporate tax revenues have helped the government's tax reduction programme which has itself contributed to macroeconomic stability and social partnership.

In theory, an over-reliance on MNCs might lead to instability if the attractiveness of Ireland as a location for foreign direct investment was diminished. The presence of foreign-owned companies can crowd out domestic firms, leading to a reduction in both output and employment in indigenous sectors. Since 1974 the indigenous sector has lost around 11.5% of its share of manufacturing employment. However, a recent study finds that 76% of this loss of share is attributable to shifts away from indigenous employment sectors as opposed to losses of employment shares of indigenous firms relative to foreign firms within the same sectors (Gorg & Strobl, 2000). Barry et al. (1997) also note that competition effects are unlikely to have been important for Irish manufacturing because Irish-based foreign MNCs largely use Ireland as an export base and do not compete with indigenous industry for the domestic market and also because, until recently at least, labour and capital were not scarce resources.

The role of industrial policy and, in particular, the very low rate of corporation tax in attracting foreign multinationals to locate in Ireland have been the subject of international controversy in recent years. Recent empirical research (e.g. Altshuler, Grubert & Newlon, 1998; Gropp & Kostial, 2000) confirms that investment-location decisions are indeed sensitive to corporate tax regimes in potential host economies. However, a favourable fiscal environment is a necessary but not a sufficient condition for attracting foreign direct investment and channelling that investment into growth.

EU Structural Funds

The Irish economy has been a recipient of structural funds from the EU since it joined in 1973. Initially payments were made through Regional Development and Structural Funds which were made available to poor and peripheral countries to prevent regional economic divergence as part of the European integration adjustment process. The broader reforms which were introduced in the late 1980s as part of the completion of the European Single Market were accompanied by a significant increase in structural and cohesion funds as part of two multi-year plans (Community Support Frameworks) which ran between 1989–1993 and 1994–1999. It has been estimated by the ESRI that total funding of the first CSF and other related programmes amounted to £3,500 million in 1994 prices[10] while estimates of the second programme suggest that structural funds for the period of the second CSF amounted to £6,100 million in 1994 prices (Honohan,1997). Assistance to much of the Irish economy has subsequently been reduced significantly for the programming period 2000–2006 in light of the considerable increase in GDP in recent years.[11] For this reason the importance of structural funds for Ireland as a whole will decrease in coming years.

In addition to the short-term demand effects of structural funds are significant longer-term supply side effects. Funds have been invested in: (1) physical infrastructure (including roads, telecommunications, ports and airports); (2) human capital; and (3) direct assistance to the private productive sector. Recipient countries are further assisted in maximizing the efficiency of their expenditure of structural funds by an institutional framework which oversees the evaluation, monitoring and financial control of programmes. In this regard Ireland is considered by the European Commission to have been one of the more effective cohesion economies in terms of administering funds.[12]

Conservative estimates of the direct impact of structural funds on Ireland's growth and convergence process suggest that they added about three to four percentage points to GNP in the late 1990s or about one half of one percentage point per annum (Honohan, 1997; Barry et al., 1997b, 1999). The same studies suggest that the long-run effects of the CSF packages will be to add a further one to two percentage points to GNP in the future. However, while the direct impact of structural funds may be relatively modest, two further points are worthy of note. Firstly, the doubling of EU structural funds after 1989 came in the aftermath of severe cutbacks in domestic public capital expenditure. In this regard they facilitated necessary infrastructural improvements without compromising the government's expenditure commitments. Secondly, the improvements in physical infrastructure and human capital, which were assisted by structural funds, have played an important role in attracting U.S. foreign direct investment. Measures of the direct impact of structural funds cannot fully account for the significance of this.

Fiscal Stabilization, Cost Competitiveness and Macroeconomic Stability

The extent and causes of the fiscal crisis of the mid-1980s have already been noted. It was not until 1987 that the turning point arrived with the decision to cut back dramatically on public spending in order to restore the public finances to order. In real terms, total current spending fell by over ten percentage points between 1987 and 1989. The success of the fiscal stabilization programme was aided by the fact that it was implemented through expenditure cuts rather than tax increases and thus did not impact negatively upon competitiveness, private investment and profitability (Honohan, 1999). A second component of the macroeconomic recovery was the re-establishment of the social partnership process, a series of pay deals in which trade unions have accepted wage moderation in exchange for tax cuts.[13] Wage restraint and peaceful industrial relations improved the cost competitiveness of the traded sectors, permitted an expansion in the level of employment and improved the incentives for both domestic and foreign investment. The number of days per year lost to strikes, for example, fell from an average of 316,000 a year between 1980–1987 to under 110,000 a year between 1988–1996 (Sweeney, 1998).

The importance of fiscal consolidation to the recovery of the economy since the mid-1980s has been much recognized. However, the success of the partnership process was boosted considerably by buoyant international economic conditions and a drop in the inflation rate. The importance of global demand conditions is confirmed by the sequence of events which precipitated the economic turnaround. As Table 2 shows it was the growth of exports, underpinned by enhanced competitiveness, which led growth and initiated a virtuous circle of increased consumer confidence and domestic demand, improved public finances and industrial relations and macroeconomic stability (Honohan, 1999, 2000; Hardiman, 2000).

Education and Human Capital

The level of skills and education of the population is an important determinant of the productive efficiency and industrial structure of an economy (e.g. Midelfart-Knarvik et al., 2000). In this regard Ireland has benefited from past investments in education, the presence of foreign multinationals and the high skill levels of returning migrants. Free second level, state-funded education introduced in 1967 improved educational participation rates up to the age of 18 such that by the late 1960s Ireland compared very favourably with other OECD countries (Tussing, 1978). In the 1960s and 1970s, the National Institutes of Higher Education and the Regional Technical Colleges were established providing a broad range of third level courses in the sciences, engineering and business studies. A means-tested grant system subsequently made third level education available to students from all backgrounds resulting in a considerable increase in participation rates. Between 1970 and 1998, the number of full time students in third level more than quadrupled from about 25,000 to 112,200. Census of Population results show that in 1971 a total of 22,000 people had scientific or technological qualifications. By 1996, this figure had increased to 158,000. The estimates of Durkan et al. (1999) of the improved education attainment of those in employment between 1981 and 1996 are set out in Table 3. The authors estimate that around 19% of economic growth between 1960 and 1992 is attributable to improvements in labour quality, particularly in the 1980s and 1990s (Durkan, Fitzgerald & Harmon, 1999, pp. 131–133). The impact of a continued rise in education is expected to continue working

Table 2. Percentage Growth in Real GDP and Components of GDP, 1987–1990.

	1987	1988	1989	1990
GDP	4.4	4.5	6.3	7.1
Government	−4.8	−4.9	−0.9	+5.4
Consumption	3.3	4.5	6.2	1.2
Investment	−4.5	−3.3	21.6	21.2
Exports	13.8	8.8	10.3	8.7

Source: National Accounts.

Table 3. Education Attainment, 1981–1996 (% of those in Employment).

	Primary	Secondary	Third Level
1981	32.8	55.4	11.9
1986	22.8	61.2	16
1991	22	57.6	20.4
1996	17	59.6	23.4

Source: Durkan, Fitz Gerald and Harmon (1999, p. 129).

its way into the labour force, enabling the education-adjusted labour force to increase at a faster rate than the measured labour supply.

There exists a two-way relationship between foreign direct investment and human capital. A skilled labour force, capable of working with the technologies of knowledge intensive multinationals, is required in order to attract foreign direct investment in the first place. The presence of foreign high-tech firms can then yield spillover effects on the domestic economy through employee training and technological and managerial advances. The ability of indigenous firms to learn from foreign companies depends largely upon the absorptive capacity of the economy which itself depends in part upon the quality of third level training in business, science and technology and also resources available for graduate research. The Irish economy has benefited in recent years from the presence of innovation-driven foreign firms. These firms have created a demand for high-skilled graduates from Irish universities and for high-tech products of domestic sub-suppliers, have themselves directly trained employees and invested in indigenous suppliers and have also served as incubators for domestic entrepreneurs.

The educational attainment of returning migrants has also facilitated the enhancement of human capital in the 1990s. High emigration of the 1980s was a drain on the productive resources of the economy as, more than during previous periods of emigration, it was the well-educated who tended to leave for overseas employment. The term "brain drain" was commonly used to describe this exodus of Irish graduates. In the 1990s, the availability of skilled employment and the overall development of the Irish economy persuaded many migrants to return to Ireland, and the economy has since benefited from their high levels of skills accrued both from their education in Ireland and work experience acquired abroad. Barrett and Trace (1998) have calculated that the bulk of immigrants in the late 1990s, both returning migrants and non-Irish immigrants, have had higher levels of education attainment than the resident population and thus added to the value of human capital and aided productivity growth.

Rapid Labour Force Growth

The Irish labour market of the early 1990s was characterized by high unemployment, a high dependency ratio and low participation rates – particularly among females. There existed a clear potential for the expansion of the economy through a more efficient use of human resources. Since 1994 this potential has rapidly been realized with an overall increase in employment of over 40%. This growth in employment reflects higher female participation rates, a natural increase in the working age population, increased inward migration and lower unemployment.

Demographic Changes

Contrary to trends across the rest of Europe, the birth rate in Ireland remained relatively stable between 1960 and 1979. A fall in the fertility rate during this period was offset by an increase in the marriage rate. However, since 1979 the birth rate has declined significantly from around 21.5 to 14.5 children born per 1,000 persons in 1998. The high birth rate prior to 1979 has ensured a plentiful supply of labour in the intervening period while the subsequent decline has liberated women to participate in the labour force. The combination of these factors has reduced the dependency rate throughout the 1990s and contributed in an important way to economic growth.

Labour Force Participation

Since 1990, the labour force participation rate in Ireland has increased from 60% to around 66%,[14] largely as a result of a significant increase in the number of women entering the labour force. The recent increase in female participation rates has been largely a one-time occurrence as rates converged with those elsewhere in the EU. Among the reasons listed by Fahey et al. (2000) for this increase are the economic shift from agriculture to industry and services, rising productivity and the consequent increase in wage rates, the sharp expansion in the demand for women's labour, rising educational levels, the emergence of the women's movement, the influence of the EU equality directives and the impact of the media (2000, p. 245).

Migration

Since before the famine, emigration has been an important feature of Irish life. While the mobility of the labour force often made overseas employment opportunities available for the unemployed, emigration was often seen as a regrettable drain of the country's population. Before 1970, emigration tended to improve Ireland's educational distribution because emigrants were disproportionately drawn from domestic service, small farming and farm labouring backgrounds (O'Gráda, 1997, p. 214). However, as already noted, the "brain drain" of the 1980s constituted a waste of much of the increased investment in human capital since the late 1960s. The net immigration which has been experienced through the 1990s has not only increased the labour force but also improved the value of the economy's human capital and has thus aided both employment and productivity over the past decade.

5. FUTURE PROSPECTS

The pace of economic growth over the past fifteen years has exceeded even the most optimistic expectations. This is reflected not only in economic conditions, most notably the convergence of living standards with the rest of Europe, the attainment of full employment and the reversal of the very long-running trend of emigration, but also in a new national self-confidence. As a small nation, Ireland has always taken pride in international recognition. In less prosperous times this pride often reflected sporting or cultural endeavours, but in recent years it has been the rate of growth of the economy which has generated most international interest. It is now important that the economy can resist attempts to prolong growth in the short-term at the expense of a realistic perspective of medium and long term prospects. The potential rate of output growth is now significantly less than it was in the late 1980s and early 1990s. This is a welcome reflection of the economy's success in employing the under-utilized resources, particularly labour, of the previous period and does not indicate a deterioration of economic performance. The immediate challenge is the consolidation of Ireland's improved economic position so that the right conditions can be established to optimize long-term economic development.

The emergence in 2002 of strong underlying inflationary pressures as well as shortages in the markets for labour, property and raw materials primarily reflected excess demand in the Irish economy. OECD estimates of an output gap in excess of 5% appear to confirm this.[15] The pace of growth over the past seven years has been quicker than could have been anticipated, and in many ways the physical infrastructure and planning system were unable to develop at a sufficient rate to accommodate such rapid growth. Since 1994, domestic demand has been increasing at an average annual rate of 13% per annum, considerably in excess of the rate of growth of supply. It is now necessary to correct this imbalance, particularly since the potential rate of expansion of productive capacity is now reduced by the attainment of full employment. Achieving this objective has been complicated by membership in EMU which has placed significant constraints on the ability of domestic policy makers to implement macroeconomic policy. The Irish Central Bank has now passed control of monetary policy to the European Central Bank which sets interest rates in the interests of the euro-area as a whole. In the absence of a single monetary policy for the euro-area, the Irish Central Bank would have had the option of raising interest rates to moderate the growth of aggregate demand. Instead, interest rates are currently negative in real terms which is exerting a strong stimulatory influence on the economy. In general terms, fiscal policy within the euro-zone is also limited by the Stability and Growth pact. At the moment it is the tax-cutting commitments of the government under the current social partnership agreements and the need to improve physical infrastructure through capital expenditure which is preventing counter-cyclical fiscal adjustment.

In the absence of the traditional tools of macroeconomic policy, other automatic adjustment processes are required to reduce the rate of growth of demand. In the Irish case this is likely to happen because a reduction in international competitiveness will reduce the attractiveness of the Irish economy for foreign direct investment and reduce demand in line with supply. In many respects this adjustment process is an inevitable consequence of economic convergence as wages and prices rise to the average of other richer countries. It also constitutes a reversal of the process which has seen the labour share of national income fall relative to the profit share since 1987. However, there is a danger that an overly rapid loss of competitiveness might result in an overshooting of wages and prices which might have a negative, lasting impact on output and employment.

In the event of an overshooting of its competitive position, the economy is also likely to become increasingly vulnerable to external shocks, the most damaging of which would be a sharp appreciation of the euro relative to the dollar and sterling or a significant downturn in the U.S. economy. As the ability to use macroeconomic policy to protect against such occurrences diminishes, the significance of microeconomic reforms increases. Enhancing the productivity and sustainability of indigenous enterprises, improving labour market flexibility and increasing standards of competition, particularly in the non-traded sectors, can help in this regard.

Competition Policy

The lack of effective competition in certain sheltered sectors of the economy can have a negative impact upon both consumer welfare (particularly through higher prices and poor quality service), and the international competitiveness of the enterprise sector, through its effect on the cost, quality and availability of factor inputs and also on incentives for innovation. In recent years the *Competition Authority* has identified several markets which can be regarded as restrictive of competition. These include public utilities and public transport, the retail liquor trade, certain sections of the media, groceries, the pharmacy sector and various business services. Increased competition and regulatory reform in these and other sheltered sectors of the economy can not only improve the productivity of the non-traded sector and help keep services inflation under control but should also ease the upward pressure on the input costs of the traded sector and thus help maintain competitiveness.

Labour Market Reforms

With the attainment of full employment, some commentators have questioned whether the current social partnership process is the best way forward for the Irish economy. The consensus-based approach to wage formation has served the economy well since 1987. Hardiman (2000) interprets the process as an experiment in "competitive corporatism" in that it combines attention to the competitive needs of the business sector with political commitment to social protection and social equity. However, the increasing tightness of the labour market, a growing feeling that the benefits of economic growth have not been fairly distributed among all groups in society, as well as tensions within the partnership process now threaten the future of centrally negotiated pay agreements.[16] At a macroeconomic level, the long wage cycles inherent in the national agreements are a form of labour market rigidity which might threaten employment in the event of an economic downturn.

If the social partnership process is allowed to lapse, it is difficult to see what it will be replaced with. A market-led approach to wage formation, similar to the U.S. and U.K. approaches, requires weak union power if industrial unrest and spiralling wage demands are to be resisted. This seems incompatible with the Irish system of industrial relations and the organized nature of the workforce (Hardiman, 2000). As already noted, it appears inevitable that labour will soon recover its share of national income relative to profits. It would seem preferable that this rise in earnings be controlled within a stable institutional framework which takes some account of macroeconomic considerations. For this reason it is important that the social partnership process can develop so as to accommodate diverse pay pressures and enable the labour market to respond in a flexible manner in the event of an economic downturn.

Industrial Policy

As noted by O'Malley (1998), the performance of the foreign sector has served to mask somewhat the revival of Irish indigenous industry since 1987 which has also been impressive in terms of employment, output and export performance and profitability. Moreover, this performance has reflected more than just the buoyant demand of the past thirteen years but has also involved an improvement in the competitive position of indigenous industry.

Nevertheless, total factor productivity of the indigenous sector lags behind that of the foreign-owned sector (though part of this difference is attributable to excess returns of "invisible" factors of production). Although structural changes in industry are part of the economic development process, it remains an important objective to improve the productivity of indigenous manufacturing. This can provide some degree of insurance against external shocks or a reduction in foreign direct investment. The National Development Plan (2000–2006) has identified a lack of scale and low productivity as the key challenges facing the indigenous sector and aims to address key information deficits relating to research and development and design, knowledge of and access to markets, and training and human resource development. It is also hoped to increase the participation of indigenous enterprises in the fastest growing, knowledge-based industries. Industrial policy relating to foreign investment can also be effective in achieving these objectives because of the positive linkages which can be developed between foreign and domestic companies.

Future strategy regarding FDI is likely to be driven by the need to increase the quality, commitment to the Irish economy, linkages with indigenous industry and spatial distribution of foreign multinationals locating in Ireland. This is consistent with the objectives of both the IDA and the National Development Plan 2000–2006 which are: (1) a strong emphasis on attracting high value-added FDI projects to the Border, Midland and Western region and the weaker areas in the South East; (2) attempting to increase the value and sustainability of overseas companies in Ireland and secure their future here; and (3) identifying and developing activities and sectors that will attract high quality inward investment.

If price stability can be restored, the medium-term prospects for the economy remain good. Long term growth will depend upon further increases in the labour supply and the average level of national productivity. The scope for further increases in the labour force is limited. Unemployment now mostly constitutes "frictional unemployment" – that amount of temporary unemployment that is inevitable in any economy due to job search activities. Anecdotal evidence suggests that the immigration of skilled workers, particularly in the Dublin area, is already being constrained by rising house prices and costs of living. Evidence of labour shortages throughout the economy is confirmed by the continued fall of the potential labour supply as measured by the CSO.

If employment is to increase further in the coming years, it might be through a higher participation rate of married women. Although female participation rates have increased significantly since 1990, the percentage of women aged between 25 and 54 who are in the labour force is still below the EU average. Recent experience has shown that the female labour supply is relatively responsive to changes in disposable income. In the medium-term, further reductions in income tax might attract more married women into the labour force though the fiscal and inflationary consequences of this strategy must also be considered. Measures to reduce the costs of childcare and public transport might also serve to encourage some of this part of the population back to work.

As the Irish economy approaches full employment, further expansion will be primarily determined by the productivity of its human and physical resources. Productivity growth in the traded sector remains strong. Having established a comparative advantage in a small number of highly innovative and productive sectors in recent years, the Irish economy can expect to benefit from a process of positive feedback which should lead to further productivity enhancement even if the rate of increase of productivity cannot be maintained at the current high levels. Experience from other countries suggests that the additional impact of new foreign direct investment eventually begins to decline. Nevertheless, the current performance of this sector augurs well for future growth. For one thing industrial policy is now oriented towards monitoring the quality rather than the quantity of incoming investment. High-tech, innovative firms in knowledge-intensive industries tend to be highly productive and also have a positive influence on the quality of domestic production and labour market skills. Furthermore, helped by the deepening linkages between multinationals and the domestic economy, indigenous start-up activity in high-tech sectors has also been accelerating. This should ensure that a greater proportion of the excess returns associated with these sectors are retained in the domestic economy.

Experience from other countries also suggests that the composition of output is likely to show a shift from manufacturing to service sectors. The lower productivity of the services sector is one of the reasons why growth rates tend to slow down as economies become more prosperous. This is because the share of services in total output increases as an economy expands. As consumers' incomes increase they tend to spend a greater proportion of their incomes on services such as entertainment, health-care, travel and eating out. Unlike traded goods, these services cannot be imported, which implies that a greater percentage of the workforce will be required to cater to this change in the composition of domestic demand. The future significance of the services sector reinforces the importance of enhancing efficiency through product market regulation, particularly perhaps for public utilities.

The increase in public investment envisaged under the National Development Plan for 2000–2006 should improve supply conditions in the medium term and facilitate economic development. Over forty billion pounds will be spent on investment categories such as economic and social infrastructure, employment and human resources, the productive sector, regional programs and the CAP rural development plan. Such a spending programme, mostly government financed, is necessary to ease some of the infrastructure bottlenecks facing the economy, including those relating to housing, roads, public transport, water supply and waste treatment, but it incurs the risk of adding to aggregate demand. For this reason parallel measures to regulate demand are of particular importance, and it must also be ensured that expenditure focuses on priority areas so as to make best use of scarce resources, particularly in the construction sector.

NOTES

1. The fact that GDP in 2000 was about 18% higher than GNP reflects the importance of foreign investment in the Irish economy.

2. A further measure of output, Gross National Disposable Income adjusted for terms of trade, measures the availability of goods and services to the economy and is perhaps the best measure of changes in living standards. Although GNDI is slightly higher than GNP (about 2.5%), its rate of growth since 1994 has been slightly lower (averaging about 7% per annum) but, even using this measure, output and living standards in Ireland have been increasing more rapidly than in any other developed economy during this period.

3. *Source:* EU Commission Services.

4. The exception was the North East of the economy – the six counties which became Northern Ireland – which had developed successful linen and ship-building industries.

5. See Kennedy et al., 1988, pp. 12–14.

6. The speed of change was dramatic. Meenan notes that in the space of a few months at the turn of 1931 into 1932, Ireland passed from being the last surviving example of a predominantly free-trading state left in the world to being one of the most heavily tariffed countries that could be found (1970, p. 142).

7. This was followed by subsequent programmes for the periods 1964–1970 and 1969–1972.

8. CSO Census of Industrial Production 1998. For current purposes high tech sectors include: (1) chemicals; (2) publishing, printing and reproduction of recorded media (including replication of computer software); (3) other foods (largely cola concentrates); and (4) manufacture of optical and electrical equipment.

9. Forfás Annual Employment Survey 1999. Irish-owned companies are defined as those with 50% plus Irish-owned shareholding.

10. ESRI: *The Community Support Framework 1989–1993: Evaluation and Recommendations for the 1994–1997 Framework,* 1993, p. 217.

11. Objective One Status still applies to the Border, Midland and Western region.

12. See European Commission: *Real Convergence and Catching Up in the EU* (2000).

13. The first agreement was the Programme for National Recovery (1987–1990) which was followed by the Programme for Economic and Social Progress (1990–1993), the Programme for Competitiveness and Work (1993–1996), Partnership 2000 (1997–1999) and the current Programme for Prosperity and Fairness.

14. *Source:* OECD Employment Outlook, Paris, 2000.

15. *Source:* OECD Economic Outlook, December 2000.
16. These tensions include conflicts between traditional and high tech and between public and private sectors.

REFERENCES

Altshuler, R., Grubert, H., & Newlon, T. S. (1998). Has U.S. investment abroad become more sensitive to tax rates? NBER Working Paper No. 6383.

Barrett, A., & Trace, F. (1998). Who is coming back? The educational profile of returning migrants in the 1990s. *Irish Banking Review*, (Summer), 38–52.

Barry, F., Bradley, J., Hannan, A., McCartan, J., & Sosvilla-Revers, S. (1997a). *Single Market Review 1996: Aggregate and Regional Aspects: The Cases of Greece, Ireland, Portugal and Spain*. London: Kogan Page.

Barry, F., & Bradley, J. (1997b). FDI and trade: the Irish host-country experience. *The Economic Journal*, *108*, 1798–1811.

Barry, F., Bradley, J., & O'Malley, E. (1999). Indigenous and foreign industry: characteristics and performance. In: F. Barry (Ed.), *Understanding Ireland's Economic Growth*. Basingstoke: Macmillan Press Ltd.

Callan, T., & Nolan, B. (1999). Income inequality in Ireland in the 1980s and 1990s. In: F. Barry (Ed.), *Understanding Ireland's Economic Growth*. Basingstoke: Macmillan Press Ltd.

Daly, M. (1992). *Industrial Development and Irish National Identity, 1922–1939*. Dublin: Gill and Macmillan.

Durkan, J., Fitz Gerald, D., & Harmon, C. (1999). Education and growth in the Irish economy. In: F. Barry (Ed.), *Understanding Ireland's Economic Growth*. Basingstoke: Macmillan Press Ltd.

Economic and Social Research Insitutute (ESRI) (1993). *The Community Support Framework 1989–1993: Evaluation and Recommendations for the 1994–1997 Framework*. Dublin: ESRI.

European Commission (2000). *Real Convergence and Catching Up in the EU*. European Commission Services.

Fahey, T., Russell, H., & Smyth, E. (2000). Gender equality, fertility decline and labour market patterns among women in Ireland. In: B. Nolan, P. O'Connell & C. Whelan (Eds), *Bust to Boom? The Irish Experience of Growth and Inequality*. Dublin: Institute of Public Administration.

European Economy (1998), pp. 80–81.

Forfás (1999a). *Annual Employment Survey*. Dublin, Forfás.

Forfás (1999b). *Annual Survey of Irish Economy Expenditures*. Dublin, Forfás.

Fitz Gerald, J. (1999). Wage formation in the Irish labour market. In: F. Barry (Ed.), *Understanding Ireland's Economic Growth*. Basingstoke: Macmillan Press Ltd.

Görg, H., & Strobl, E. (2000). *Multinational companies and indigenous development: Panel data evidence for Ireland*. Mimeo.

Gropp, R., & Kostial, K. (2000). The disappearing tax base: is foreign direct investment eroding corporate income taxes? Working Paper No. 31, European Central Bank, September 2000.

Hardiman, N. (2000). Social partnership, wage bargaining, and growth. In: B. Nolan, P. O'Connell & C. Whelan (Eds), *Bust to Boom? The Irish Experience of Growth and Inequality*. Dublin, Institute of Public Administration.

Honohan, P. (Ed.) (1997). EU structural funds in Ireland: a mid-term evaluation of the CSF 1994–1999. Policy Research Series No. 31. Dublin, The Economic and Social Research Institute.

Honohan, P. (1999). The European dimension: the single market and the structural funds. In: F. Barry (Ed.), *Understanding Ireland's Economic Growth*. Basingstoke: Macmillan Press Ltd.

Honohan, P. (2000). Ireland in EMU: Straitjacket or skateboard? *Irish Banking Review*, (Winter), 15–32.

Kearns, A., & Ruane, R. (1999). The tangible contribution of R&D spending by foreign owned plants to a host region: A plant level study of the Irish manufacturing sector (1980–1996). Trinity Economic Paper, No.7.

Kennedy, K., Giblin, T., & McHugh, D. (1988). *The Economic Development of Ireland in the Twentieth Century*. London: Routledge.

Lane, P. (1988). Profits and wages in Ireland. *Trinity Economic Papers*, No. 14.

Meenan, J. (1970). *The Irish economy since 1922*. Liverpool, Liverpool University Press.

Midelfart-Knarvik, K. H., Overman, H. G., & Venables, A. J. (2000). Comparative advantage and economic geography: estimating the location of production in the EU. CEPR Discussion Paper No. 2618.

National Development Plan 2000–2006 (2000). Government Publications Office.

OECD (1999). *Economic Outlook*. Paris: OECD.

OECD (2000). *Economic Outlook*. Paris: OECD.

OECD (2000). *Employment Outlook*. Paris: OECD.

O'Gráda, C. (1997). *A Rocky Road: The Irish Economy Since the 1920s*. Manchester: Manchester University Press.

O'Malley, E. (1995). An analysis of secondary employment associated with manufacturing industry, General Research Paper No. 167. Dublin, The Economic and Social Research Institute.

O'Malley, E. (1998). *The Revival of Irish Indigenous Industry 1987–1997*. Dublin: Economic and Social Research Institute.

Ruane, F., & Görg, H. (1997). Reflections on Irish industrial policy towards foreign direct investment. *Trinity Economic Papers*, No. 3.

Sweeney, P. (1998). *The Celtic Tiger: Ireland's Economic Miracle Explained*. Dublin: Oak Tree Press.

Tussing, A. D. (1978). *Irish Educational Expenditures – Past, Present and Future*. Dublin: Economic and Social Research Institute.

(Ireland) (handwritten annotation)

3. FOREIGN DIRECT INVESTMENT: THE CASE OF THE ELECTRONICS AND PHARMACEUTICALS INDUSTRIES

F23 F21 L63 L65 (handwritten annotation)

Joe Durkan

1. INTRODUCTION

This chapter looks at the rationale and experience of Ireland in relation to Foreign Direct Investment and within this broad framework examines the Electronics and Pharmaceutical Industries. The chapter considers the historical background, explaining the emergence of FDI as a development strategy, then examines the difficulties, both real and imagined, that arose as a result of FDI, while the final part of the chapter looks at the modern period where FDI is now seen as part of the globalisation process.

2. FDI AS A DEVELOPMENT STRATEGY

Although FDI has been an important feature of the Irish economy for 40 years it has not always been so. Prior to its emergence as a development strategy there was a commitment to protectionism that lasted from the thirties. Protectionism itself was a product of exceptional circumstances following the breakdown of the old free trade world that prevailed before the 1914–1918 Great War.

The Irish Economy in Transition: Successes, Problems, and Prospects, Volume 85, pages 33–49.
Copyright © 2002 by Elsevier Science Ltd.
All rights of reproduction in any form reserved.
ISBN: 0-7623-0979-2

At Independence there was a commitment to free trade. In effect this meant free trade with the U.K., as this was both the principal destination of exports and the source of much of imported goods. The country has a natural advantage in grass-based production (cattle and milk), so that the objective of policy was to maintain free trade, with a view to maximising output in agriculture, and to minimise farm input costs and consumer costs. Since the majority of the population depended directly or indirectly on agriculture this policy appeared eminently successful. In a free trade world it could have been expected that the economy would develop initially on the basis of cattle and milk, thereafter in the primary and secondary processing of these products, in the provision of goods and services to the farming sector, and finally in the provision of consumer goods to farmers.

In the event, this development did not take place. The initial factor was the Great Depression, but this was followed by an Economic War with Britain and then by the Second World War. The Great Depression led to the spread of protectionism across industrial countries, and created a climate that was favourably disposed to protectionism within Ireland – a climate that a new government was only too eager to respond to, beginning a process that was to shift the economy from a free trade environment to one of the most protected in Western Europe, over a period of a decade. Keynes is often quoted as being favourably disposed to early Irish protectionism, but it is not clear if this was simple politeness or a result of analysis. The Economic War with Britain (1934–1938) disrupted trade with Britain, for both exports and imports, and gave a further stimulus to protectionism. The Economic War with Britain arose as a result of the government withholding payments to Britain on foot of obligations associated with land reform in the previous century. As a consequence Britain imposed tariffs and quotas on Irish exports, mainly cattle, beef, milk and dairy products. The conclusion of the dispute is generally seen as being favourable to Ireland, but did require exports of live animals from Ireland to Britain. Although trade previously was primarily in cattle, rather than in beef, the requirement for cattle reduced the possibility of developing the beef industry. The Second World War, with the associated shortages as a result of Britain's war effort, made it essential to increase domestic production of a range of goods, and made a virtue out of import substitution.

The introduction of protectionism was eagerly seized by local business, the most classic case being Irish Steel, whose conditions of operation included the lease of state property at favourable rates, tariff protection, an embargo on scrap metal exports, and an exclusive licence. Hence the producer simultaneously succeeded in excluding competition both from imports and from a domestic producer, and managed to influence costs by preventing the export of scrap metal (Barry & Durkan, 1996).

A consequence of protectionism was a proliferation of very small plants, serving a very small market, covering a wide range of goods previously imported. This was the classic import substitution strategy, and generally involves producing goods domestically where all the evidence is that there is no comparative advantage. As a consequence, costs everywhere were greater, and the economy remained static, though it is difficult to disentangle the separate factors at work during that period. For the rural community, protectionism rendered some agricultural production unprofitable, and reduced real farm incomes.

While it could be argued that special circumstances could be used to justify the introduction of protectionist measures, protectionism was continued too long after the end of the war. The post-war reconstruction period in Europe could have provided the necessary favourable climate for industry to experience lower protection and to learn to respond to external competitive pressures, given the supply constraints in Europe. However, protected industry was small scale, widely dispersed, meeting local markets, and very high cost. Not only was it not in a position to benefit from European reconstruction, but it required increased tariffs simply to prevent a loss of sales to imported goods. Thus, in the 1950s when Europe was experiencing the period of fast growth that ended in 1973, the Irish economy was characterised by low growth, high emigration, high unemployment, and fiscal and balance of payments imbalances. Agribusiness had not developed. The cheap food policies pursued by Britain turned the terms of trade decisively against agricultural products (particularly beef and dairy products), so that at prevailing prices agricultural output was static. Furthermore, low agricultural incomes forced people off the land and, given the integrated labour market with the U.K., into Britain. In order to deal with the poor economic performance, the industrial development body, the Industrial Development Authority (IDA), was in 1956 empowered to grant aid outside the "undeveloped areas" – the objective being to increase industrial employment via import substitution.

At this time an attempt was made to encourage exports via a tax concession on additional profits from exports. This represented the first break with the inward looking tradition of import substitution, begun 25 years earlier, but was still focused on existing firms. A more significant break occurred with the publication of the "Programme for Economic Expansion" in 1958. This explicitly recognised that a more outward looking strategy was needed if the economy was to develop. Industrial growth needed to be based on export growth, as the domestic market was too small to allow firms to realise economies of scale. In order to achieve export growth a dual approach was adopted:

(1) new industry was to be promoted
- foreigners were allowed to set up business;
- Export Sales Relief (ESR) was adopted.
(2) existing industry was to be made more competitive
- grants for rationalisation were given;
- reductions in tariffs took place, forcing firms to become more competitive.

Once existing industry was made more competitive, it was expected that domestic firms would begin selling in overseas markets.

This dual approach to industrial development – viz. the promotion of new industry and the improved competitiveness of existing industry – has been at the centre of the industrial policy debate in Ireland since the outward looking policy was first articulated. The outcome of the policy, in terms of the mix between new and existing industry, was not anticipated.

There can be little doubt that in the period from 1958–1973 outward-looking policies were very successful. In a study published in 1967 ("Survey of Grant Aided Industry") it was shown that total employment in grant-aided industry by 1966 was 17,000, of whom 13,600 were in overseas industry. There were also some overseas firms that had been established prior to the era of protection and some others established without grant whose primary focus was the domestic market, amounting in employment terms to some 4,000. Together overseas firms accounted for just under 10% of employment in manufacturing. The essential difference between the grant-aided overseas firms and non-grant-aided overseas firms was not the issue of grant, but the focus of activities. Grant-aided overseas firms exported the bulk of output. Among the first companies to establish was Pfizer, whose presence has continued and deepened.

It was in the period from 1966 to 1973 that a very rapid expansion of overseas firms occurred. By 1973 there were 576 overseas companies employing some 68,000 people in manufacturing. This compares with 3,994 Irish firms employing 150,000. Employment in overseas firms had quadrupled since 1966, while employment in Irish firms had fallen by 10%. Total manufacturing employment had increased by about one-sixth.

By 1973 the economy was fully employed and had experienced its fastest sustained period of economic growth (4.4% p.a. from 1960–1973). Net immigration was being experienced, participation rates in education had risen, and the state had set in place increased social expenditure in education and health-care. Thus it would be fair to say that the outward-looking policies had proven remarkably successful. The shape of this success was very different than what had been expected. The main emphasis in the policy had been on indigenous firms, as it was not expected that overseas firms would locate in Ireland given the small size of the market. The outcome (and this has continued over the next three decades), was that overseas firms proved to be the main growth area in manufacturing, shifting from what was random success in attracting companies, essentially opportunistic, to a more strategic approach to firms and sectors. In the early 1970s the emphasis shifted to considering sectors that were expected to be a long-term success. In particular, the pharmaceutical, healthcare and electronic sectors were targeted. This was not an attempt to pick winners, but a judgement about sectors. In fact the approach was to encourage leading firms in each sector to locate in Ireland. The basic idea was that leading firms had already established their credentials, the objective was to establish the credentials of Ireland as a location. There can be no doubt that this was successful, and a list of overseas pharmaceutical and electronics companies in Ireland reads like a list of leading U.S. companies.

There was insufficient attention given to the nature of the success with overseas firms, and this led to much debate about the strategy throughout the 1970s and 1980s. It is possible to identify those factors that were important in the initial success.

First, at the time outward-looking policies were implemented, the industrial world was fully employed. There were shortages of labour and capacity in the OECD area. This had the effect of encouraging inward migration to the OECD group of countries, and of encouraging industry to locate outside traditional regions. Ireland had the advantage of location in Europe, of a plentiful supply of labour, and, with the introduction of outward-looking policies, a favourable climate for investment. To the very first companies to locate in Ireland the fact of available labour was critical.

Second, there was ready access to the U.K. market, particularly after the signing of the Anglo-Irish Free Trade Agreement, and this encouraged location in Ireland of firms whose main focus was the U.K. market.

Third, the grant system, and the existence of Export Sales Relief (ESR) under which firms paid no corporation tax on profits from exports, were very favourable incentives to location. From the point of view of industrial countries, these incentives were not perceived as a threat at that time, as these countries were fully employed. The "Survey of Grant Aided Industry" concluded that the tax and grant incentives were more important than any inherent attractions offered by the country. For the majority of companies the ESR was more important than the grant in influencing location, though differential grants were used to influence regional location. In a recent paper (Durkan, 1999), it was shown that the situation is more complicated than this, and that taxes, grants and relative local costs are all relevant in determining the post-tax rate of return and hence the location in one country rather than another. Furthermore, it can also be shown that capital-intensive firms favour tax concessions, while labour-intensive firms favour grants. For the majority of firms that located in Ireland during this period, the present value of the ESR far outweighed the once-off value of the grant, but of course the ESR favoured the location of capital-intensive firms. There were also no restrictions on the repatriations of profits.

Over the period under discussion, employment in domestic manufacturing declined. Opening up firms to competition did not generate the improvement in competitiveness that had been expected. Many firms proved uncompetitive in the face of the operation of the Anglo-Irish Free Trade Agreement. These firms were marginal even within the framework of a supply constrained industrial world. Their position was probably worsened by the advent of overseas firms, as this caused upward pressure on wage rates. However, since the economy was fully employed, this process of change was the vehicle for improving real incomes; and given that many of these firms derived their rationale from import substitution, it is not surprising that they went into decline. It would be fair to say that the process of industrial change engineered by foreign investment was unanticipated, but once underway the primary emphasis' of those involved with promotion turned to overseas companies. Increasing employment in existing indigenous firms or even maintaining employment in the face of competition was inherently more difficult than attracting a single new firm from the U.S. to locate some additional capacity outside the U.S.

The oil price increase of 1973/1974 and the further increase in 1979/1980 marked the end of the fast growth era in the industrial world. That world was now characterised by lower growth in output and high unemployment. Industrial investment in the major industrial countries weakened, but firms were experiencing reductions in profitability and hence looking for overseas low cost, high profitability locations, a process that has continued since that time. As a consequence there was a shift in investment to overseas locations, most obviously to the newly industrialising countries of East Asia; but there was also continued growth in output and employment in overseas firms in Ireland. The number of overseas firms increased from 576 employing 68,500 in 1973 to 939 employing 87,600 in 1983. That period also witnessed some attrition among firms that had located in Ireland in the 1960s as they were not immune to the two world recessions. There was also a sharp decline in employment in indigenous industry. This decline was a continuation of the process underway prior to 1973, but was exacerbated by the two recessions, a failure by some industry to adapt to EEC entry, and the impact on costs of fiscal and incomes policies pursued in the period from 1973 to 1983.

Over the same period there was a very significant increase in the labour force. This was a result of an increase in the adult population, immigration, and increased participation in the labour force by married women following the removal of restrictions on employment of married women in the public service and some service industries. The combination of the weakness in domestic firms and the growth in the labour force resulted in an increase in unemployment and led to a reconsideration of industrial policy. At its crudest this reconsideration was based on a naïve view that there should be full employment since the state had spent so much by way of grants to foreign firms and that the failure to realise full employment was due to foreign firms. In reality there was little analysis of the impact of foreign firms or the legitimate expectations a society could have of foreign investment.

3. BACKWARD AND FORWARD LINKAGES

One criticism of overseas firms was that they had poor backward and forward linkages with the rest of the economy. While there was no explicit policy, it is clear that firms locating in Ireland were not expected to be competing for materials with indigenous firms or competing in final product markets. In policy terms this was certainly a mistake. Agribusiness had failed to develop prior to entry to the EEC for reasons already discussed. Even after entry, agribusiness remained commodity production. Competition for basic inputs by secondary producers could have led to a more rapid development of this sector. The sector is not impervious to change, but generally requires some additional agent to demonstrate the viability of change.

In the same way there were few forward linkages from production in Ireland. Foreign plants were essentially production units. They were integrated in the production process of their parent company, typically using inputs from the parent and shipping product to the parent or to subsidiaries for further processing. Until quite recently the pharmaceutical industry was engaged primarily in the production of bulk fine chemicals, mainly the active ingredient used in medicines, though some were producing the final product from imported active ingredients. (Strictly speaking, the chemicals sector includes a significant proportion of the production of bulk fine chemicals by the pharmaceuticals industry, so that the distinction between these two sectors in not so clear in practice in Ireland.) Hence the likelihood that these would be sold on to local firms was remote, as these firms would then be competing with the parent. Furthermore, subsidiaries in Ireland had generally no sales function. They were simple production units.

This weakness in backward and forward linkages did not just reflect some implicit policy or the place of companies in the production process of the parent; it was also influenced by the tax regime. The ESR (replaced by a 10% tax on profits of manufacturing companies) encouraged firms to locate the maximum amount of profits in Ireland, as this minimised their tax liabilities. Hence the incentive is to "purchase" from the parent at artificially low prices and to "sell" the output at artificially high prices, thus maximising profits located in Ireland. Such internal pricing (transfer pricing) limits the extent to which overseas plants will engage in local transactions. Thus, it is not surprising that the bulk of production is exported. For the pharmaceuticals sector the proportion is 95%, while for electronic equipment the proportion is almost 92%.

Of course the extent of transfer pricing is not unlimited. The U.S. Internal Revenue Service (IRS) has an interest in internal pricing arrangements between the parent and subsidiary. Ideally it requires arms-length pricing; but in the absence of this, particularly in the pharmaceuticals area, where there may be no arms-length transactions anywhere because of patent protection, the U.S. IRS agrees prices on transactions within related companies. The U.S. IRS did not have an arms-length relationship with plants overseas, as they tend to visit to ensure that they are not simple warehouse operations.

Even with this there may be some additional profits located in Ireland. The extent of this is not obvious. Attempts have been made to compare implied profitability between plants in Ireland and overall profitability, but they seem to take insufficient account of the relative newness and capital intensity of the plants in Ireland.

Transfer pricing distorts national data, by overstating exports and understating imports, but from Ireland's perspective increases government revenue. And of course to the extent that it encourages investment that would not otherwise take place in Ireland, it achieves the objective. The more interesting aspect of this is the extent to which the tax advantage distorts location or is just a signalling device. One way to consider this is to look at costs in Irish plants and the decisions on new investment. While, as indicated above, the location decision is influenced by taxes, grants and local costs, the critical aspect of the operation for local management is the extent to which the operation will continue once the location decision is made.

For local management the immediate threat is from competition within the worldwide company for new investment and the possibility that shareholders will seek to reduce costs by shifting production to low cost producers elsewhere. One way to avoid this is to ensure that costs are contained and that the plants are competitive within the organisation, without the benefit of the tax advantage. Some, though not all, pharmaceutical companies have sought to realise this objective, on the basis that the tax advantage may not be maintained, and have engaged in process development to ensure competitive costs. Local production plants also face the possibility that over time new investment will locate elsewhere, other than on cost grounds, so that it is necessary to remain at the forefront of new developments and to locate some basic research at the local organisation. This has the effect of changing the role of the production unit within the overall organisation. The classic example of this in Ireland is Bristol Myers Squibb, where local management saw the Irish plant becoming a commodity producer, with possibly no long-term future against competition within the company from lower cost locations in poorer countries, and directed the local operation into a major research facility.

Where the product life cycle is short, local staff must constantly be anticipating and linking directly to developments in the product range and seeking to expand that range. This pattern has been followed by many subsidiaries of multinationals, and is one explanation of the continued growth in output and maintenance of employment in these firms.

This issue is very different from that of backward and forward linkages, which was at the forefront of the policy debate in relation to multinationals in Ireland from the 1960s and which was a major concern in the early 1980s. The issue remains the extent to which the location of a firm in a country is permanent, but this must be seen in the context of the current stage of globalisation.

The traditional concern has given rise to the concept of *embeddedness*. In its simplest form this refers to the extent that a firm is integrated into the domestic economy, depending on the local economy for material supplies (backward linkages), and where the local market is an important one for sales, either to final consumers or to other producers who use the output of the firm as a material input into their own production process (forward linkages). It is possible to measure these effects through input-output tables, and it can be shown that for the overall multinational sector in Ireland, backward linkages have increased over the past 30 years, though these linkages remain relatively low.

With the restoration of globalisation of production from the mid-1970s – a process that was a normal feature of the pre-1914 world – and in particular the opening of China to overseas firms and to the world market, the links between materials, production and markets have become more complex. Firms will seek to realise in each location the benefits of that location. Hence they may be willing to produce different stages of the production process at different locations, depending on the relative advantage of each location. Thus, traditional measures of linkages may not be important. Firms may have weaker linkages over time, but the source of the location may be stronger; and the firm is therefore more embedded in the sense that the location is important to the overall operation of the parent.

Hence the relevant issue is to consider the extent to which the operation of the firm depends on the local economy, essentially asking how important is the location to the firm. This is the direct opposite of backward and forward linkages, which sought to show the importance of the firm to the economy. To develop this concept requires individual company data and data for local production units. A series of indicators has been developed from one unpublished specific company study to capture this concept. These indicators cover:

- Capital embeddedness (Capital Stock in Ireland percent overall capital stock, New Investment in Ireland percent New Investment, Investment per employee in Ireland percent overall investment per employee);
- Profit Importance (Post tax profits in Ireland, percent overall post tax profits, profits per employee);
- Educational Attainment of staff in Ireland relative to educational attainment in other locations, use of local staff in other locations, and use of head office staff locally; and finally,
- Importance of the local plant to technology development within the organisation.

These indicators will provide measures of the extent to which location in a country is likely to be maintained, at least in the medium term.

The poor backward and forward linkages between overseas and domestic firms has been criticised by comparison with experience in the Newly Industrialising Countries (NICs) of East Asia, where government pursued a more active role in establishing links between domestic and overseas companies, with the expectation that local firms would develop more rapidly and then become sources of growth in their own right. The objective in Ireland was to encourage location, often of companies that required no local inputs beyond labour. Forcing companies to develop local links, where costs are higher, reduces profitability and makes it more difficult for overseas firms to establish that low-cost base that justifies the investment without the tax concession. Firms did establish links, but on the basis of relative costs.

Thus, at least as far as most pharmaceutical companies and some of the electronics firms are concerned, it is fair to conclude that while the initial attraction may have been the tax and grant incentives, there are cost advantages also. These advantages are now not all internal to the firms. There are significant external economies associated with both sectors, particularly the pharmaceutical sector, that encourage further investment by existing and new firms.

External Economies

Until recently the pharmaceutical industry was primarily involved in the production of the active ingredient that went into finishing plants in other countries. The first firm to establish itself in Ireland was Pfizer, producing chemical products, and it located in the south of the country 40 years ago. Within the region the technical expertise associated with building the physical plant was developed, the local authority established the necessary expertise for regulating the physical environment through planning and other controls (fire safety, water management, waste disposal); and there are sufficient people who can be employed with skills necessary for the sector. As a consequence, the area is the natural location for similar plants; and while similar plants are located elsewhere, the bulk of production of active ingredients is carried out in the south of the country.

The electronics sector is more complex. In the computers sub-sector, a mid-range industry existed up to the mid-1980s, mostly consisting of DEC, Prime and some other smaller producers. There was also a local software industry producing customised software for the domestic market and a software publishing sector, much of whose output was won on contract independently of software development in Ireland. Taken together this looked like an integrated activity; yet there were very few direct links between these agents, with the possible exception of IBM and ICL neither of which had a production facility in Ireland and some software houses. IBM had no manufacturing presence, yet was most important in terms of mainframe installations, and software companies. Since the mid-1980s this sector has been transformed with the advent of PC producers (Dell and Gateway) and the location of Intel; and the non-computer sub-sector has expanded rapidly. There are clear external economies associated with Intel's operation, and the continued growth and development of the plant and the continuous change in the product range produced at the site all attest to the factors referred to earlier. In addition to having many of the characteristics of a conglomerate, Intel also has significant backward linkages in the economy and has been strengthening them over time.

The Indigenous Sector

From the mid-1970s to the early 1980s the characteristics of overseas companies were seen as a weakness in industrial policy, so much so that overseas firms were blamed for the failure to maintain full employment in the face of the two oil-based recessions. In fact, the real failure of industrial policy in Ireland was the failure of indigenous firms to develop. It would have been very difficult for firms to develop in any event as the period was characterised by the lack of a consistent general economic policy for domestic firms to operate within. The failure of general economic policy in the 1970s makes it difficult to see how industrial policy could have been successful – industrial policy was expected to counteract the effect of poor economic policy. Thus, it is easy to see how employment in indigenous firms continued to decline, in spite of the very significant degree of support given by way of grant. When it is remembered that many of these firms owed their origin to protectionism, their continued decline becomes more explicable.

In the 1980s there was a shift in policy following a report by Ira Magaziner, who had carried out similar work in East Asia, and which is popularly known as the Telesis Report. This report recommended a fundamental shift in policy towards indigenous firms. The most important insight was the recognition that the correct approach to indigenous firms was to identify the constraints they faced and then to apply resources to deal with these constraints. Previously capital grants were the main instrument used, but capital grants are inappropriate where the constraints are in management, in marketing, or in product development. Once firms consider the question of constraints, they are already adopting a strategic approach to their business and on the way to possible development. Grants, if necessary at all, can then be applied to dealing with constraints.

The Telesis Report also recommended that industrial policy for local companies should concentrate on a small number of firms in order to build strong indigenous companies that could compete internationally. These firms could then become a focus for other local industry. The origin of this approach lies in the East Asian experience. In effect this involves picking winners – not winning sectors, but winning firms. The principal concern with this approach is that concentrating on a small number of firms will inhibit the development of other potentially successful companies. The counterfactual is difficult to test, as the favoured companies are likely to be successful, and the unfavoured may have disappeared. In relation to overseas firms the main recommendation was to reduce the grant rate, as the main benefit arose from the tax concession, and there was clearly some deadweight loss associated with the grant system (and indeed with the tax rate).

While government never formally accepted the recommendations of the Telesis Report, it had a major impact on policy. There was a definite concentration on some firms in terms of resources, particularly in the beef sector. The folly of this was evident in the eclipse in this sector of those not supported, where even export credit guarantees were lost, and in the failure of the sector to develop beyond commodity production. The most successful indigenous companies (Smurfits and Roadstone) received little or no support under this policy. Outside of these selected firms, policy was designed to build up the capacity of firms to think strategically about their business as a whole, rather than seeking capital grants for new investment. Firms would then be given assistance to overcome the constraints. In effect the Telesis recommendations of the early 1980s were precisely the type of measures that should have been followed when the outward-looking strategy was first devised. These measures were strengthened in the early 1990s following another review of industrial policy. The basic underlying message of this review was not about industrial policy but about policy in general: growth in output depends on efficiency and competitiveness, and public policy should be directed to realising both. Hence, the recommendations covered all aspects of economic policy, including taxation, infrastructure, environment education and training support for industry and institutional change. In effect the approach was to get good general economic policy, and within this industrial policy could operate more efficiently. This is very different from a situation where industrial policy was expected to overcome the negative impact of bad economic policy. The focus of the recommendations was to improve the environment for indigenous firms, though the implementation of the recommendations has improved the competitive environment for all firms. This reinforced other policies and together they formed the basis of the remarkable growth of the 1990s. Measures of competitiveness have improved dramatically since the late 1980s so that the location by new firms is not just based on tax and grant incentives. There is now an excess competitiveness problem.

4. GLOBALISATION AND THE SINGLE MARKET

The objective of the Single Market Programme was to improve the performance of the European economy by establishing a single market, where previously there were individual markets. Although there was a common market, there were border controls between members affecting product markets, and the movement of people, and there were also capital controls in some member countries. Technical regulations and standards also differed among countries, imposing additional costs on firms. Since the markets were seen as separate, many firms maintained production units in several countries, none of which realised potential economies of scale. Country-specific regulation of the financial sector limited competition in the sector, and in some cases maintained a cartel. There was also substantial price discrimination among countries by firms, which existing arrangements helped to maintain. The overall costs of not having a single market were estimated (Cecchini et al., 1988), and these estimates were the basic justification of the Single Market Programme, with EMU being its logical successor. The estimates were based on two static exercises (micro and macro) and have been criticised. Baldwin (1989) suggests that focusing on static effects seriously under-estimated the economic impact of the single market programme, as the growth rate could be permanently raised. If this were so, then the growth impact would very soon outweigh the static impact.

The Cecchini study made no effort to estimate the impact of the single market programme by country. There was, however, a debate about the distribution of these static gains, with peripheral and poorer regions likely to see a weakening of their position or possibly an improvement. This debate was very similar to the Krugman and Frankel-Rose debate about differential shocks between countries in the monetary union. However, separate individual country studies did indicate that the static effects differed by country; and this formed one, though not the only basis, for substantial transfers between EU members. In the case of Ireland the estimated effect of the single market programme was significantly less than the EU effect, so that the debate in Ireland was in relation to the amount of the compensation the country should receive for not opposing the changes, even though the country was expected to make some static gains. (Interestingly the East African Common Market collapsed in the 1960s on just such an issue, with all countries losing out. It has now begun again.) The critical issue was not the static gains.

Within the EC the greater part of the finished products of the pharmaceuticals sector were purchased directly, or reimbursed in whole or in part, by public health authorities. Public procurement procedures and prices differed across the EC and influenced (and were influenced by) the location of finishing plants and the nature of the pharmaceuticals industry within each member country. In the U.K., the pharmaceuticals industry was research-based, so that pricing policy for drugs under patent involved ensuring that firms recovered overall research investment. Hence prices involved industrial and health departments. In France, finishing capacity was an unstated requirement for reimbursement. In addition to these characteristics, public health authorities had differing procedures for the certification and approval of products. There were also differing dosage requirements for patients and in the range of goods that could be sold over the counter (OTC). As a consequence the EC had a highly fragmented sector, with serious overcapacity in the finishing end of the business. In the Cecchini Report it was estimated that the industry was operating at just 30% of capacity. Hence the finished product industry offered the greatest opportunity for rationalisation of plants between countries, with the most efficient becoming the major site for finishing. The internal market programme therefore created an opportunity for downstream development in Ireland. The plants, producing bulk fine chemicals, in general are low cost, for reasons discussed earlier, and the country still maintains the low tax regime. The critical issue for pharmaceuticals companies was the extent to which the single market programme was implemented. In particular the question is the extent to which public procurement policies no longer seek to favour national production. Over the period since the programme was begun, there has been a more general acceptance of the principles of the single market programme (though there are still bizarre exceptions, e.g. the automobile market, where the potential for revenue losses by government has maintained price discrimination by auto companies). Hence change in the pharmaceuticals sector is underway. Most attention is focused on mergers in the industry and the impact this will have on costs and the efficiency of research, and hence on overall profitability. However, on the ground there has been a shift to rationalisation of plants, and from Ireland's perspective, the movement to locating finished product activity in Ireland. The most obvious have been the cases of Pfizer, which has extended its activities further, and Wyeth, which is in the process of commissioning its second finishing plant in five years.

The electronics sector is much more global in nature, and not so heavily reliant on government purchases; but there were still concerns that Europe would establish barriers to trade with other countries in order to protect European manufacturing. This may have been behind the location decisions of some U.S. companies and the expansion of others in the EU, and specifically in Ireland with the advantages referred to earlier. The electronics sector cannot be separated from software activities, so that in some respects it is better to think of the whole ICT sector. Dell, Gateway, Compaq, Hewlett-Packard, Intel, 3COM, Xerox, Microsoft all have a presence in Ireland, but the focus of their activity is not the domestic market. In its broadest sense covering computers, electrical and instrument engineering, and software, the sector experienced a doubling in employment over the period 1993–2000 and now employs almost 100,000, or 6% of total employment in Ireland. The gross output of the sector is about one-sixth of GDP, though its value added is considerably less. However, while the bulk of the output is exported, the real impact of the sector will come in the way ICT investment and usage occurs and raises total factor productivity, particularly outside the sector itself. The data in relation to this are poor, but some work (Raven, 2001) indicates that the Irish economy exhibits more new-economy characteristics than other EU countries, with Finland a very close second.

5. CONCLUSION

The conclusion of this chapter has been that the current mix in industry was almost accidental. The initial impetus from the adoption of the outward-looking approach was expected to come from local firms. In the 40 year period since, the overseas sector has come to dominate manufacturing while the indigenous sector has declined in absolute and relative importance. The overseas sector was initially attracted by the availability of labour as well as by a favourable tax and grant regime. The domestic market was and remains irrelevant to the majority of overseas companies, while the availability of materials for further processing has not been important. The pharmaceuticals sector and the associated chemicals sector have tended to import their required materials. The modern electronics sector is dominated by U.S. firms, and for them the issue has been the availability of highly skilled labour, as well as the tax and grant regime and access to EU markets.

The tax and grant system played an important part in this development. However, while these are clearly important, many overseas firms have an incentive to make plants in Ireland cost-competitive within the organisation. In addition, the competitive position of all firms, both local and overseas, has improved significantly over the 1990s, due to shifts in economic policy and the continued impact of changes in the institutional arrangements for settling pay, overcoming many of the cost disadvantages and difficulties associated with doing business in Ireland. The Single Market Programme instigated in the EU in the early 1990s has given an additional impetus to location of downstream activities in Ireland.

The tax and grant systems have the effect of influencing location. The majority of firms taking advantage of these incentives are American. This, coupled with full employment, massive budget surpluses, and rapid growth, has led to pressure from other EU countries for harmonising tax and grant systems within the EU. While it is obvious that a different approach is needed in Ireland, given full employment, eliminating tax and grant differences cannot be undertaken in isolation as there are very significant differences in other areas of costs, with significant product subsidies and factor market subsidies in some countries. It is also naïve to believe that eliminating tax and grant distortions will re-distribute a fixed amount of U.S. investment among EU countries. The problems of many EU countries are more fundamental than this.

REFERENCES

Baldwin, R. (1989). The growth effects of 1992. *Economic Policy*, 9.

Barry, F., & Durkan, J. (1966). Team Aer Lingus and Irish Steel: an application of the declining high-wage industries literature. *Irish Business and Administrative Research*, 17.

Cecchini, P., Catinat, M., & Jacquemin, A. (1998). *The European challenge: 1992, the benefits of a single market*. Commission of European Communities.

Durkan, J. (1999). *Corporation tax and tax competition: a review of the issues.* Foundation for Fiscal Studies Annual Conference.

Durkan, J. (1991). The impact of economic and monetary union: the internal market and the reform of the CAP on the economy. Mimeo.

Irish Government Publications (1990). 1992 and the electronic, electrical and instrument engineering sectors – a report for the European Bureau.

Irish Government Publications (1990). 1992 and the pharmaceutical, healthcare and chemicals sectors – a report for the Europen Bureau.

O'Sullivan, M. (1998). Manufacturing and global competition. In: J. W. O'Hagan (Ed.), *The Economy of Ireland: Policy and Performance of a Small European Country.* Gill and MacMillan.

Raven, J. (2001). A new economy in Europe. In: *European Economic Outlook.* PriceWaterhouse Coopers.

DATA APPENDIX 1998

	All Industry	Chemicals	Pharmaceuticals	Electronics
Gross Output	£48,427 m	£11,728 m	£2,027 m	£13,831 m
% Turnover Exported	72.9	94.7	95.3	90.6
U.S. firms output %	54.1	74.5	38.9	76.3
Employment	242,772	21,432	7,231	59,830
Net Output per person	£0.109 m	£0.443 m	£0.200 m	£0.086 m
Net Output per person, U.S. firms	£0.258 m	£0.762 m	£0.261 m	£0.116 m

Source: Census of Industrial Production, 1998 (Irish CSO, 2000).

4. NURTURING INDIGENOUS ENTREPRENEURSHIP IN IRELAND: THE CASE OF THE IT SOFTWARE SECTOR

Connell Fanning and Ciaran Murphy

1. INTRODUCTION

Ireland has achieved unprecedented economic success over the past 10 years. This phenomenon has seen Ireland sustain dramatic growth rates, drop from very high unemployment rates, to virtually eliminating unemployment and searching the world for skilled workers, become a role model for Europe and enjoy unprecedented confidence throughout a once stagnant economy and society. Much of the reason for this success is attributed by the media and others to the performance of the "high-tech" sector (including pharmaceuticals, chemicals) in Ireland and, especially, to the Computers/IT element of the sector.

We were asked to consider the issue of nurturing indigenous entrepreneurship in Ireland's IT sector, and for this paper we focus specifically on the software sector. We do this, first, because the number of indigenous Irish companies in the IT hardware industry is very low and, second, because Ireland has become the largest exporter of software in the world.

The latter is in itself a remarkable story. How could a country with a population of 3.7 million reach such a pre-eminent position in the information economy of today? What does it mean? And what does it say about nurturing

The Irish Economy in Transition: Successes, Problems, and Prospects, Volume 85, pages 51–84.
© 2002 Published by Elsevier Science Ltd.
ISBN: 0-7623-0979-2

indigenous entrepreneurship in a small country and, if nurturing is possible, who can do it and how?

In seeking a direction for answering these types of questions, we attempt to evaluate the role played by the Foreign Direct Investment (FDI) software companies, venture capitalists, and government policy in nurturing entrepreneurship in the indigenous software sector. To do this, we first need to describe the software sector in Ireland and examine the general economic environment in which entrepreneurship occurs in Ireland. Having reviewed the three aspects just identified, we outline the nature of competition in the IT area so that we can then draw some implications for policy-thinking in the future.

2. THE IRISH SOFTWARE SECTOR

To begin, the Irish software industry must be described. The official message about Ireland being the largest exporter of software does not describe the full picture. Much of the software that is exported from Ireland is software that has been developed elsewhere (typically in the U.S.) and has been localized in Ireland into the languages of different European countries. Therefore, the measured value/volume of software exports is based on a virtually invisible import base. The best example of this is Microsoft. While employing about 1,500 people in Ireland, Microsoft has only a very small development group based in the country, with probably fewer than 50 employees. The precise figure cannot be obtained from either Microsoft or from official sources.

Thus, much of the software exported from Ireland has been developed elsewhere so that the operation of a number of software multinationals here is akin to a basic, factory-type, production operation. While the success of Ireland in attracting these localization operations must be acknowledged, it is significant that there has not been the same success in getting such firms to locate R&D operations in the country. This contrasts with Microsoft setting up its first R&D facilities outside of the U.S. in Israel, another small country.

The indigenous and foreign components of the Irish software sector for the period of our study are compared in Tables 1 and 2.

The data show that there are very significant differences between the foreign and indigenous components of the Irish software sector. There are far more indigenous companies, but these are much smaller in terms of revenue and employees than the foreign companies. Almost all of the revenues generated by foreign companies come from exports.

As a report prepared for the National Software Directorate suggested, "Ireland has several policy and economic-based "competitive advantages" which have enabled it to attract key international players to the country. These include

Table 1. Profile of Irish Indigenous Software Companies.

	No. of Companies	Employment	Average No. of Employees	Revenue	Exports as % of Revenue
1993	336	4495	13	–	49
1995	390	5773	15	617 m	58
1997	561	9200	16	796 m	69
1999	670 (e)	17,984 (e)	27 (e)	–	–

(e): estimate.

Table 2. Profile of Foreign Software Companies Located in Ireland.

	No. of Companies	Employment	Average No. of Employees	Revenue	Exports as % of Revenue
1993	81	4448	55	–	98
1995	93	6011	65	4171 m	99
1997	108	9100	84	5926 m	98
1999	174 (e)	24,572 (e)	149 (e)	–	–

(e): estimate.

supportive State strategy resulting in employment grants for inward investment, a skilled English-speaking workforce with what is perceived to be a strong work ethic, and a stable economic environment. These have enabled Ireland to establish a strong multinational-based software localization sector" (Price Waterhouse Coopers, November 1999).

Key indicators of entrepreneurship in the Irish software sector show that there are major differences between the profiles of the indigenous sector and the FDI companies. For example, much of the latter sector can be characterized as assembly and low level factory production with the knowledge content of the product and operations processes generated elsewhere. By contrast, the indigenous software sector is characterized by companies developing software products and services.

According to the analysis for the National Software Directorate:

> [the] IDA's success at persuading major U.S. software vendors to site localization in Ireland has distorted the popular perception of the software industry. The critical weakness is that these high profile U.S. companies are to a great extent not involved in serious creative and development work – the software activity with the greatest economic value (Price Waterhouse Coopers, November, 1999).

This is further confirmed by the fact that, while over 90% of indigenous software companies are in the packaged software or customised software business, only 20% of foreign companies are in those high value creation categories, suggesting that many multinational software companies do little knowledge creation or development in Ireland.

In the same way as the Bahamas, the Cayman Islands and Switzerland became major financial centres in earlier times, Ireland is now promoted as the "software capital of the world" similar to these earlier examples. This image of Ireland is, in reality, based on attracting foreign software companies through a series of clever government measures rather than through any coherent and comprehensive policy to promote large numbers of entrepreneurial indigenous companies.

The points at issue emerging from the comparison above is that entrepreneurship is not a primary feature of the Irish software sector and that indigenous entrepreneurship in the sector is limited. This allows us to refine the questions to be addressed in this contribution to the Conference.

The specific questions lurking in the two points noted is: Is there is a strategic dilemma, if not possibly an inherent contradiction, in having public bodies attempting to nurture entrepreneurship in the software sector by trying to "pick winners," and directly influence them *or* is it more appropriate for government to approach entrepreneurial nurturing by seeking to remove obstacles, some of which government itself puts in the way of entrepreneurs, because it cannot actually nurture software entrepreneurship directly?

The next step in approaching this question is to outline the indigenous software sector.

A Brief History of the Indigenous Software Sector

The history of the indigenous software sector can be roughly split into three waves. Based on the previous work of Murphy (1998) we have characterised each of these waves in Table 3.

As the table shows, there were few software companies prior to 1985. These were primarily focused on meeting the accounting, payroll and production needs of U.S. manufacturing companies located in Ireland. Some of them realized that there was a large degree of similarity in the systems they were providing for different companies and began to produce packaged solutions. The founders of these companies had to depend on cash flow and their own personal guarantees to banks to grow their companies. These were the instigators of an entrepreneurial culture focused on product development and selling into the export markets that later came to typify the indigenous software sector.

Table 3. Three Waves of Irish Software Companies.

Characteristic	First Wave Before 1985	Second Wave 1985–1995	Third Wave After 1995
No. of Companies	< 100	350–450	> 500
No. of Employees per Company	< 25	< 40	< 60
Focus	Application Software and Services Indigenous Market	Product Export (U.K.) (70% of companies exporting)	Product Export (U.S.) (80% of revenue from exports)
Marketing Strategy	Direct Sales	Direct Sales (85 Overseas Offices)/ Agents/Distributors	Direct Sales, Agents/Distributors World Wide Web
R&D Financing	Very Little Cash Flow Personal Guarantees	Some Cash Flow Business Angel Business Expansion Schemes	Relatively Large Business Angels Venture Capital IPOs
Growth Strategy Role of Government	Slow and Organic Non-Specific Industrial Promotion Policies	Organic Employment Grants R&D Support Marketing Assistance Preference Shares National Software Director	Very Rapid R&D Support Preference Shares Marketing Assistance
Financial Strategy	Stay Profitable	Profitability	Pursue Market Share at any cost

Source: Developed from Murphy (1998).

The decade 1985–1995 saw a rapid expansion in the number of indigenous software companies. While the size of these companies was still small, the companies in the wave broadened the product spectrum from business applications to a very diverse technology constituency. This decade also witnessed a significant focus on the export market.

The third wave of software companies has been characterised by those facing the need to grow fast and be global. The emphasis has been on developing technical software companies and finding the resources to pursue rapid growth strategies. Companies have put great emphasis on penetrating the U.S. market, and a number of companies have raised finance through capital public offerings in the U.S. and U.K. as well as Ireland. The size of companies has also become larger. By 2001, the stage was reached where the largest of the indigenous companies were having to meet the demands of the global financiers in Wall Street.

At this point, and with this picture of the three waves of development in mind, particularly the stage now reached in the last wave, we turn to examine the context in which the IT explosion took place in Ireland. We do so at two levels: the general economic conditions prevailing and three aspects of the specific business supports available.

3. THE MACROECONOMIC ENVIRONMENT: THE "CELTIC TIGER"

The extraordinary change in the macroeconomic environment of the Irish economy in the last few years is the first aspect of the context against which any view about nurturing indigenous entrepreneurship generally in Ireland and in the software sector in particular must be placed.

The starting point is with the question: what kind of phenomenon is the so called "Celtic Tiger"? The term "Tiger," although evocative and extensively used in the media, is ill-defined economically and for explanatory purposes would need to be related to analytically grounded notions. There are, alternatively, different types of historical experiences of rapid growth across many countries which can be used to characterize the recent macroeconomic performance of the Irish economy. Broadly these are:

- Transformation (or development in the Schumpeterian sense);
- Re-construction (e.g. post-World War II re-building);
- Catch-up/Convergence (exploiting technologies of leading countries);
- Spurt (temporary coincidence of favourable conditions);
- Re-structuring/Adjustment (sectoral shifts and fiscal re-balancing); and
- Business Cycle (boom phase).

Each of these has obviously different meanings and, therefore, implications for policy thinking. Looking at it non-historically and non-analytically, the media like to see the Irish economy as being a "Tiger" or even as going through a "Renaissance." Whatever about the former, the latter is quite fanciful in terms of any historically meaningful use of the term. There is not space here to consider the various elements and their complex interaction and, although we should mention that it is still an area which is very much open to debate,[1] we offer two points for understanding the general economic context.

First, for our purposes we can confine ourselves just to noting that, from a comparative perspective, there appears to be elements of most, if not each, of the historical experiences in the recent Irish experience, including the slow, but on-going, liberalization of the economy and society, which is usually referred to as "openness," "export-orientation," and transformation and restructuring, underlying the performance overall. Viewing the recent experience as comprising a complex of elements suggests caution about simplifying the experience into something impressionistic and ill-defined like a "Tiger."

Second, the main elements in what can be termed the standard explanation or model of the Celtic Tiger are summarized in Table 4. The table is organized to reflect the time spans – broadly divided as "long," "medium" and "short" – over which the forces generally regarded as underpinning and generating the recent growth phenomenon have had time to work their effects. The division roughly corresponds to: (i) those that are slow acting but fundamental; (ii) through a grouping of intermediate acting factors which affect general economic conditions for entrepreneurship; and (iii) down to those that are more transitory and fluctuating. The latter, although having more immediate and visible effects on economic change, are also more contingent or variable in existence.

A number of key outcomes emerging from the consistency of policy commitments by successive governments leading into and during the "Tiger" phase and the interaction of the factors listed are particularly relevant to our topic and should be highlighted from Table 4. These are:

(1) reduction of price inflationary pressures and replacement of inflationary reputation by a credible commitment to monetary stabilization in line with international trends;

(2) competitiveness through exchange rate devaluations replaced by national wage agreements with exchange rate stability reducing risk of premium and easing of pressures from fiscal borrowing lowering interest rates;

(3) perception of shift towards a more "business friendly" culture with greater acceptance of need for incentives and rewards for risk-taking and innovativeness;

(4) enhancement as a location for multi-national companies and in profitability of foreign direct investment;

(5) availability, including return, of skilled, educated and experienced Irish labour especially from U.K. and U.S.; also an "open" labour market allowing labour flows within EU; and

(6) beginnings of institutional reform in public administration and in ownership/direction of the state commercial companies which controlled energy, transport and communications sectors to improve national competitiveness.

Table 4.   Standard Explanatory Model of the "Celtic Tiger."

Long-Term Factors (from 1960s)

(1) Demographic Trends	• Education-Investment and Increasing Participation → Human Capital Accumulation • Age Profile • Labour Market Participation – untapped pool of labour in low female participation
(2) Industrial Policy Consistency	• Fiscal Regime – Tax Expenditures on Foreign Companies: low rates of corporation tax and grants and subsidies • Adaptive Targeting – selection from established "Winners," and growing sectors, esp. in U.S. economy • English speaking country in Europe • Selling of Demographic "Dividend" and Educational Investment Promotion of "young," "flexible" and "adaptable" (incl. non-unionized) workforce
(3) Outward Orientation	• Anglo-Irish Free Trade Area • European Community Membership • Single European Act – the "Single Market" project • European and Monetary Union – Maastricht Treaty

Medium Term Factors (from mid-late 1980s)

(4) Fiscal Correction	• Public Spending Controls • Public Debt and Borrowing Stabilization and Reduction • Public Sector Wage Controls in Context of "Social Partnership"
(5) Monetary Stabilization	• Decoupling from Sterling Zone • Anchoring to Strong Currency Policy of Euro-core Zone (DM) • Competitive Exchange Rate Devaluations (1986, 1993) • Commitment and Membership of Single European Currency (Euro)
(6) Social Partnership	• Institutional Consensus on Employment Growth • Incomes Policies – re-distribution towards profit share with tax reductions to bolster take-home wages

Table 4. Continued.

	• Some Liberalization of Economy – tentative "privatization" and de-monopolization under EU requirements of the "Single Market" etc.
Short-Term Factors (on-going)	
(7) European Union	• Structural & Cohesion Funds: Pump-priming investment in physical infrastructure and training; Income support for farming sector
	• Commitment and General Drive towards European Union Convergence
(8) International Conditions	• Buoyancy of U.S. Economy and Stock Markets

Source: This summary is based on what appears to be the consensus around which analysis within Ireland is converging. As it is an impression from many writers, some of whom have modified their thinking over time, it would be inappropriate to single out any author for responsibility. However, without putting anyone on the spot for the selection and presentation above, it should be noted that the work of the economists and sociologists located at the Economic and Social Research Institute in Dublin has been the most extensive and useful to date, in particular, the Medium Term Review series and various papers by Fitzgerald (for example, 1999, 2000). McAleese (forthcoming) is also a useful review of key elements of what we summarize as the standard model.

This overview of the preconditions of the "Celtic Tiger" period shows that the general economic environment was highly attractive to investment by foreign multinationals especially from the U.S., with much of it in the IT sector. FDI, in turn, played a role causing the "Celtic Tiger."

The overall impact of FDI in creating the "Celtic Tiger" is indicated by the data in Table 5 on output, employment, and export shares of manufacturing industries classified by ownership. Foreign-owned firms exported 93% of their output while having a 70% share of output.

The significance of this impact is further borne out by the data in Table 6 which shows the U.S. FDI inflow to a number of countries and the relatively strong position of Ireland as suggested by comparisons of average investment/employee ratios.

The high investment/employee ratio relative to other countries was also, of course, very significant relative to existing Irish industry.

Perhaps the "Tiger" metaphor is appropriate after all. Tigers are not indigenous to Ireland. Nor is a main driver of the recent growth experience indigenous. The tiger is also an endangered species – a warning for Ireland?

The outstanding result of the factors outlined in Tables 4, 5 and 6 is the higher output growth rate and rapid expansion of employment, with a dramatic take-off around 1994/5, initially in output and then in employment. The

Table 5.   Output, Employment and Export in Shares (%), Foreign and
Indigenous, 1998.

Shares (%)	Foreign	Indigenous	Total
Exported Output	93	47	83
Output Share	70	26	100
Employment Share	46	49	100

Source: Doyle, Gallagher and O'Leary, 2000, p. 4, Table 1.

Table 6.   Average U.S. Direct Investment per Employee Manufacturing, on
Historical Cost Basis, U.S.$, Selected Years.

Country	1983	1992	1996
Ireland	14,417	19,846	29,948
U.K.	2,306	3,763	6,423
France	823	3,137	4,042
Germany	1,195	1,939	2,381
Spain	619	2,040	3,042
EU15	1,273	2,627	4,189

Source: Barry, F., Bradley, J. and O'Malley, E. (1999). Indigenous and Foreign Industry:
Characteristics and Performance. In: F. Barry (Ed.), *Understanding Ireland's Economic Growth*
(pp. 45–74). London: Macmillan.

increasing material standard of living, as the numbers employed and the rates
of net-of-taxes incomes have improved, created a liveliness, confidence and
awareness of the possibilities of Ireland in total contrast to the dourness and
fatalism of the 1950s and 1960s and the hesitancies of the 1970s and 1980s.
From being a small, backward economy suffering the almost constant hemor-
rhage of emigration, Ireland now appears to have become a modernized
economy in the extraordinary situation of requiring substantial inflows of labour
– including unskilled – to sustain its pace of development.

The question which next arises is: what is the relationship between this
phenomenon and an active government policy of nurturing domestic entrepreneurship? This requires going somewhat deeper in the processes underlying
growth and beyond the standard model of the Celtic Tiger. Three points are
immediately relevant to the matter of nurturing indigenous entrepreneurship
generally and in IT software in particular.

The first point is that the lower personal taxation rates possibly helped and, more certainly, won't have hindered the phenomenon. More likely the role of taxation was to encourage skilled, including entrepreneurial, labour to stay in Ireland rather than emigrate and be available as a pool of educated and skilled labour. This will have facilitated entrepreneurship generally and in the software sector in particular, given the attractiveness of alternative employment in the U.S., in the software sector especially.

The second point is that the slowly changing attitude towards business in Ireland generally and by governments and public administration, in particular, probably figured as large as any quantifiable cause of the "Tiger" phenomenon. This was reflected in the shift away from a protectionist mentality towards an acceptance, if not yet understanding and appreciation, of the role of competition, except in so far as publicly administered business undertakings are concerned. This, too, will have affected entrepreneurship in the indigenous software sector.

The third, and most general point, is that the overall buoyancy of the economy has lifted almost all sectors, and this will have encouraged and supported the formation and growth of indigenous firms generally.[2] This process will also have applied to the indigenous software sector and will have had an effect aside from any specific government measures for promoting entrepreneurship in the indigenous software sector, the next topic which arises.

In conclusion, the general environment for business, foreign and indigenous, and thereby, for software entrepreneurship improved greatly with the so-called "Celtic Tiger." The next step in our inquiry is, therefore, to consider some factors relating specifically to indigenous software entrepreneurship and the apparent take-off in software.

4. POLICIES AND SUPPORTS FOR INDIGENOUS ENTREPRENEURSHIP

The three factors explored here – the presence of multinational companies, the venture capital process in Ireland and government policies – are generally regarded as being relevant to the promotion of entrepreneurship in the indigenous software sector and each are briefly examined to shed light on the question being pursued.

Role of Multinational Software Companies

The analysis so far suggests the question as to whether the indigenous sector has spun off from the FDI software companies or not? From interviews with a number of key software entrepreneurs in Ireland, the answer is that it has not. Furthermore, none of the founders or CEO's of the largest indigenous software companies (Iona, Baltimore, CBT, etc.) worked for foreign software companies.

The view of the key software entrepreneurs interviewed for this study is that Foreign Direct Investment software companies have contributed little to the development of the indigenous entrepreneurship in the Irish software sector. They point to the emphasis on localization and duplication in the FDI companies – attributes that have little to do with the creation and establishment of an entrepreneurial culture for software development and international competitiveness. Furthermore, many of the employees in multinational software companies actively engaging in development work enjoy very good working and living conditions, and have little incentive to risk setting up their own companies or for taking on the demanding task of building a business in highly competitive areas.

Interestingly, however, a number of indigenous software entrepreneurs suggested that the development of the industry had been generally helped by the arrival in the 1970s and 1980s of the U.S. companies in *manufacturing*. These companies needed software to operate their European-oriented businesses located in Ireland. Typically, this software was required to work on mid-range IBM and DEC computers. Encouraged perhaps by government policies, they offered this software business to indigenous fledging software companies. The best of the indigenous companies found this a profitable market. Some also used the opportunity as the base from which to launch themselves internationally. Many of the highest profile software entrepreneurs in Ireland started their careers in this way.

A number of these entrepreneurs pointed specifically to the *broad* experience that they received in these companies as a key factor in their later success. As one of them put it, "We learned an awful lot about software development and the selling of our products. We were in Sweden one week and the next week we were in the U.S., the next in Japan. We learned a lot about the different aspects of this business and having proved that we could meet the demanding requirements of U.S. manufacturing companies gave us the confidence to consider competing in global markets."

These views are generally consistent with Porter's work (1985, 1990, 2000) and in line with previous findings in Ireland (O'Gorman, O'Malley & Mooney, 1997, Section 4) on internationally competitive firms showing that successful companies benefited from having to meet the standards of highly demanding and sophisticated customers with its implications for a country/region becoming profitable location for an industry.

Finance and Venture Capital

Venture capital companies play a key role in the world-leading U.S. software industry. Success in the software development industry is dependent on the ability to get the new product to market quickly and to obtain reasonable market share with sufficient returns to resource further product development. While the underlying process will be considered in the following section, it should be noted here that the time to market has decreased significantly and, thereby, the resource needs have greatly increased. Availability of venture capital is, therefore, extremely important to achieve rapid early growth.

A key reason given by software entrepreneurs for the relatively low number of major indigenous software companies has been the absence of venture capital resourcing in Ireland. Borrowing money from banks, who were perceived to be very risk adverse, was seen to be difficult, slow and insufficient. Also, finance being knowledge and not just funds, government grants and tax breaks do not have the same business effects as venture capital financing.

Even the establishment of a number of VC funds in the mid-1990s has not made a significant difference. The reason given for this by software entrepreneurs was that much of the VC finance was coming from banks and pension funds who were still seen to be very conservative in their behaviour. Furthermore, Irish VCs were perceived by a number of the software entrepreneurs as having little to add to the software companies. This contrasts with the situation in the U.S. where VCs "are partners and not just accountants. They help the software companies open doors to lucrative markets and to recruit top people (i.e. with key skills, knowledge, experience and contacts). On the other hand, if you are not performing there they will look for heads to roll."

The data in Table 7 shows that the Irish VC sector is still very much in its infancy. The table represents the total investment by all full members of the Irish Venture Capital Association. It shows that the scale in absolute terms, which is what matters to entrepreneurs seeking to found and build companies, is very small.

Furthermore, the data in Table 8 for VC investment by the same group in high tech companies shows a very low involvement in the high-tech sector. The figures in these tables exclude investment by some private individuals and stockbrokers which however, is estimated to have been less then £20 m.

While revealing that there are indications of a growing VC investment in high technology companies, the conclusion one can draw is that VC funding of high tech companies in Ireland is only beginning.

It is interesting to compare these figures with the situation in Israel with a population of 5.5 million, compared to Ireland's population of 3.7 million. In

Table 7.   Venture Capital Investment by Financing Stage, All Companies, Ireland 1997–1999.

Financing stage	1997		1998		1999	
	No. of Companies	Amount Invested	No. of Companies	Amount Invested	No. of Companies	Amount Invested
Early Stage	16	6.2 m	27	9.4 m	52	23.3 m
Expansion	39	19.1 m	38	18.2 m	66	41.5 m
MBO/MBI	3	5.4 m	7	13.2 m	10	74.8 m
TOTAL	58	30.6 m	72	40.7 m	128	139.6 m

Table 8.   Venture Capital Investment in High Tech Companies in Ireland, 1997–1999.

	1997		1998		1999	
	No. of Companies	Amount Invested	No. of Companies	Amount Invested	No. of Companies	Amount Invested
Computer related (non-Internet)	10	2.4	17	7.4	29	13.5
Computer related (Internet)	3	1–3	4	3.3	14	5.8
Electronics related	1	0-4	3	0.8	5	8.4
Medical, Health	2	0.8	0	0	1	0.8
Biotechnology	1	0.4	3	0.8	3	0.5
Communication (non-Internet)	7	4.1	5	3	11	5.2
Communication (Internet)	0	0-0	1	0.1	13	17.6
TOTAL	24	9.4	33	15.4	76	51.8

Note: IR£1 = Euro 1.27.
Source: First Annual Report of the Irish Venture Capital Association, 2000.

Israel over *$1.5 billion* has been raised by venture capital companies with the target of financing start-up companies in various high-tech sectors, the majority of which are involved in the development of software products. It should be noted that most of these venture capital companies have been financed by foreign investors. Over 500 companies have received significant funding.

Israel has also been successful in forming a number of bilateral agreements with countries such as the U.S., Canada, Britain and Germany aimed at enhancing R&D in Israel. Of those the most significant is the U.S. – Israel BIRD foundation established in 1977. Since then, almost $200 million has been invested in more than 400 projects with the greatest investment being in the software sector. Significantly, BIRD employs a full-time Director of U.S. Operations in California. BIRD actively recruits potential strategic U.S. partners for Israeli firms. It is reckoned that one of BIRD's successes has been that to combine the marketing expertise, distribution network and global leverage of U.S. companies with the innovation and high standard of production capabilities in Israeli companies.

Irish software entrepreneurs have been starved of venture capital in comparison to their international competitors. This has meant that very few of them could have become significant players in the global software market. One immediate implication for nurturing entrepreneurship which can be noted here is that, if indigenous venture capital continues to be inadequate, then governmental programmes to attract foreign venture capital will need to be put in place.

Role of Government

Since the Second World War democratic governments have been held increasingly accountable by electorates for "managing" the economy, and they have put themselves in that position by competing for votes through "promises" in elections. Among other things, this requires promoting an internationally competitive business sector. This applies to the situation in Ireland as much as the U.S., U.K. and other European Countries. Measuring the role of government in encouraging the development of rapidly growing industries is, however, a difficult exercise. Furthermore, there is the more fundamental issue of whether government can actively nurture, i.e. make happen, entrepreneurship in general and, specifically, in the IT software sector.

The direct linkages between government policy and operational impact can be hard to discern even if they exist. However, it has been a clearly articulated policy of Irish governments in the 1990s to "create jobs".[3] This is reflected in announcements by government ministers continually emphasizing "promised" numbers of "jobs." Successive governments took the view that this could best be done by attracting foreign direct investment. Government policy in the software sector was consistent with its policy in most other internationally traded sectors.

This emphasis on fast job creation was not conducive to the long-term growth of indigenous software companies, and indeed entrepreneurs would argue, that it made life unnecessarily difficult. One entrepreneur gave the example that in the early 1990s it was impossible for him to get employment grants to recruit extra staff to his company to undertake development work for a multinational company. In contrast, however, that same multinational company was being offered employment grants for undertaking the work themselves.

One key fact about government and software is that in almost every country, government is the single largest purchaser of software. Therefore, should it choose, it can have a direct impact on the development of the software industry in Ireland by ensuring that it purchases a significant amount of innovative software from competitive indigenous companies and that it encourages local companies to purchase innovative software from the same source.

It is virtually impossible to get information on this issue from Irish official sources. Software entrepreneurs who were interviewed were, however, extremely critical of the lack of vision in this regard displayed by government departments. They assert that state departments and agencies have a propensity to use multinational companies for their software needs.[4] It was put to the interviewees that they could be accused of "sour grapes" and not understanding that civil servants are measured in terms of the "value for money" which they obtain for "the taxpayer." Their response was that they would wish to see government being extremely demanding as a customer but that government could realistically be expected to take a strategic interest in the development of the software industry. They contrasted the Irish situation with the U.S., India and Israel. While government is perceived to be constantly urging Irish software companies to be innovative they have seldom if ever entered into a partnership with Irish companies to determine ways in which information management and technology in the Irish public service could be more innovative, and give the added benefit of encouraging a strong and competitive indigenous software sector.

In terms of broader policy issues, the government has had mixed success. Expenditure on Research and Development in Ireland, in general has been relatively small by international standards. In the early 1990s, Ireland had the lowest government funding for basic research (at 0.05% of GDP) of any country for which data were available. Table 9 shows that data for expenditure on R&D paint an equally poor picture. Ireland is very much down toward the bottom of the league ladder in terms of promoting R&D. However, it should be pointed out that expenditure on R&D is increasing.

Research and Development expenditure is a key element in a knowledge-intensive society and is an indicator of the commitment and investment by government and business investment in this area. Where R&D has occurred with the help of government funding it has largely been produced in the universities or with some university funding linkage. The emphasis in Universities in

Table 9. Irish Expenditure on R&D as Percentage (%) of GDP with International Comparisons, 1996–1998.

	1996	1997	1998
Ireland	1.42	1.43	–
Australia	1.68	–	–
Austria	1.52	1.52	1.55
Canada	1.6	1.6	1.6
Denmark	2.01	2.03	2.06
Finland	2.59	2.78	2.92
France	2.32	2.23	–
Germany	2.3	2.31	2.33
Italy	1.02	1.08	1.11
Japan	2.83	2.92	–
Netherlands	2.09	–	–
Norway	–	1.68	–
New Zealand	–	–	1.1*
Portugal	–	0.65	–
Spain	0.87	0.86	0.88
Sweden	–	3.85	–
U.K.	1.95	1.87	–
U.S.	2.67	2.71	2.79

Source: OECD, Main Science and Technology Indicators 1999, p.1.

most cases has been on the "Research" rather than the "Development." The question that needs to be asked is whether this has been sufficiently successful. The answer is no. The resulting number of patents has been low. By contrast, in the U.S. it is estimated that over 70% of R&D funding now goes for development rather than research. Development grants in Ireland are not directed towards the creation of specific software products led by the software industry responding to perceived customer needs and opportunities. Neither the universities nor the state agencies have the expertise to develop commercial products; nor are they entrepreneurial entities.

The inherent difficulty with state funding of such projects/products is that some of them will fail. Allied to the R&D issue is the question of locating incubator units in universities. The model that is often put forward in public debate in Ireland is the MIT one where it is quoted that MIT receives in excess of $150 m per annum from companies that develop out of MIT. Yet interestingly, MIT does not have campus companies. When anyone there wishes to set up a company they are encouraged to leave MIT. The university gets its revenue from agreed licensing arrangements for any R&D work that was carried out on campus and that subsequently resulted in successful commercial exploitation.

Indeed the success of MIT "related companies" can be explained by the very fact that these companies have not been protected from day one. They have been business ventures from the start. Ireland, as yet, does not have this type of culture but has the potential.

Ireland has a large pool of suitably qualified personnel entering the industry which is the foundation for having a growing software industry with an increasing number of entrepreneurs. This is an area where government policy has been very successful. Table 10 shows that Ireland heads the list of OECD countries in terms of percentage of third-level students taking third level-IT courses.

This is a situation that will continue to improve as the government has given significant funding to increase the number of IT graduates. We estimate that the number of IT graduates will have doubled between 1998 and 2002.

In conclusion, we suggest that the role of multinational software companies in the development of indigenous software entrepreneurship has been very limited, that of the venture capital process inadequate and that of the government largely ineffective, except in so far as its long-term educational policies were concerned.

Table 10. International Comparison of Third Level Students Taking IT Related Courses (%).

Country	Type A (degree)	Type B (Cert/diploma)
Ireland	5.7	10.3
Australia	3.7	–
Austria	–	–
Canada	2.3	4.9
Denmark	–	–
Finland	2.1	4.1
France	–	–
Germany	3.1	0.4
Italy	1.1	–
Japan	1.4	–
Netherlands	1.4	3.3
Norway	1.2	5.9
New Zealand	0.9	0.7
Portugal	–	–
Spain	2.8	7.8
Sweden	–	–
U.K.	4.2	7.2
U.S.	2.1	3.1

To move our analysis forward towards an answer to our question we need a perspective on the entrepreneurial process in the software business. We develop this in the next section.

5. A PERSPECTIVE ON SOFTWARE ENTREPRENEURSHIP

To think about supports and, in particular, government policies for directly nurturing entrepreneurship in the software sector – whether in evaluation or formulation mode – requires identifying a conceptual apparatus through which the questions and issues can be identified and addressed. It is now widely accepted that the work of Joseph Schumpeter (1883–1950) provides a powerful method of conceptualising the driving forces of economic change and characterizing policy challenges in conditions of market competition.

In this section we first summarize the immediately relevant points from Schumpeter's analysis and, second, use them to describe the nature of competition in the IT sector as it relates to policy thinking in Ireland. This will then provide the basis for commenting in the final part of the paper on the current situation in Ireland, and in particular about the software development sector, in the light of the preceding analysis.

Schumpeter's Concept of "Creative Destruction"

Schumpeter created a powerful theoretical analysis of economic development and the growth of social product in the capitalist/market economic system. He logically located the economic sources of change in entrepreneurship as the agent of change; innovation as the act of change; profit as the reward for bearing uncertainty; and credit finance as the means for acquiring the required factors of production (1912, 1911). This provided the analytical framework for his major historical study of business cycles in which the clustering of innovations and investment was a significant phenomenon (1939).

Arising from, and using this sequence of analysis, Schumpeter memorably encapsulated "the essential fact about capitalism" in his conception of competition as a "process of creative destruction" (1943, 1954, p. 83). This conception, although generally recognized for its insightfulness and aptness, took some time to become part of mainstream economic thinking. But Schumpeter had no doubts about the importance of this process, describing a neglect of it as "like *Hamlet* without the Danish prince" (1954, p. 86). In the last decade or so it has become one of the core ideas in growth theory and analysis. This has been due to a large extent to the impact of the "IT Revolution" on businesses, competition and country performance.

In brief, Schumpeter's model of the process of creative destruction in the capitalist, market-economy is grounded on two inter-related ideas.[5] Schumpeter starts from the "essential point" about capitalism, namely, that "we are dealing with an evolutionary process" (1954, p. 82). By its very nature, capitalism is "a form or method of economic change and not only never is but never can be stationary" (1954, p. 82). For Schumpeter, the "fundamental impulse that sets and keeps the capitalist engine in motion comes from the new consumers' goods, the new methods of production or transportation, the new markets, the new forms of industrial organization that capitalist enterprise creates" (1954, p. 83).

The second feature is that of qualitative changes that fundamentally alter "the economic structure *from within*, incessantly destroying the old one, incessantly creating a new one" (1954, p. 83; 1934, pp. 63–64). In another of his memorable epigrams, Schumpeter conveyed the essence and the inevitability of the impact of qualitative change "Add successively as many mail coaches as you please, you will never get a railway thereby" (1954, p. 64, *fn.* 1). This process of creative destruction is, in Schumpeter's view, the "essential fact" about capitalism.

> It is what capitalism consists in and what every capitalist concern has got to live in (1954, p. 83).

These features give rise to a number of implications, one of which is particularly relevant for our topic generally and for evaluating and formulating government policies to nurture entrepreneurship, in particular. As Schumpeter points out, we are dealing with an "organic process." Viewing any particular part of it in isolation must be done carefully since

> every piece of business strategy acquires its true significance only against the background of that process and within the situation created by it. It must be seen in its role in the perennial gale of creative destruction; it cannot be understood irrespective of it, or on the hypothesis that there is a perennial lull" (1954, p. 84).

The danger for policy thinking lies in accepting "the data of the momentary situation as if there were no past or future to it . . ." (1954, p. 84). He points out that

> . . . the usual government commission's report practically never try to see that behaviour, on the one hand, as a result of a piece of past history and, on the other hand, as an attempt to deal with a situation that is sure to change presently – as an attempt by those firms to keep on their feet, on ground that is slipping away from under them. In other words, the problem that is usually being visualized is how capitalism administers existing structures, whereas the relevant problem is how it creates and destroys them (1954, p. 84).

In other words, public administration thinking and insights are not the same as commercial or market thinking and insights. This is underpinned by

Schumpeter's notion of "creative responses," in contrast to "adaptive responses," to changes in economic conditions. He sees creative responses as having three essential characteristics, one of which is immediately relevant to the topic of this paper: namely, a creative response can be understood afterwards by an observer in full possession of the facts, but it can practically never be "understood" beforehand, i.e. "be predicted by applying the ordinary rules of inference from the pre-existing facts" (1947, p. 216). That is, government agencies, accountable for the proper and correct use of taxpayer funds, would have to have the same insight as the entrepreneur and, hence, would *repeatedly* be entrepreneurial, in which case there should not be a problem about entrepreneurship. This points to the nub of the issue about government directly "nurturing" entrepreneurship.

Therein, as we shall see, lies the challenge for devising policies for nurturing entrepreneurship in Ireland. What kind of policies can a government in a small economy like Ireland formulate to cope with the "perennial gale of creative destruction," to use Schumpeter's memorable phrase. Indeed, the crucial question which this perspective requires one to address is: how can the Irish government formulate an active, interventionary policy to *destroy and create*?

There are two fundamental questions that have to be answered first and to ignore them – as is usually done – is to presume and leave implicit answers that may be seriously inadequate and misleading for formulating public policy. These are: (1) is the process of creative destruction not a phenomenon of the market process? and (2) if the answer to the first is in the affirmative, does it not mean that government policies should promote the general (e.g. the process) not the "particular" (e.g. a company)?

This problem is further complicated by the implications of two observations made by Schumpeter on the basis of his conception of creative destruction as the essence of the capitalist process of development. The first is that the competition which counts is less about price competition – a point not widely recognized at the time Schumpeter was writing – than

> the competition from the new commodity, the new technology, the new source of supply, the new type of organization . . . which commands a decisive cost or quality advantage and which strikes not at the margins of the profits and the outputs of existing firms but at their foundations and their very lives (1954, p. 85).

This kind of competition is, according to Schumpeter, much more important: it is "the powerful lever that in the long run expands output and brings down prices" (1954, p. 85). He likens it to a "bombardment" in comparison to price competition which is like "forcing a door" (1954, p. 84).

The corollary of this type of competition is that it "acts not only when in being but also when it is merely an ever-present threat. It disciplines before it

attacks" (1954, p. 85).[6] Again the problem posed for government policy making
is stated well by Schumpeter:

> The businessman feels himself to be in a competitive situation even if he is alone in his
> field or if, though not alone, he holds a position such that investigating government experts
> fail to see any effective competition between him and any other firms in the same or a
> neighbouring field and in consequence conclude that his talk, under examination, about his
> competitive sorrows is all make-believe (1954, p. 85).

Schumpeter uses retailing as an example to paint "a picture of stagnating
routine." Avoiding price competition, retailers in an area try to improve their
relative position by "service and 'atmosphere'." Others, drifting into the trade,
bring disruption but not in a way that benefits customers. As the "economic
space around each of the shops" narrows, livelihoods are undermined.
Attempts will be made to raise prices by tacit agreement which will result in
further reduction of sales. By "successive pyramiding" a situation will evolve
"in which increasing potential supply will be attended by increasing instead
of decreasing prices and by decreasing instead of increasing sales" (1954,
p. 85).

Schumpeter notes that such cases are "fringe-end cases to be found mainly
in the sectors furthest removed from all that is most characteristic of capitalist
activity" (1954, p. 85), a characterization that applied virtually to all sectors of
the Irish economy for a long time.

This "picture of stagnating routine" conveys the business atmosphere of
Ireland from independence in the 1920s to well into the 1960s and, for many
sectors, into the 1980s.

But such cases are "transient by nature" and in the case of retail trade taken
by Schumpeter as an example, he notes that

> The competition that matters arises not from additional shops of the same type, but from
> the department store, the chain store, the mail-order house and the supermarket *which are
> bound to destroy those pyramids sooner or later* (1954, p. 85, emphasis added, fn. omitted).

An economy, being made up of "sectors," i.e. the groupings of businesses,
faces the same process. This was a reality that came late to Ireland and was
forced upon it by external pressures from increasing internalization of trade
and the internal frustrations of social and economic stagnation. It would be
optimistic to say that it has been "discovered" and that it is understood
generally. It would be more true to say that the result has been a behavioural
response in Ireland rather than a purposeful act. It is at this point that Ireland
has plunged into the perennial gale of creative destruction in embracing the
IT sector.

Competition and Quality Ladders

The notion of "quality ladders" is useful for capturing a key aspect of the process of creative destruction as it manifests itself in the personal computer market and products. It reflects the importance of quality upgrading of products and continuity in the process of innovation. As Grossman and Helpman put it,

> An essential aspect of quality competition . . . is the continual and cyclical nature of the process whereby each new product enjoys a limited run at the technological frontier, only to fade when still better products come along. Almost every product exists on a *quality ladder*, with variants below that may already become obsolete, and others above, that have yet to be discovered (1991, p. 43).

In accordance with Schumpeter's insight into the capitalist process of development, we see that nothing is static or stationary. There is a process of repeated quality innovations and product improvements across a continuum of products with each having its own quality ladder (Grossman & Helpman, 1991, pp. 43–44). In this model of competition

> entrepreneurs target individual products and race to bring out the next generation. These races take place *simultaneously*. In any time interval, some of the efforts succeed while others fail. Successful ventures call forth efforts aimed at still further improvement, with each innovation building upon the last (Grossman & Helpman, 1991, p. 44).

Working in the tradition of endogenous growth theories, recently given an impetus from the models of Romer (1986) and Lucas (1988), in which the source of sustained growth is the accumulation of knowledge, Aghion and Howitt formalize a description of simple growth process inspired by some of Schumpeter's ideas about creative destruction (1992). Having noted some of the many channels through which societies accumulate knowledge – formal education, on-the-job training, basic scientific research, learning-by-doing, process and product innovations – Aghion and Howitt model a channel which they consider had received little attention in this growth tradition, namely, that of industrial innovations which improve the quality of products (1992, p. 323). This model focuses on obsolescence, whereby better products render previous ones obsolete, which in the view of the authors "exemplifies an important general characteristic of the growth process, namely that *progress creates losses as well as gains*" (1992, p. 323; emphasis added). This occurs especially when "individual innovations are sufficiently important to affect the entire economy" (1992, p. 324), a situation applying to the introduction of, for example, personal computers.

The innovation process is driven by the prospect of "monopoly" profits (or "economic rents").[7] Uncertainty attaching to the process arises from two sources. The first is the usual one of not knowing whether an attempt at innovation will be successful, i.e. accepted by customers, and the investment outlay justified by profitable returns. The second is the randomness, from the perspective of any individual firm, with which a superior and successful product can arrive to compete in the market. Therefore the "monopoly" profits will only last until the next innovation which renders the knowledge underpinning those returns redundant.

This "business stealing" effect (Aghion & Howitt, 1992, p. 325), by which the creativity of the innovators destroys the profits of competitors, is the reality for businesses of the process of creative destruction. Furthermore, innovations or threatened innovations by a firm may force other firms to stop or to move on to the next improvement (Grossman & Helpman, 1991, p. 54).[8] Customers benefit in this process of continual innovation when successful innovators provide a product of higher quality at the same price as before; cost reductions and quality improvements being two different ways for firms supplying more services at a given price (Grossman & Helpman, 1991, pp. 51, 55, fn. 1).

The PC Market: A Paradigm[9] for Policy Thinking

The competitive process of creation and destruction identified by Schumpeter has been a feature of the personal computer sector from its outset and, for some time, of information technologies in general, including telecommunication services and equipment such as mobile phones. The reality of this process is brought home to every parent and child at virtually every Christmas shopping season with the widespread publicity attending the launch of new video games machines, such as Sony's Playstation and, most recently, Playstation 2. Such are the ways that widespread public awareness, understanding and acceptance emerge and become embedded in social culture.

For our purposes we will take the personal computer (hardware and software) as the paradigm to help identify some important issues for policy thinking about the IT sector, and, specifically, software products. Even a casual inspection of a sequence of hard-disk drives for PCs vividly demonstrates the emergence and evolution of this key PC component within a process of creative destruction. The rapid shrinkage in physical size and weight alone tells the story of creation resulting in destruction, of the "leapfrogging competition," as Nakamura (2000, p. 21) terms climbing the quality ladder, and the precarious-ness of the grounds on which companies compete. This process of creative destruction driven by competition promotes the phenomenal growth in power and speed of personal computer products, reflected in "Moore's Law," and is the essence of entrepreneurship in the PC market.

All across the PC market, from final products and services, through intermediate products and services to basic materials, knowledge, capabilities and organization, there is no certainty. But the "rules" of the competition are relatively simple:[10]

(1) participation requires investment in "creating new, faster and smaller versions of the component," e.g. modem, memory;
(2) the result of this must "leapfrog the competition by creating a new generation";
(3) the bulk of the profits can often be captured by "the first firm to market with the new generation";
(4) to survive, the out-paced firm must be able to find and create an innovation, to leapfrog to the next generation and capture enough profits to survive.

Competing in this market is not compatible with a quiet, orderly business life and while much quality improvement arises from investment in on-going technical problem-solving, the joker-in-the pack for promoting entrepreneurship is creativity, the imaginative leap which reshapes an industry. For all the resources poured into any direction there are no guarantees of success. Fundamentally the competition is about ideas, and ideas can spring up at any time, surpassing earlier ideas and rendering the results of earlier ideas obsolete.

The development of products on the basis of generating ideas affects both sides of the market, suppliers and customers. The effect on customers is no less important than that on suppliers and, indeed, contributes significantly to the uncertainty facing firms investing in innovation activities. Customers also make commitments to a product or service, and this commitment may involve substantial investment of money, staff time and other resources (Nakamura, 2000, pp. 22–23). They must try to select the "winners" in the product race. As Nakamura points out:

> This effect becomes sharper when the number of consumers investing in a given system influences its value for each consumer, for example, the more of your friends who have email, the more useful email is to you (2000, p. 23).

The consequence of these two aspects of the competitive software market is that, while prospective costs can be counted, the anticipated value of creativity is hard to measure:

> Because we learn about the true value of new products only with experience, and because consumers invest in new product systems only over time – and in doing so enhance their

value – it takes a long time to know how valuable any given piece of creativity is (2000, p. 23).

Yet creativity is the pivot on which everything turns. It affects customers, producers and investors. It also impinges on governments attempting to devise policies for nurturing entrepreneurship in the IT software sector.

This understanding of entrepreneurship in the software sector can be summarized using the classification of the nature of entrepreneurship summarised in Table 11. In terms of this classification, the type of entrepreneurship that drives the software industry is best described in terms of the third type. Yet most indigenous software entrepreneurships in Ireland would still fall into the first category, which characterized the first wave of software companies. During the second and third waves, some firms established by indigenous software entrepreneurs reached into the second category and began to anticipate future needs rather than respond to existing gaps in the market. Nevertheless, the truly innovative stage has yet to take hold in Ireland and the question which arises is whether existing strategies for nurturing entrepreneurship can create or effectively support Irish companies.

6. NATURE-NURTURE: STRATEGIC DILEMMA?

A number of implications emerge from, first, the development of the Irish software sector, second the perspectives on the "Celtic Tiger," third, the review of

Table 11.   Market-Based Classification Of Entrepreneurship.

(1) ARBITRAGEURS	• Look for gains from *perceived* price or price-cost differences • Oriented towards *present* • *Information* → Exchange
(2) SPECULATORS	• Look for gains from *expected* (intertemporal) price or price-cost differences • Oriented towards *future* • *Expectations* → Exchange
(3) INNOVATORS	• Look for gains from *creating* intertemporal price or price-cost differences • Oriented towards future • Expectations → *Production Strategies*

Source: Developed from Lachman (1986, pp. 125–126; 1976, p. 131).

supports for the Irish software sector and, finally, the perspective on the process of entrepreneurship in the software industry – in particular seeing the PC market as a paradigm for thinking about elements of the IT sector. Taking the key word from the topic we were given for this conference, these implications could be seen to revolve around what might be termed the "nature-nurture" quandary.

By "nature" we mean the nature of the economic system, that is market competition and, in particular, innovations as both the outcome of the competitive process and as a means by which individual firms seek to compete. By "nurture" we mean the active promotion of entrepreneurship by government through discriminatory measures, in particular fiscal measures such as tax-concessions and subsidies targeted at specific firms or sectors. As we shall see, a number of these implications suggest strategic dilemmas requiring resolution and in some cases may involve outright tradeoffs or even logical contradictions and also politically difficult options.

A generally unrecognised dichotomy in Irish policy thinking is that a government policy focussed on job creation – most effectively through FDI – is not one that will obviously nurture the domestic entrepreneurial process. The buying-in of stages of the production process to "create" jobs – when the entrepreneurship and knowledge work is done elsewhere – is not nurturing entrepreneurship. Nor does current discussion about the need for Ireland to "move up the value chain" represent the change in thinking and better understanding to take that jump. Such discussions reminds one of the psychologist Abraham Maslow's aphorism: if the only tool you have is a hammer, you'll see every problem as a nail.

Furthermore, although the job creation measures to attract FDI have benefited enormously in recent years from the educational policies initially started for quite separate reasons over three decades ago, the entrepreneurship process itself is not one that is a feature of high levels of education in Ireland. In Ireland one can spend most of the first twenty years or so of life in state funded and controlled education prompting the question: how could students find the characteristics and abilities for entrepreneurship of the "Innovator" type? Putting "business appreciation" proper programmes into schools and universities is commendable for creating educated citizens, but these are not evidence-based policies for creating entrepreneurship of the necessary type.

The idea, widely promulgated by government itself at every opportunity, that government is responsible for (i.e. in some – unexplained – sense is to be credited with) job creation is a widespread but seriously flawed perception of business. To say, as many people do in Ireland, that one person's perception or opinion is as good as another's is nonsense when it conflicts with evidence from external reality. The eminent management thinker, Peter Drucker, stated this about business in terms of the testing of opinion against reality (1970, p. 147). Irish evidence suggests that so-called "job creation" measures are not entrepreneurship nurturing policies.

A long time ago Drucker also pointed out that what gets measured gets done (1989, p. 61). In this he was reflecting the propensity to focus effort on what shows up in information and in the information that reaches those "who matter." The role and performance of state agencies who, purportedly, are in the "business" of business promotion are measured by the number of jobs that *they create*. Of course this is public relations stuff. These agencies don't create jobs. Again, as Drucker said, customers create businesses. So those who find the customers "create" the jobs (1979, p. 56; 1989, pp. 34–35). Thus, the dilemma for nurturing entrepreneurship in software is posed by the fact that agencies would have to be held accountable for and measured against ideas. But the political risks involved in committing significant amounts of taxpayer funds to what may appear to the voting public to be ephemeral ventures are too great.

This dilemma is a difficult one to resolve, although it need not be insur- mountable. However, it is compounded by another problem, which arises from the types of competition and entrepreneurship in the software sectors.

To recognize the process of creative destruction poses the most serious dilemma, if not an outright contradiction, about the type of policies pursued in Ireland. The meaning of a competitive process involving "creative destruction" for state agencies is that promoting and supporting investors in a new idea could lead to, and indeed requires, the elimination of an earlier idea currently existing in another firm which had previously been supported with taxpayer funds. It is difficult to envisage an Irish government explaining that to the employees, the local community and the public, especially within range of an election.

Another way of putting it is in terms of Drucker's warning that good decision making for business requires starting with a diversity of views (1970, p. 151). The same would seem to apply to good decision making *about* business, including "nurturing" entrepreneurship and supporting projects in the software sector. It is difficult to see how policies to promote a diversity of ideas and competition among businesses and in the same sector to "manage" creativity to generate new ideas could be operationalized in government measures. If there are any doubts about the implications of this paradigm for formulating administratively-feasible direct interventions to nurture entrepreneurship, some reflection on the origination of ideas will help.[11]

Even in indirect support, through general R & D resourcing, with large amounts of money poured into research, state funded vested interests inevitably win the battle. Thus, to date the R&D expenditure has been given mainly to universities with the emphasis placed on the "R" rather than the "D." This hasn't worked as demonstrated, for example, by the Irish performance measured by the number of U.S. patents compared, for example, to Israel. This is seen as a competitive disadvantage for the Celtic Tiger (Porter, October 2000). The question raised by this issue is whether a country the size of Ireland can afford to fund "R" as an end in itself, i.e. as a base for directly generating "D" opportunities, rather than investing in development with the research drawn from the best all over the world.

These implications at least raise the question (if they do not actually point to the answer) of whether there is a direct role for government in nurturing entrepreneurship in the software sector. This is the hard question arising from competitive process and nature of entrepreneurship in the globalised software market.

7. CONCLUSION

The current strength of the Irish economy is enjoying an unprecedented and lengthy period of growing prosperity. The general climate for business has greatly improved. This includes business start-ups, and the Irish indigenous software sector has been naturally developed in line with these general improvements.

The major driving force in the last few years has been the arrival and expansion of foreign direct investment companies, especially from the U.S. and especially in the IT sector, both hardware and software. This makes the "Celtic Tiger" vulnerable to the U.S. business cycle and stock market performance, worries that didn't exist in Ireland even a year ago. We have to see how that shakes out in the years to come.

Furthermore, the FDI companies have generated little direct or spill-over effects for entrepreneurship in software, and effectively neither Irish venture capitalism nor government job creation policies have added value in that regard.

The requirement for continuous and rapid innovation, with destruction as well as creation at the heart of the competitive process, implies that it is ideas, not information, which need to be measured in designing state policies for promoting entrepreneurship in the Information Technology sector.

The dilemma for government seeking to nurture entrepreneurship in software, and also IT hardware, is that it cannot, it would seem, be involved or be seen to be involved in the competitive process. It must appear to be "neutral." But neutral means neither going forward or (perhaps) backward, and software is not a business where anyone can stay in the one place.

Therefore, the questions facing Ireland, at least in so far as entrepreneurship in the software sector is concerned, are: whether a government can nurture entrepreneurship; whether it should try to nurture entrepreneurship; what "nurturing" would mean in practice in Ireland in today's competitive and glob-alized environment; or whether it should pursue its objectives more obliquely by removing obstacles and letting entrepreneurship flourish. The latter requires: trust in the people; the right moral, legal and financial framework; and, overall, doing more while governing less, i.e. it requires leadership, not administration.

The subtitle of the conference is "success," which we have reviewed; "problems," which we have identified; and "prospects," which is the hardest part of the task assigned by the organizers. In summary, we suggest from the foregoing arguments that the prospects for Ireland in IT software depend, *first*, on how positive the environment remains for entrepreneurship in general and, *second*, how fast government can take on board the practical implications of the nature of the competitive process in software when deciding goals and, designing policies.

The point we are making in conclusion can be put another way. Depending on how one views the world, one may see things differently. If the starting position is a belief that "government manages (i.e. controls) the economy," then it will seem reasonable and even natural that government can intervene directly to "nurture" entrepreneurship. If, in contrast, the starting position is a belief that "the future is inherently unknowable and uncertain," then it will follow that implica-tions drawn from the alternative position is fundamentally problematic. The first position has long characterized government industrial development policies and measures in Ireland. There is little sign yet that policy thinking in the basis of this position is sufficiently tested against the implications of the second position. To work out effective policies for nurturing indigenous entrepreneurship in IT software would seem to require asking different questions, re-balancing the terms of the debate, and learning to use other perspectives.

NOTES

1. A very useful account from a historical perspective which touches on some of the issues in this debate is given by Fitzgerald, (1999). Another useful account, using Porter's "Diamond Model of National Competitiveness" to organize their analysis, is by Doyle, Gallagher and O'Leary (2000).

A historical sense of Irish economic development can be acquired from a sequence of reading from the following writers: O'Grada (1994) covers well the long background from 1780–1939; Kennedy's books (1971, 1975, 1988), as well as many articles, provide a thoughtful and balanced perspective on the twentieth century experience. These can be supplemented by the useful "snapshot" of the structure of the economy at the edge of modernization in the 1960s by O'Mahony (1964, 1967); the much-underestimated review by Meenan (1970) of thinking, issues and policies from independence in 1922 to the 1960s; and for comparative analysis papers by Bradley (for example, 1995 and 2000) are helpful. The series edited by O'Hagan (1st ed. 1975 and subsequent editions) provides a convenient tracking of current descriptions and analyses of the main aspects and issues of the economy as it changed in the last quarter of the twentieth century.

2. It is cautionary to reflect on the obvious expansion in the sale and production of "old fashioned" products, for example, candles of all sorts – aromatherapy, religious, decorative, celebratory, etc. – in recent years to remind oneself that there are ultimately no "old sectors," only strong and weak companies that are cautious against thinking about policy in terms of the causally imprecise classification of sectors.

3. Previously Irish governments used the state-owned companies in, e.g. energy, telecommunications and transport, to "create" jobs, i.e. to use their monopoly positions to carry over-manning, with the cost shifted to customers and other businesses either through prices or taxation to fund subsidies.

4. Recall the old adage: "Nobody ever got fired for hiring IBM"; the culture of the Irish public service is that mistakes are not tolerated.

5. This outline is based on Schumpeter, 1954, Ch. 7. This chapter is a compact statement of the vision of market competition and the resulting process of innovation outlined by Schumpeter in *Business Cycles*, 1939, Chapter 3/B.

6. This idea is represented in contemporary analysis by the concept and terminology of "contestable markets" (Baumol, Panzar & Willig, 1988) which has had a significant impact in policy thinking about regulation in recent years.

7. The terminology is unsatisfactory. Kay tried calling such returns "added value" (1993, pp. 19–30; 1996, 192–218) arguing that they are the best performance measure of corporate success, before conceding and returning to "economic rents" (2000, pp. 7–8).

8. There is also the effect of "initiative innovation," i.e. copying, which can limit the potential for exploiting new ideas and for earning economic rents from investing in new ideas.

9. A "paradigm" in the sense of Kuhn (1996, pp. 10, 187; 2000, p. 168): exemplar, practice, model, standard examples.

10. Based on Nakamura (2000, p. 21) from which the quoted phases are taken.

11. Hannah Arendt, the philosopher/political scientist, among others emphasizes that a "characteristic of human action is that it always begins something new" (1973, p. 10). Her theory of "natality" or "beginning" is founded on the insight that human plurality implies that each life is a new beginning, in recognizing the possibility of new beginnings, in understanding that people can always make a choice, and in the belief that human action can change the world. (1955, 1958, 1963). This position on the origination of ideas and the role of imagination in business is most closely shared by the economist George Shackle (for example, 1986).

The difficulty for directly interventionist policy design is increased by the inevitability, (and social necessity) of divergent, expectations which is emphasized by Lachman (for example, in 1977, p. 187). Public policy geared to "picking winners" is implicitly based on assuming convergent expectations. Two comments, one from Von Mises and the second from Loasby, which re-inforce each other, serve to convey the points about the link between entrepreneurship and uncertainty and suggest the difficulties uncertainty poses for nurturing entrepreneurship:

That man acts and that the future is uncertain are by no means independent matters. They are only two different modes of establishing one thing (Mises, 1963, p. 104).

To be genuine, choice must be neither random nor predetermined ... If knowledge is perfect, and the logic of choice complete and compelling, then choice disappears; nothing is left but stimulus and response ... If choice is real, the future cannot be certain; if the future is certain there can be no choice (Loasby, 1976, p. 5).

Furthermore, the difficulty of breaking a "monopoly mindset" was also noted by Druker (1993, p. xii). The Irish economy is still heavily monopolized and cartelized, with state owned organizations controlling key sectors. The "privatization" agenda – the form in Ireland for attempts to de-monopolize and commercialize these sectors – would seem to be stalling again.

REFERENCES

Aghion, P., & Howitt, P. (1992). A model of growth through creative destruction. *Econometrica*, *60*(2), 323–351.

Arendt, H. (1973). Lying in politics: reflections on the Pentagon papers. In: *Crises in the Republic*. Harmondsworth: Penguin Books.

Arendt, H. (1955). *Men in Dark Times*. New York: Harcourt Brace.

Arendt, H. (1977[1963]). *Eichman in Jerusalem*. Harmondsworth: Penguin Books.

Arendt, H. (1998[1958]). *The Human Condition* (2nd ed., with Introduction by M. Canovan). Chicago: University of Chicago Press.

Arora, A., Gambardella, A., & Salvorte, T. (2000). International outsourcing and emergence of industrial clusters: the software industry in Ireland and India. Paper for the Silicon Valley and Its Imitators Meeting. Stanford University.

Baumol, W. J., Panzar, J. C., & Willig, R. D. (1988). *Contestable Markets and the Theory of Industry Structure* (revised ed.). Jovanovich, San Diego, CA: Harcourt Brace.

Bradley, J. (1995). Economic aspects of Ireland: an overview of the two economies. In: J. Bradley (Ed.), *The Two Economies of Ireland: Public Policy, Growth and Employment* (pp. 7–34). Dublin: Oak Tree Press.

Bradley, J. (2000). The Irish economy in a comparative perspective. In: B. Nolan, P. O'Connell & C. T. Wheland (Eds), *Bust to Boom? The Irish Experience of Growth and Inequality* (pp. 4–26). Dublin: Institute of Public Administration.

Cullinane Group (1997). *Israel: A Model for Indigenous High-Tech Development in Ireland*. Dublin: The Cullinane Group.

Doyle, E., Gallagher, L., & O'Leary, E. (2000). The Celtic Tiger: the 51st state in Europe. Working Paper Series: No. 01-01. Department of Economics, University College, Cork.

Drucker, P. (1970[1967]). *The Effective Executive*. London: Pan Books.

Drucker, P. (1979). *Management*. London: Pan Books.

Drucker, P. (1989[1955]). *The Practice of Management*. Oxford: Butterworth Heinemann.

Drucker, P. (1993). Introduction to the transaction edition. In: *The Concept of the Corporation* (pp. ix–xii). New Bunswick: Transaction.

Fitzgerald, J. (1999). Understanding Ireland's economic success. Working Paper Series: No. 111. ESRI, Dublin.

Fitzgerald, J. (2000). The story of Ireland's failure – and belated success. In: B. Nolan, P. O'Connell & C. Whelan (Ed.), *Bust to Boom? The Irish Experience of Growth and Inequality* (pp. 27–57). Dublin: Institute of Public Administration.

Grossman, G. M., & Helpman, E. (1991). Quality ladders in the theory of growth. *Review of Economic Studies, 58*, 43–61.

Ireland (1995). *Report of the Science, Technology and Innovation Advisory Council.* Dublin: Stationery Office.

Ireland (1993). *Making Knowledge Work for Us: A Strategic View.* Dublin: Stationery Office.

Kay, J. (1993). Foundations of Corporate Success: How Business Strategies Add Value. Oxford University Press, Oxford.

Kay, J. (1996). *The Business of Economics.* Oxford: Oxford University Press.

Kay, J. (2000). Strategy and the delusion of grand designs. In: *Financial Times*, Mastering Strategy: The Complete MBA Companion in Strategy (pp. 5–10). Harlow: Pearson Education.

Kennedy, K. (1971). *Productivity and Industrial Growth: The Irish Experience.* Oxford: Clarendon Press.

Kennedy, K., & Dowling, B. (1975). *Economic Growth in Ireland: The Experience since 1947.* Dublin: Gill and Macmillan.

Kennedy, K., Giblin, T., & McHugh, D. (1988). *The Economic Development of Ireland in the Twentieth Century.* London: Routledge.

Kuhn, T. (1996[1962]). *The Structure of Scientific Revolutions* (3rd ed.). Chicago: University of Chicago Press.

Kuhn, T. (2000). *The road since structure: philosophical essays, 1970–1993* (with an auto-biographical interview). J. Conant & J. Haugeland (Eds). Chicago: University of Chicago Press.

Lachman, L. (1976). On the central concept of Austrian economics: market process. In: E. G. Dolan (Ed.), *The Foundations of Modern Austrian Economics* (pp. 126–132). Kansas City: Sheed and Ward.

Lachman, L. (1977). *Capital, Expectations, and the Market Process.* Kansas City: Sheed and McNeel.

Lachman, L. (1986). *The Market as an Economic Process.* Oxford: Basil Blackwell.

Loasby, B. J. (1976). *Choice, Complexity and Ignorance: An Inquiry into Economic Theory and the Practice of Decision Making.* Cambridge: Cambridge University Press.

Lucas, R. E., Jr. (1988). On the mechanics of economic development. *Journal of Monetary Economics, 22*, 3–42.

McAleese, D. (Forthcoming). *The Celtic Tiger: Origins and Prospects.*

Meenan, J. (1970). *The Irish Economy Since 1922.* Liverpool: Liverpool University Press.

Murphy, B. (1998). The next wave of software companies. Presentation at University College, Cork, Ireland.

Nakamura, L. I. (2000). Economics and the new economy: the invisible hand meets creative destruction. *Federal Reserve Bank of Philadelphia Business Review*, 15–30.

National Software Directorate (1999). Strategic Development of Internationally Traded Service Industries Throughout Ireland. National Software Directorate, Dublin.

OECD (1999). Main Science and Technology Indicators. Paris.

O'Gorman, C., O'Malley & Mooney, J. (1997). Clusters in Ireland: the Irish indigenous software industry: an application of Porters cluster analysis. National Economic and Social Council Research Series Paper No. 3. Government Publications Office, Dublin.

O'Grada, C. (1994). *Ireland: A New Economic History 1780–1939.* Oxford: Clarendon Press.

O'Hagan, J. W. (Ed.) (2000). *The Economy of Ireland.* First published as *The Economy of Ireland: Policy and Performance* (1st ed., 1975). Dublin: Irish Management Institute. (6th ed., 1991) *The Economy of Ireland: Policy and Performance of a Small European Country.* (7th ed., 1995) Dublin: Gill and Macmillan.. *The Economy of Ireland: Policy and Performance of a European Region* (8th ed.). Dublin: Gill and Macmillan.

O'Mahony, D. (1967[1964]). The Irish Economy: An Introductory Description (revised ed.). Cork: Cork University Press.

Porter, M. E. (1980). *Competitive Strategy: Techniques for Analyzing Industries and Competitors.* New York: The Free Press.

Porter, M. E. (1985). *Competitive Advantage: Creating and Sustaining Superior Performance.* New York: The Free Press.

Porter, M. E. (1998). *On Competition.* Boston: Harvard Business School Press.

Porter, M. E. (1990). *The Competitive Advantage of Nations.* London: MacMillan.

Porter, M. E., Takeuchi, H., & Sakakibara, M. (2000). *Can Japan Compete?* London: MacMillan.

PriceWaterhouseCoopers (1999). *Strategic Development of Internationally Traded Service Industries Throughout Ireland.* Dublin: National Software Directorate.

Romer, P. M. (1986). Increasing returns and long-run growth. *Journal of Political Economy, 94,* 1002–1037.

Romer, P. M. (1990). Endogenous technologies change. *Journal of Political Economy, 98,* S71–S102.

Schumpeter, J. A. (1934). *The Theory of Economic Development: An Inquiry into Profits, Capital, Credit, Interest, and the Business-Cycle.* (German ed., 1911). R. Opie (Trans.). Oxford: Oxford University Press.

Schumpeter, J. A. (1967). *Economic Doctrine and Method: An Historical Sketch* (German ed., 1912. English ed., 1954). Oxford: Oxford University Press.

Schumpeter, J. A. (1939). *Business Cycles: A Theoretical, Historical, and Statistical Analysis of the Capitalist Process.* NY: McGraw-Hill.

Schumpeter, J. A. (1991). The creative response in economic history. Originally in *Journal of Economic History,* 149–159, November 1947. Republished 1951, in: R. V. Clemence (Ed.), *Essays of J. A. Schumpeter* (pp. 216–226). Cambridge, Mass: Addison-Wesley. Also published, and as part of, Comments on a Plan for a Study of Entrepreneurship.In: R. Swedberg & J. A Schumpeter (Eds), *The Economics and Sociology of Capitalism* (pp. 406–428). Princeton: Princeton University Press.

Schumpeter, J. A. (1954[1943]). *Capitalism, Socialism and Democracy* (4th ed.). London: Unwin University Books.

Venture Capital Association of Ireland (2000). *Report on Venture Capital Investment Activity 1999.* Dublin: Matheson, Ormsby Prentice.

Von Mises, L. (1963[1949]). *Human Action: A Treatise on Economics* (3rd revised ed.). Chicago: Henry Regnery.

(Ireland, EMU)

5. MONETARY AND FISCAL POLICY IN EMU

Rodney Thom

E52 E62
F36 F31

1. INTRODUCTION

The euro has radically altered the rules governing macroeconomic policy in the participating countries. Since January 1999 control over interest rates has passed to the European Central Bank (ECB) and the Stability and Growth Pact imposes constraints on national fiscal policy. Central banks can no longer set interest rate levels which may be best suited to the needs of their domestic economies and are denied the ability to manipulate the external value of their currencies to correct for threats to either competitiveness or inflation. Rather, they must accept the one-size-fits-all policy as dictated by the ECB. Likewise, the Stability and Growth Pact limits government deficits to 3% of Gross Domestic Product, which in practice implies that countries should run at least a balanced budget over the normal course of the business cycle. In short, the complete loss of monetary independence and the limitations on fiscal policy imply that national policy makers are now constrained in their ability to use the traditional instruments of macroeconomic policy when faced with short-run stabilization problems such as a rise in unemployment or a sudden surge in inflation.

The challenges imposed by these new constraints may be more significant for Ireland than for other participating economies. First, as a substantial proportion of trade is with non-euro economies, Ireland is particularly exposed to changes in the external value of the euro. Currently about 57% of exports and 78% of imports are with non-euro area countries, which in the aggregate account

The Irish Economy in Transition: Successes, Problems, and Prospects, Volume 85, pages 85–105.

for approximately 65% of total Irish trade.[1] Second, heavy reliance on American multinationals as a source of foreign direct investment (FDI) has increased Ireland's exposure to cyclical variations in the U.S. and, by implication, the world economy. In short, because the Irish business cycle is not synchronised with the core economies, the one-size-fits-all monetary policy imposed by the ECB may be inappropriate to deal with Irish stabilisation problems. Third, the structure of the Irish centralised wage bargaining process, or social partnership, puts an additional constraint on discretionary fiscal policy by requiring government to pre-commit, or trade off, income tax reductions for wage moderation. All of these have been features of the Irish economy in recent years. Starting from almost full employment in 1999–2000, the combination of a weak euro and relatively low interest rates increased the demand for Irish output leading to labour shortages and inflationary pressures. Unambiguously this situation required higher interest rates and a stronger currency. However, the ECB sets interest rates to achieve a target inflation rate for the euro area and, despite several dramatic interventions in 2000, has, by and large, followed a policy of benign neglect towards euro exchange rates. Also, the current social partnership agreement, known as the Program for Prosperity and Fairness or PPF, added a further stimulus to demand by committing government to tax reductions in the December 2000 budget. More recently, the U.S. downturn and the events of September 11, 2001 have slowed the growth of world trade leading to a number of downsizings by multinationals located in Ireland.

This chapter discusses ways in which Ireland can face up to these challenges. The following section outlines the current state of the Irish economy and suggests that from a macro perspective the important issues are excessive growth and an inflation rate that is currently above the euro area average. Section 3 discusses adjustment in a small overheated euro area economy and argues that wage and price inflation should be viewed as part of the solution rather than the problem. Section 4 considers the role of fiscal policy. The final section addresses the issue of the euro participation and its implications for stabilisation policy.

2. THE IRISH MACRO ECONOMY

By any standards the Irish economy has experienced a remarkable transformation since the late 1980s. Between 1960 and 1990 Irish GDP was at best only 70% of the EU average. However, during the 1990s GDP doubled in size leading to full catch-up with the rest of Europe. At the same time the unemployment rate declined from a high of 17% in 1987 to 4% in 2000. To a large extent these trends reflect a convergence process driven by FDI-induced productivity gains and increases in labour force size via immigration and female participation rates.[2] In the absence of external shocks, adjustment problems and stabilisation issues only arise when the actual growth rate differs from the sustainable rate – that is, when demand for the economy's output differs from its ability to supply. This difference is commonly referred to as the output gap, defined as the percentage deviation of actual from trend growth.[3] The Department of Finance (2001) estimates that the output gap increased from 0.5% in 1998 to 4.5% in 2000 indicating that the Irish economy was operating above its long-run sustainable growth path. As a consequence, the economy also experienced an inflation rate greater than that in the euro area as a whole.[4] In 1998 Irish inflation was 0.9% above the euro area average. In 1999 this divergence increased to 1.4% and then accelerated to 3.3% in 2000.

There are at least two reasons why a positive output gap and associated inflationary pressures emerged in the late 1990s. The first relates to competitiveness and is discussed in detail in the next section. The second is mostly down to euro participation and lax fiscal policy. Since the euro's launch in January 1999, high Irish equilibrium growth has been reinforced by a series of demand shocks emanating from low interest rates, an undervalued currency and lax budgetary policy. Although the ECB increased euro interest rates over 2000, Irish rates are below pre-euro levels and also below the levels which would probably pertain if Ireland were outside the euro-system. More importantly, Fig. 1 documents the dramatic depreciation in the effective Irish pound nominal exchange rate since the euro was launched in January 1999. It should be noted that while a euro depreciation affects all participating economies, the impact is highly asymmetric with respect to Ireland. This point is emphasised by recent Bank of England (2000) estimates of the two-year impact of a 10% euro depreciation. For Germany, inflation rises by 0.4% in year one and by 1.1% in year two. The impact on French inflation is similar (0.6 and 1.6%), but the Irish estimates are 1.8% in the first year and 4.5% in the second year. The stance of fiscal policy is more ambiguous and, given the recent controversy between the Irish Government and the European Commission, more controversial. However, two Irish Central Bank economists, Cronin and Scally (2000), have recently produced estimates for the structural budget balance, the correct indicator of the strength and direction of fiscal policy. They conclude that the evidence suggests, "a significant loosening of fiscal policy." Hence, an economy very close to full employment and growing at a rate well above the OECD and European averages was required to accommodate a large stimulus to aggregate demand from both external and internal sources. The result was that high but sustainable growth turned into an inflationary boom presenting Ireland with an adjustment problem but zero ability to take the first best policy actions – higher interest rates and a stronger currency.

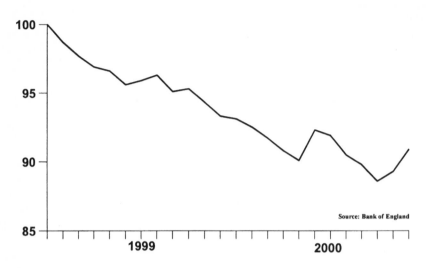

January 1999 = 100

Fig. 1.   Nominal Effective Exchange Rate.

It is clear, and commonly agreed, that the current situation cannot be sustained in the medium term. This does not necessarily imply a dramatic slow-down or that the Irish economy must move into recession. It simply implies that the actual growth rate must converge to the sustainable long-run path, which over the medium term could be as high as 4% to 5% per annum. The key issue is not a slowdown in the growth rate. Rather, it is whether convergence will be characterised by a "hard" or "soft" landing and whether macroeconomic policy can play a role in smoothing the adjustment process. Although economists frequently use the terms "hard" and "soft" landings they are rarely defined in any precise way. This paper uses the following simple but plausible distinction. A soft landing is an adjustment process whereby the actual growth rate converges to, but does not breach, the sustainable or trend level. Conversely, a hard landing is an adjustment in which the growth rate temporarily falls below the sustainable path before convergence is achieved. The issue which the rest of this paper addresses is the role of macroeconomic policy in ensuring a soft rather than a hard landing for the Irish economy. It should be noted that the U.S. recession, the slowdown in world trade and the events of September 11, 2001, all militate against the probability of a soft landing. However, these events are all outside the control of the Irish authorities. What is at issue is the ability of policy makers to cushion the effects of these external shocks on the domestic economy.

3. ADJUSTMENT IN A SMALL EURO-ECONOMY

Prior to mid-2001 when most economists finally accepted that the U.S. slow-down would have a significant impact on the European economy, debate on Irish macroeconomic policy had focused on excess inflation and the government's ability to deal with it. In particular, the success of social partnership requires that actual inflation does not exceed expected inflation and that anticipated increases in real wages are actually realised. Unfortunately the rise in inflation from under 2% to more than 5% in 2000 was unanticipated when the PPF was agreed. Hence, average real wages fell below what was promised, leading to uncertainty, industrial unrest, and eventual renegotiation of the wage package by government, employers, and labour unions. To a large extent discussions surrounding renegotiation of the PPF and the implied relationship between inflation and economic growth reflected confusion about two key issues. The first concerns perceived differences between the underlying causes of infla-tion and the arithmetic by which the Consumer Price Index (CPI) is calculated. The second relates to inflation and competitiveness.

The first area of confusion is best illustrated by attitudes towards interest rate changes and their effect of housing costs. The Irish CPI uses a payments approach to measuring the costs of home ownership with mortgage interest accounting for approximately 4% of the total basket. Hence, when the ECB increases interest rates, as it did throughout 2000, the CPI automatically increases and government and media interpret this as inflationary. While it is correct that higher interest rates must, other things equal, lead to a once-off rise in the price index, they also reduce discretionary incomes leading to a revi-sion of household expenditure patterns and lower inflationary expectations. That is, higher interest rates should be considered as anti-inflationary which is, of course, exactly the reason why the ECB decides to raise them in the first place. Unfortunately, this confusion is reflected in the government's "Anti-Inflation Package" as outlined in the Minister's December 2000 Budget Statement.[5] In essence this package consists of reductions in indirect tax rates including the valued added tax and excise taxes on fuel. As with a change in interest rates, cuts in consumption taxes will have a once-off impact on the CPI but other things being equal will also fuel demand leading to higher inflation in the future. Hence while the ECB combats euro area inflation with higher interest rates, the Irish government attempts to offset the impact on the Irish CPI by reducing consumption taxes.

More fundamentally, this approach reflects an additional confusion between inflation and competitiveness. Unambiguously the Irish government along with the media and many economic commentators interpret both wage and price inflation as a loss of competitiveness, a threat to prosperity and something to be avoided at all costs. However, an alternative and more rational approach sees excess inflation as part of the adjustment process and a key mechanism in ensuring a soft-landing for the Irish economy. Apart from demand shocks, there are at least two reasons why Irish inflation might have accelerated in recent years. First, labour is not perfectly mobile within the European Union or between the Union and other countries. Hence, as the economy moves closer to full employment, aggregate supply becomes more inelastic, and rising real disposable incomes feed into aggregate demand leading to an increase in the average level of prices. This is the frequently cited "Massachusetts" or "Northern California" effect. That is, if a large integrated economic area such as the United States or the European Union experiences significant disparities in regional growth rates, then, with less-than-perfect labour mobility, we would expect to see changes in relative prices with average price levels in the faster growing regions increasing relative to those in the more depressed regions.

Second, the Balassa-Samuelson effect predicts a real appreciation or loss of competitiveness as an equilibrium phenomenon. Consider an economy which produces two types of goods, tradable and non-tradable. The first is typically represented by manufacturing and the second by services. Now suppose that productivity growth is higher in the former, leading to increases in both nominal and real wages in tradable industries. In the Irish case this disparity in productivity rates is normally explained by relatively large inflows of FDI into manufacturing and export-orientated sectors. However, if non-inflationary wage increases in the tradable sector spill over into the less dynamic non-traded sector, then prices in the latter will rise at a rate faster than that which would be justified by productivity gains. That is, for a given nominal exchange rate the economy will, relative to its trading partners, experience inflation and a real appreciation.[6] There is nothing inherently damaging in this. It is simply part of the adjustment process or, in an Irish context, a consequence of living standards catching up with those of our more prosperous partners.

Two points are important here. First, available estimates suggest that the Balassa-Samuelson effect accounts for at most one to one and a half percentage points of the difference between Irish and euro area inflation. In its Summer 2000 *Quarterly Bulletin*, the Irish Central Bank estimated that the three percentage point gap between underlying Irish inflation and average euro area inflation, which then existed, could be decomposed as follows: 0.5% was due to Ireland's greater exposure to non-euro imports; 1% was due to higher Irish traded-sector productivity growth or the Balassa-Samuelson effect discussed above; the remaining 1.5% was "mainly attributable to cyclical considerations. This essentially reflects strong domestic demand conditions" (p. 27). In addition

Blanchard (2001), using upper bound figures for productivity growth, estimates that at most 1.5% of Ireland's excess inflation can be attributed to the Balassa-Samuelson effect. Second, Balassa-Samuelson assumes that wages in the traded sector keep pace with productivity growth. In the case of Ireland this is unambiguously not the case. Figure 2 uses the index of relative unit labour costs to provide a picture of competitiveness in Irish manufacturing from 1990 to 1999. This index is measured in a common currency and depicts competitive gains relative to Ireland's trading partners. Changes in the index reflect three factors – increases in nominal wages, productivity gains, and changes in the nominal exchange rate. Given the latter, the index would be relatively constant if wage increases reflected productivity growth. However, this is obviously not the case. Over the decade the index falls by almost 50%. Between 1994 and 1998, or between the 10% devaluation of the Irish pound in 1993 and euro participation, the decline is approximately 30%.

As shown in Walsh (1999) productivity gains resulting from FDI inflows have "not been captured by workers through higher wages" but have resulted in a "rapid growth in employment combined with low wage inflation." Starting from the high unemployment of the 1980s, this effect was unambiguously beneficial. At that point the problem was low productivity and unemployment.

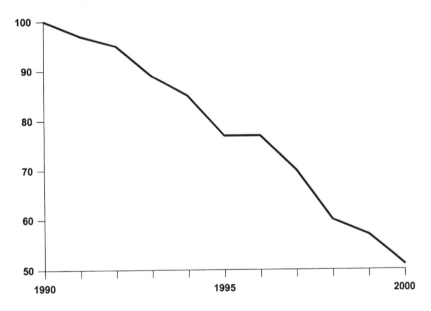

Fig. 2. Relative Unit Labour Costs (IR£).

However, by 2000, Ireland was at full, or even over-full, employment, and additional competitive gains were more likely to result in an excess demand for labour leading to overheating, bottlenecks and intensified inflationary pressures rather than in ever-increasing employment. In this situation the correct approach is surely to eliminate excess demand by permitting wages to rise. Despite this, the official view appears to be that high growth can be maintained by recruiting additional workers from overseas and by providing tax incentives to encourage higher labour force participation. However, as argued in Durkan (1999) the latter can only succeed at the cost of reducing participation in third level education, which is detrimental to future growth, and the former can only lead to greater stresses on public infrastructure and a housing market which is already experiencing significant excess demand. In addition, we cannot rule out the possibility that capacity constraints and an over congested economy could at some point reduce the attractiveness of Ireland as a profitable location for FDI.

In terms of its ability to accommodate further increases in the labour force, the Irish economy at the end of 2000 was at full capacity with additional expansion more likely to exacerbate congestion and infra-structural problems rather than to maintain economic growth and employment above that which is sustainable in the longer run. Hence, rather than continuing to secure further competitive gains, the optimum strategy is to bring domestic costs into line with those in competitor economies: that is, adjustment to the sustainable growth path via higher wages and reduced competitiveness. Once this happens and in the absence of external shocks, Ireland can still maintain a relatively high growth rate providing, productivity that does not decline and that subsequent wage increases are consistent with maintaining full employment. Indeed, to a large extent adjustment through higher wages simply implies a higher real living standard which is after all supposed to be the reason why we want economic growth in the first place. Or, as a friend once put it in casual conservation: those who argue for continued pay restraint as a means of securing further competitive gains are like Japanese soldiers still guarding their posts on remote Pacific islands twenty odd years after WWII had ended. Whereas the soldiers needed to be told that the war was over and that they could return home to enjoy the peace, some Irish commentators need to be told that the "unemployment war" has been won and economic growth must now be realised in terms of higher living standards rather than in ever-increasing employment. Given the absence of adverse shocks, this relatively benign scenario implies a soft landing for Ireland's overheated economy. The mechanism involved (a gradual loss of competitiveness) would presumably not be welcome in official circles and by those who hope for a further decade of extremely high growth rates; but common sense and historical experience tell us that a growth slowdown will occur regardless, implying that such a loss of competitiveness is, in fact, inevitable.

While this argument has considerable merit, it may be a mistake to be excessively sanguine about adjustment via wage and price inflation. First, there are the standard costs of inflation. These costs include the blurring of the information conveyed by the price system and arbitrary redistributive effects. People on fixed incomes lose and savers are penalised while borrowers gain. This effect is potentially more severe than in an independent monetary regime, since outside the euro a rise in inflation would lead to higher nominal interest rates. However, with interest rates fixed in Frankfurt, higher inflation lowers real interest rates, giving an additional stimulus to borrowing and consumption.

Second, there can be no guarantee that wages will rise only to the point at which the loss of competitiveness is just sufficient to choke off the excess demand for labour. Prolonged inflation can feed into the wage setting process by raising inflationary expectations and lead to real wages in excess of those consistent with full employment. That is, overshooting of the real wage and the real exchange rate may be a distinct possibility. Third, there is always the possibility of an adverse shock occurring at some time in the future. For example, a strong euro depreciation against the dollar and sterling has a disproportionate effect on Irish inflation, leading to higher inflationary expectations and increasing the chances of overshooting the real wage levels mandated by sustainable full employment growth. Conversely, a euro appreciation or a serious U.S. recession could erode competitiveness to the point at which unemployment becomes an issue and real depreciation rather than appreciation is required to stabilise the economy. In a monetary union, such depreciation would have to come about through lower-than-average Irish inflation rates. However, if inflation has gathered sufficient momentum and is still ongoing when such a shock hits, then competitiveness might well move in the wrong direction for some time, increasing the adjustment ultimately required and exacerbating Ireland's stabilisation problems.

To summarise, higher wages and an erosion of competitiveness are a necessary part of the adjustment process. But, as argued above, there is a potential downside related to the costs of inflation, possible overshooting and adverse shocks. Indeed, in the December 2000 Update for Ireland's Stability Programme, these dangers are recognised by the Department of Finance:

> Even in the absence of an external shock, the rapid pace of growth requires vigilance . . . Ireland's real exchange rate is appreciating and will continue to do so until equilibrium wage rates consistent with sustainable growth are reached . . . [however] . . . tightness in the labour market creates a risk that the economy could overshoot this equilibrium rate – significantly if that tightness was exploited to pursue excessive expectations. The ensuing

loss of competitiveness would damage economic and employment growth, push up unemployment and undermine capacity for further social progress. That is why reaffirmation of
the PPF is so important (Page E.14).

Can this downside risk be reduced by conventional macroeconomic policies?
Without doubt the ability to raise interest rates and let the currency
appreciate would have been the best option in 2000. Higher interest rates and
a stronger currency could have a dramatic effect on inflationary expectations,
lower the probability of overshooting, and permit the authorities greater
flexibility in engineering a soft landing. To our detriment, membership of the
euro precludes this option, but it does not imply that government is powerless.
Indeed, the standard textbook Mundell-Fleming model tells us that with
irrevocably fixed exchange rates fiscal policy can be an effective stabilisation
instrument.

4. FISCAL POLICY

Fiscal policy is a means by which government can attempt to stabilise the level
of economic activity around the sustainable or full-employment level. Other
things being equal we would reasonably expect fiscal policy to be counter-
cyclical. That is, fiscal tightening would occur when the economy is overheating
and fiscal loosening during recession. However, Leddin and Walsh (1998) show
that fiscal policy in the 1990s has been pro-cyclical rather than counter-cyclical.
More recent estimates of the structural, or cyclically adjusted, government deficit
reach much the same conclusion. In addition to the Central Bank study
mentioned above, the Economic and Social Research Institute (2000) considered
eight alternative measures of the direction of fiscal policy and found that five
suggested that the 2000 budget was expansionary. This view has also been
expressed by the European Commission which has also censored the Irish
government for what it considers to be an over-expansionary 2001 budget.
Finally, the Department of Finance (2001) estimates that the cyclically adjusted
budget balance will deteriorate by –0.7% in 2001 and by –0.2% in 2002. In
short, Irish fiscal policy continues to be pro-cyclical.

   This apparent fiscal laxity stems from commitments under the PPF and from
the previously mentioned confusion surrounding the fundamental causes of inflation and the calculation of the CPI. Under the social partnership process, of
which the PPF is the latest instalment, successive Irish governments have pre-
committed to income tax reductions in order to secure industrial peace and
wage moderation. In addition, and as explicitly stated in the 2001 Budget
Statement and in the Updated Stability Programme, this policy is also aimed
at increasing labour force participation.[7] Regardless of whether these incentives

are effective in encouraging greater participation, the overall budgetary strategy is unbalanced in that the government has chosen to reduce taxation per se rather than to shift the burden from direct to indirect taxation. In particular, the government has been reluctant to offset income tax reductions with higher excise duties on tobacco, alcohol, and gasoline. As such tax increases would result in a once-off increase in the CPI, the social partners view them as inflationary. Indeed, the government's response to the inflationary surge in 2000 was to reduce value added tax (Europe's equivalent to sales tax) from 21% to 20% and to cut the excise duty on auto-diesel by 6%.[8]

Taken at face value this fiscal laxity appears irresponsible. Given that the economy was at full, or even over-full, employment, tax reductions can only stimulate demand, further leading to intensified inflationary pressures. If anything, the balance of evidence appeared to be on the side of fiscal contraction and tax increases. This, of course, runs counter to the view that domestic policy is irrelevant in a small open economy (SOE) because purchasing power parity (PPP) dictates that the price level and its rate of change are externally determined. This is, at best, a naive view of the world. All the evidence we have suggests that while PPP *may* hold in the long run, it *only* holds in the long run. A more realistic version of the model recognizes that even SOEs have substantial non-traded sectors, and that non-traded prices are determined by domestic supply and demand. Also, where Irish and European industries are characterised by monopolistic rather than perfect competition, traded products may be differentiated implying that producers, even if they are located in very small economies, may have some market power. In what is generally considered the leading text in international macroeconomics, Obstfeld and Rogoff (1996) go so far as to suggest that "the law of one price fails dramatically in practice, even for products that commonly enter international trade." Also, despite a high propensity to import, participation in the euro actually enhances the effectiveness of fiscal policy because it cannot be offset by pro-cyclical movements in either interest or exchange rates. Hence, over those time horizons relevant to politicians and other social partners, fiscal policy can be an effective stabilisation instrument. Therefore, we cannot simply brush off the possibility that by adding a stimulus to aggregate demand an overly lax policy has contributed to inflationary pressures in Ireland. By the same argument fiscal contraction can ease inflationary pressures.

However, there is also a potential downside to active counter-cyclical fiscal policy. First, the well-documented decision and implementation lags imply that fiscal policy is, at best, a relatively blunt stabilisation instrument. Second, in a high growth environment political realities suggest that fiscal contraction may be a non-starter. Put simply, tax increases at a time when the economy is booming and revenues are buoyant are impossibly hard to sell to the electorate. Again, interest rate increases and a strong Irish pound would be more palatable and effective, but they are, unfortunately, excluded by euro membership. Third, it is plausible to argue that tax increases or even reneging on promised tax cuts could destroy Ireland's social partnership arrangements, which are commonly credited with having played an important role in the Irish growth miracle of the 1990s, just as they were important in the European growth miracle of the 1950s and 1960s.[9] Fourth, if the efficacy of tax increases is dubious, the scope for expenditure reductions is equally limited. As with tax increases any failure to deliver on public sector pay could have the same political implications and the same consequences for social partnership. Also, excess demand for labour is now evident in the public as well as the private sector, leaving little scope for cutbacks in numbers employed. Likewise, downsizing major public sector infra-structural projects such as Dublin's proposed metro system may be attractive from a demand management point of view, but would also involve a supply-side cost by intensifying congestion, housing problems and transportation bottlenecks. Not only can congestion, etc. lead to higher inflation, but as argued by McHale (2000), "The problem of congestion ... has, like excessive wage increases, the potential to undermine Ireland's competitive edge in attracting overseas investment, not to mention the deleterious effects on the quality of life." Hence, while it may be useful to defer unproductive projects such as the proposed national sports arena, which have a high opportunity cost and little supply-side benefit, additional cutbacks in infra-structural investment could lead to more problems than they solve.

While this does not excuse misguided reductions in consumption taxes or profligate and politically motivated expenditure on high profile but unproductive capital projects, it does suggest that fiscal contraction may be difficult to implement and a serious threat to social partnership. However, in a fully employed economy it may be that social partnership has run its course. In a nutshell, its principal contribution was to deliver a mechanism whereby wage moderation and enhanced competitiveness could be traded off against employment growth and tax concessions. But in the current situation the case for additional competitive gains, continued employment growth and further tax reductions is far from convincing. Ireland does not have a competitiveness problem or an unemployment problem. If anything, the problem today is that the economy is too competitive, resulting in excess labour demand that may be best dealt with by a market-driven wage setting process rather than centralised negotiations under a social partnership arrangement.

There is, of course, a downside to this scenario. In the absence of an exchange rate option it will be more difficult to deal with asymmetric shocks which, other things being equal, may increase the chances that wages will overshoot the level required to maintain full employment. Hence, social partnership may still have a valuable role to play by delivering wage moderation in adverse circumstances. More fundamentally, Calmfors and Driffill (1988) have shown that macroeconomic stability is best guaranteed either by a highly centralised social partnership type system or by a flexible market-based approach to wage setting. In the former social partners set wages to avoid higher taxes required to finance unemployment benefits and react to adverse shocks by restoring wage levels consistent with full employment. In the latter the emergence of excess demand or supply is eliminated by appropriate wage adjustment which is clearly appropriate in the current Irish situation. However, there can be no guarantee that social partnership would be replaced by an American-style flexible labour market. Rather, there is every chance that we would see the re-emergence of decentralised unions and employers bargaining on a bilateral basis. This, as shown by Calmfors and Driffill (1988) and emphasised by Durkan (1999), is a sub-optimal outcome if both sides transfer the responsibility for unemployment away from the wage bargaining process and towards government. Hence social partnership is probably more valuable than the most likely alternative. Retaining the present system, albeit in a more flexible form which targets the maintenance of full employment rather than continuous job creation, can only increase the chances of a soft landing.

Further, social partnership may have greatest value in recession. If the slowdown in the U.S. economy persists and, as is likely, its effects are asymmetrical with respect to Ireland, then wage restraint will be of crucial importance. In its *Medium Term Review 2001–2007,* the ESRI (2001) acknowledges that "despite our historic links with the U.K. changes that have occurred in the Irish economy now mean that Ireland is more exposed to events in the U.S. economy" (p. 39). This exposure takes two forms. First, the U.S. is now a major export market for Ireland, and a recession has a direct impact on the demand for Irish output. Second, many Irish-based multinationals export primarily to the EU. Hence, to the extent that a U.S. slowdown adversely affects the European economy, it leads to reduced exports and job losses in Ireland. While events in both the U.S. and the EU are immune to Irish policy decisions, wage moderation and continued social partnership may be of crucial importance to prudent economic management in the face of an external downturn.

5. IRELAND AND THE EURO

It is often forgotten that Ireland's golden age of economic growth has coincided with dramatic changes in the exchange rate regime. When the European

Monetary System (EMS) was launched in March 1979 Ireland decided to participate in the Exchange Rate Mechanism (ERM) while the United Kingdom opted
out of the latter. As a result the long-standing 1:1 parity link between sterling
and the Irish pound was severed. This switch was motivated by the perception
of sterling as a weak inflation-prone currency whereas the ERM centered on
the deutsche mark (DM) was perceived as a "zone of monetary stability."
Initially these hopes went unfilled. Following Mrs. Thatcher's election in May
1979, sterling appreciated strongly and the British inflation rate declined.
However, due to a combination of sterling volatility and fiscal profligacy, which
was inconsistent with a strong currency regime, the Irish pound depreciated by
approximately 30% against the DM over 1979 to 1986. When order was restored
to the public finances in the late 1980s, Ireland was able to maintain a more
or less constant exchange rate against its ERM partners. This period of stability
was, in no short measure, aided by sterling joining the ERM in 1990, inflation
convergence both within and outside the EMS, and a marked lack of turbulence
on international money markets. Unfortunately this stability was shattered in
September 1992 when sterling was forced out of the ERM and depreciated
against the DM. As Ireland continued to operate a quasi-, but thankfully not
irrevocably, fixed exchange rate against the DM, the manufacturing sector
suffered severe competitive losses on British markets and against imports from
the United Kingdom. After four months of futile and costly resistance, the Irish
pound was devalued by 10% within the ERM.

Following the currency crises the EMS abandoned its 2.5% and 6% fluctu-
ation bands and adopted wider 15% bands. Although the move to wide bands
did not require any ERM participant to abandon a DM-peg, the Irish authorities, either by accident or design, used this flexibility to great advantage.
Rather than peg to any currency, the Irish pound was permitted to partly
accommodate movements in sterling by offsetting movements against the
offsetting DM thereby keeping the average, or effective, exchange rate
relatively stable.[10] Figure 3 depicts exchange rate volatility by plotting 60 day
moving averages of the absolute value of the daily change in Irish pound
exchange rates against sterling, the dollar and the DM while Fig. 4 illustrates
the same series for the effective exchange rate defined as a weighed average
of the three bilateral rates.[11] All three bilateral rates exhibit considerable
volatility relative to the effective rate. Prior to the euro's launch there is a
marked increase in volatility against sterling and the dollar while the DM series
trends towards zero. Hence, pegging to one currency does not automatically
reduce overall volatility. As Fig. 4 illustrates, Irish pound volatility is
relatively low for most of the period but increases as the currency approaches
its irrevocable link with the euro.

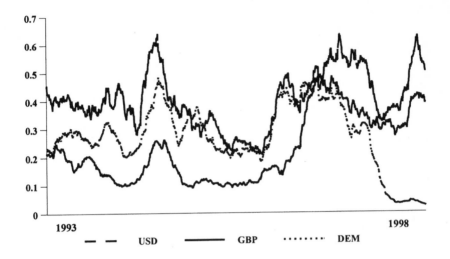

Fig. 3. Volatility, 1993–1998, Bilateral Exchange Rates.

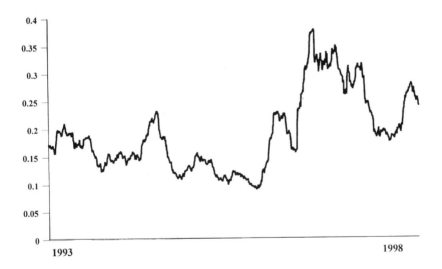

Fig. 4. Volatility, 1993–1998, Effective Exchange Rate.

Most significantly, this was the first time since the foundation of the State
that Ireland came close to having an independent currency and an independent
exchange rate policy. Over the same period real GDP grew at an annual average
rate of 8.5%, unemployment fell from 14.1 to 7.4,% and the numbers employed
increased from 1.2 to 1.5 million. This may, of course, be coincidental; but it
would be extremely difficult to argue that the exchange rate regime and what
appeared to be an independent policy had any detrimental impact of the real
economy. Indeed, it may be more plausible to argue that against the background
of high productivity growth and wage moderation leading to significant competitive gains, a neutral exchange rate policy targeted at stability of the effective
exchange rate was highly appropriate.

This raises the obvious question: if it wasn't broke why did we want to fix
it? The simple answer is that the decision to participate in the euro was
politically motivated and taken without any *prior* economic assessment.[12]
However, political decisions have economic consequences, and the most obvious
effect of euro participation is the surrender of exchange rate policy. What,
however, is the appropriate role of exchange rate policy? Specifically, do we
view the exchange rate regime as a means to promote growth and trade, or do
we regard it as a means to stabilise the economy? Euro advocates tend to take
the former view while defectors take the latter.

The first view is articulated by McAleese (2000) who argues that "studies
of the economics of introducing a flexible exchange rate regime in Ireland
have repeatedly concluded that ... exchange rate uncertainty ... would
impose excessive costs on our trade and foreign investment" (p. 100) and that
"over the long run, EMU could result in a fusion of the benefits of fiscal
consolidation, low inflation and fast growth ..." (p. 101) None of these
arguments hold up against the evidence. First, the conclusions reached by the
(uncited) studies are inconsistent with the performance of the Irish economy
between 1994 and 1998. Figure 3 suggests that bilateral volatility was
relatively high during these years. However, given that over the same period
real GDP increased by 8.5% per annum and unemployment fell from 14% to
7%, it would be difficult to conclude that exchange rate uncertainty, as proxied
by volatility, had a detrimental effect on economic growth. Further, recent
econometric studies by Morgenroth (2000) and Thom and Walsh (2001) report
that the exchange rate regime has no significant effect on Anglo-Irish trade.
Second, while it is probable that the Maastricht Convergence Criteria and
adherence to the Stability and Growth Pact have had a disciplining effect on
Irish fiscal policy, it is simply erroneous to argue that the former was responsible for restoring order to the public finances. The government deficit reached
12.7% of GDP in 1981, 10.5% in 1986 but declined to 2.3% by 1990. Hence,

fiscal correction was well under way long before the Maastricht Treaty was negotiated. Also, the hypothesis that commitment to the euro was a necessary condition underlying fiscal stability in the 1990s is tantamount to claiming that democratically elected governments cannot be trusted to manage the Irish economy. While the experiences of the late 1970s and early 1980s would lend support to this view, the evidence of the 1990s clearly suggests both the electorate and their representatives now accept that irresponsible budgetary policy militates against economic growth. Indeed it is probable that Ireland would have complied with the Maastricht debt and deficit criteria by 1988/1989, some four years before they became binding for euro aspirants.[13] Third, the asymmetric effect of the euro's depreciation over 1999–2000 is evidence that the euro can impose high inflation on the Irish economy. This, of course, could have been avoided if we had retained the freedom to let the currency to compensate for sterling's strength by appreciating against the euro. McAlesse also asserts that "Ireland's economic prosperity and competitive exchange rate up to 1998 were the consequence of the government's commitment to EMU" (p. 100). On the contrary, the relatively stable effective exchange rate was the consequence of a policy which permitted considerable variation against euro currencies rather than a commitment to a DM/euro peg.

More correctly, international macroeconomics typically treats the exchange rate as a stabilisation instrument. If Irish trade was closely integrated with the core economies and if fluctuations in economic activity were in line with the European business cycle, then the issue of euro participation would, from a stabilisation perspective, be of little consequence. However, Ireland is not a core European economy. More than 60% of Irish trade is with non-euro countries, and business cycle activity is more closely correlated with the United States and the United Kingdom than with France or Germany. Put simply, the one-size-fits-all monetary policy is targeted at euro averages and is unlikely to be appropriate to Irish stabilisation needs. During our period of monetary independence, the Irish Central Bank successfully minimised the impact of volatility on the effective exchange rate. Having surrendered the exchange rate option and tied ourselves irrevocably to just one currency, accounting for just 22% of our total imports, we cannot avoid volatility in the effective exchange rate. Hence, if anything, the euro is likely to increase the probability of a hard landing for Ireland's runaway economy. In short, even if domestic policy is exemplary, stabilisation issues are likely to be more severe than in the recent past but will be beyond the control of the Irish authorities. This is bad news from any perspective but especially depressing for the euro propagandists who appear to believe that exchange rate stability promotes economic growth.

However, in a series of papers Frankel and Rose have produced evidence to suggest that integration via a common currency promotes trade between partner countries and that bilateral trade leads to closer synchronisation of business cycle activity. Using a standard gravity model, Rose (2000) estimates that *countries with the same currency trade over three times as much with each other as countries with different currencies* while Frankel and Rose (1998) find that correlation between business cycles is significantly related to the intensity of bilateral trade. If correct, this hypothesis implies that while countries such as Ireland may not be closely integrated with the European economy ex ante, they will be ex post. Hence, Ireland's decision to participate in the euro may be justified on the grounds that further integration with the European core leads to more intra-EU trade and, as a result, greater synchronisation with the European business cycle. In addition to the empirical evidence on Anglo-Irish trade as cited above in Morgenroth (2000) and Thom and Walsh (2001), there are two caveats to this hypothesis. First, Krugman (1991) argues that integration makes it possible to exploit scale economies leading to higher industrial special-isation and regional concentration which increases the incidence of asymmetric shocks and lowers synchronisation between national economies. Second, and on a more normative note, even if the Frenkel and Rose hypothesis is correct, it raises the question of whose business cycle is best for a small economy. If, as is probable, the international monetary system becomes increasingly dominated by the dollar and the euro, then small countries will have to choose which form of dollarisation they prefer. For euro countries such as Belgium and Austria, the choice is clear. However, for Ireland with significant trading interests in each camp, the choice is more difficult, especially if the United Kingdom continues to opt out of the euro-system. Unfortunately Ireland has already decided. We can only hope that future generations will not have to suffer the consequences of a political decision which, at best, lacks a clear economic rationale.

6. CONCLUSIONS

Ireland does not have a growth problem, an employment problem, or a compet-itiveness problem. If anything the problem is that growth is currently above the rate which is sustainable in the longer run and that the economy is over competitive, resulting in labour shortages and inflationary pressures. Put another way, Ireland is now faced with a stabilisation problem that requires that the economy converge to the sustainable growth path in a smooth and orderly manner. Restoring competitiveness to levels consistent with full employment is an essential element in this adjustment process. However, in the absence of the exchange rate option it would be a mistake to be complacent about automatic convergence via wage and price inflation. Adverse shocks and exchange rate volatility increase the probability that competitiveness may overshoot its equilibrium level, leading to a more rapid decline in the growth rate and a hard landing. Also, reducing aggregate demand by fiscal contraction would be relatively inefficient and a potential threat to social partnership which is worth preserving given the most likely alternative of bilateral wage bargaining by decentralised unions and employers.

Without doubt recourse to exchange rate policy would ease these problems and improve the chances of a soft landing. This is not to say that the exchange rate is a highly efficient stabilisation or fine tuning instrument. However, it must be recognised that non-euro currencies are important to the Irish economy and that sudden movements in the euro's value against sterling and the dollar can be destabilising. In these circumstances an independent currency is valuable and, as the policy followed between 1993 and 1998 demonstrates, can be used to enhance stability and prevent external shocks from creating cyclical deviations in growth and employment. Exchange rate policy, whether flexible or an irrevocable peg, is not a means to promote growth. Rather it is an instrument which, when used properly, can help stabilise output around its full employment level. Hence, participation in the euro is best regarded as a stabilisation issue rather than a growth issue. In the longer run Ireland's economic growth is unlikely to improve or deteriorate as a consequence of the euro membership. What is certain is that given high trade dependency on non-euro currencies and low synchronisation with the European business cycle, the euro will increase the incidence of demand shocks, leading to greater cyclical variation in economic activity and inflation. This was also true of the European Monetary System, but that regime permitted currency realignments and, in its final years, considerable flexibility which Ireland used to its advantage. In the euro these options are closed forever.

NOTES

1. Recent (July, 2000) CSO data gives the following distribution for total Irish Trade: Euro area 35%, United Kingdom 26%, United States 16% and rest of the world 23%.
2. See Barry (1999) for a comprehensive analysis of Irish economic growth.
3. Estimating sustainable growth rates is fraught with conceptual and practical difficulties and most efforts are largely ad hoc. However, the evidence suggests an upper limit of approximately 3% for mature economies. See O'Gráda and O'Rourke (2000).
4. O'Rourke and Thom (2000) suggest that excess Irish inflation may have been present prior to 1999.
5. See Department of Finance: *Budget 2001*, page A7.
6. See European Central Bank (1999) and Blanchard (2001).

7. In his reference to income tax changes the Minister states, "I have cut [income] tax rates to improve the incentive to work" (page A.17).

8. In the case of tobacco, the excise duty was raised to compensate for the VAT reduction.

9. See Eichengreen (1996) and O'Gráda and O'Rourke (2000).

10. As shown by O'Rourke and Thom (2000) volatility measured by the weighted average of Irish pound exchange rates against sterling, the DM and the dollar was lower over 1994 to 1998 than during the first two years of euro membership.

11. The weights are: DM.40, Sterling 0.35, Dollar 0.25. The DM is used as a proxy for the euro.

12. The government subsequently commissioned a favourable economic analysis, Baker et al. (1996), which was released some four years after the Maastricht Referendum and, by coincidence of course, at the start of Ireland's EU Presidency in mid-1996.

13. Although the 1989 debt/GDP ratio was well in excess of the 60% reference value, a country could be deemed to comply with the criterion providing that the ratio was "sufficiently diminishing and approaching the reference value at a satisfactory pace." This was the let-out clause that applied to both Belgium and Italy who had debt ratios in excess of 100% in 1998.

REFERENCES

Baker, T, Fitzgerald, J., & Honohan, P. (1996). *Economic Implication for Ireland of EMU*. Dublin: ESRI.

Barry, F. (Ed.) (1999). *Understanding Ireland's economic growth*. MacMillan Press.

Calmfors, L., & Driddill, J. (1988). Bargaining structure, corporatism and macroeconomic performance. *Economic Policy, 6,* 14–61.

Cronin, D., & Scally, J. (2000). Assessing Irish fiscal policy in EMU: the role of the structural budget balance. *Central Bank of Ireland Quarterly Bulletin*, 65–77.

Department of Finance (2000). *Budget 2001*.

Durkan, J. (1999). *The role of budgetary policy in social consensus, Budget Perspectives*. Dublin: ESRI.

European Central Bank (1999). Inflation differentials in a monetary union. *Monthly Bulletin*.

Eichengreen, B. (1996). Institutions and economic growth: Europe after World War II. In: N. F. R. Crafts & G. Toniolo (Eds), *Economic Growth in Europe since 1945*. Cambridge: Cambridge University Press.

Economic and Social Research Institute (2001). *Medium-Term Review: 2001–2007*. ESRI.

Frankel, J. A., & Rose, A. K. (2000). An estimate of the effect of currency unions on trade and growth. NBER Working Paper No. 7875.

Krugman, P. (1991). *Geography and Trade*. MIT Press.

Lane, P. (1998). Irish Fiscal Policy Under EMU. *Irish Banking Review*.

Leddin, A, Walsh, B. (1998). *The Macro-Economy of Ireland* (EMU ed.). Dublin: Gill & Macmillan.

McHale, J., (2000). Options for inflation control in the Irish economy, ESRI Quarterly Economic Commentary.

McAleese, D., (2000). Twenty-five years "a growing." In: R. O'Donnell (Ed.), *Europe: The Irish Experience*. Dublin: Institute of European Affairs.

Morgenroth, E. (2000). Exchange rates and trade: the case of Irish exports to Britain. *Applied Economics, 32,* 107–110.

Obstfeld, M., & Rogoff, K. (1996). *Foundations of International Macroeconomics*. Cambridge, Mass.: MIT Press.

O'Gráda, C., & O'Rourke K. (2000). Living standards and growth. In: J. O'Hagan (Ed.), *The Economy of Ireland: Policy and Performance of a European Region*. Dublin: Gill and Macmillan.

O'Rourke, K., & Thom, R. (2000). Irish inflation: Appropriate policy responses. *Irish Banking Review*.

Thom, R., & Walsh, B. M. (2002). The effect of a common currency on trade: Lessons from the Irish experience. *European Economic Review*, 6, 1111–1123.

Walsh, B. (1999). The persistence of high unemployment in a small open labour market. In: F. Barry (Ed.), *Understanding Ireland's Economic Growth*. MacMillan Press.

6. FISCAL POLICY AND THE PUBLIC FINANCES: CREATIVE APPROACHES TO PENSION FUNDING

John McHale

1. INTRODUCTION

As the Irish budget surplus continued to soar in early 2001, it was ironic that concerns about Ireland's *expansionary* fiscal policy were giving an early test to the workability of fiscal cooperation under Economic and Monetary Union (EMU). Although fiscal policy has fallen out of favor as a demand management tool, it was widely recognized at the start of EMU that counter-cyclical fiscal policy would have an important role to play given the constraint of a "one size fits all" monetary policy. Of course, fiscal demand management is only needed if cyclical conditions diverge. Unfortunately, there was considerable evidence of divergence between the fastest and slowest growing euro-zone members, with OECD projections for output gaps in 2001 ranging from a high of 4.1% in Ireland to a low –0.7% in Italy (OECD, 2000).

In this context, then, Ireland's expansionary budget for 2001 caused understandable consternation among its European partners, and ultimately a formal "recommendation" to tighten its fiscal stance. As a matter of demand management, there was much to complain about. Yet critics did not always appreciate how hamstrung Irish fiscal policy was by its ties to incomes policy.[1]

The Irish Economy in Transition: Successes, Problems, and Prospects, Volume 85, pages 107–141.
© 2002 Published by Elsevier Science Ltd.
ISBN: 0-7623-0979-2

Starting in 1987, Irish governments have pursued a set of widely praised national agreements with unions and employers that achieved wage restraint in return for tax cuts. This formula worked very well in the relatively depressed conditions of the late 1980s and early 1990s. It also helped to scale back onerous tax distortions and to underpin the strategy of making Ireland an attractive destination for foreign – especially American – direct investment. The most recent agreement – the Programme for Prosperity and Fairness (PPF) – was already under considerable strain in the closing months of 2000, however. The cause of the strain was inflation. The headline CPI inflation rate peaked at 7% in November, the month before the 2001 budget was announced.[2] This inflation rate compared with annual wage increases of 5.5% under the PPF. Difficult talks were taking place on re-negotiating the partnership agreement in the days before the 2001 budget. It is noteworthy that though a provisional agreement was made, the union leadership announced that it was reserving its final decision until after it heard the Minister's speech. This timing dramatized how entwined fiscal and incomes policy had become, and must be borne in mind in evaluating the contents of the budget.

Thus, the government faced a dilemma: offer a (clearly cyclically inappropriate) budget with substantial tax cuts and spending increases, or risk the collapse of the social partnership framework.[3] Both options ran the risk of intensifying the inflation spiral that was taking hold.

The problem is that the government has more targets than instruments. At the risk of oversimplifying, there are two targets – stable inflation and low structural unemployment, but essentially a single instrument – fiscal policy. Before EMU the government could use monetary policy to stabilize the economy, allowing some room to use fiscal policy to secure wage moderation through social partnership. Under EMU the government has lost control over monetary policy, leaving fiscal policy to be pulled in different directions.

In this chapter, I argue that one way out of the dilemmas of this kind is to adjust the social partnership framework to allow for deferred compensation in the form of contributions to worker retirement accounts. Instead of offering cyclically inappropriate tax cuts, the government could make concrete contributions to these accounts in return for wage restraint. The key requirement for such deferred compensation to work is that it is substantially valued by workers but has a limited impact on current consumption.

Later I argue that borrowing constraints or self-control problems that lead to under-saving by otherwise reasonably sophisticated economic actors are enough for this requirement to be met.

Any proposal that mixes macroeconomic management policy with pension policy is open to the objection that it subordinates long-term needs to short-term contingencies. I will argue, however, that introducing a system of individual accounts would provide a significant improvement on present pension policy in any case. The combination of flat rate pensions and limited occupational coverage does not ensure adequate income replacement for many middle and higher income workers in retirement. Moreover, because pensions are not linked to earnings or contributions, workers view the contributions required to pay the pensions bill as pure taxes.

The rest of the chapter is structured as follows. In the next section, I provide a brief description of the Irish pensions system, examine the long-run fiscal strains caused by population aging, and describe plans to set up a National Pensions Reserve Fund (NPRF) to pre-fund future social welfare and public sector pension obligations. Section 3 reviews the relationship between Irish fiscal and incomes policy in light of the constraints imposed by EMU. Here I show that the dilemma facing the government is that it has too few instruments. (A simple model of the instruments problem is also developed in the Appendix.) In Section 4, I propose a system of individual accounts with negotiated government contributions as a means of providing the needed second instrument. In Section 5, I contrast this proposal with competing proposals such as pension bonds, tax incentives for saving, and the government's new special savings incentive scheme. Section 6 concludes.

2. THE IRISH PENSIONS SYSTEM

First Pillar: Social Welfare Pensions

When compared with its European partners, the outstanding fact about state pension provision in Ireland is the absence of an earnings-related pillar. Throughout most of the last century, the Irish pension system loosely followed developments in the United Kingdom.[4] When the State Earnings-Related Pensions (SERPs) were introduced in the United Kingdom in the mid-1970s, however, the Irish government did not follow, leaving Ireland and the Netherlands as the only countries without state-earnings related pensions in Western Europe (Kalisch et al., 1998).[5]

Ireland has a two-tired sytem of flat-rate state pension provision:

- "Social assistance" pensions are non-contributory, means tested, and payable to those aged 66 and over. These pensions are paid on a flat-rate basis, with a standard weekly payment of £95.50 from April 2001. The payments are not indexed to either earnings or prices, making Ireland the only EU country apart from Portugal without automatic pension indexation.[6]

- "Social insurance" pensions are contributory, non-means tested, and payable to those aged 65 and over. A "retirement pension" is payable at 65 to those meeting the contribution conditions, *but payment is conditional on retirement.* An old age (contributory) pension is payable *without a retirement condition* from age 66. Both of these pensions are paid on a flat-rate basis, with a standard weekly payment (Class A) of £106.00 from April 2001. Like the non-contributory pensions, these pensions are not indexed and are thus subject to discretionary changes at budget time. Given the flat rate structure and a weak relationship between the number of contributions and benefits, the link between total contributions and total benefits is weak (Franco & Munzi, 1996). Contributions are made in the form of Pay Related Social Insurance (PRSI) premiums, which are levied at fixed percentages on employees and employers, and entitle contributors to a range of benefits in addition to contributory pensions. The PRSI rates for the year beginning in April 2001 are:

  - Employees – graduated with a top rate of 6% up to an earnings ceiling of £28,250;
  - Employers – graduated with a top rate of 12% and no earnings ceiling (an earnings ceiling of £36,600 was eliminated in the 2001 budget);[7]
  - Self-employed – 3% contribution rate (reduced from 5% in the 2001 budget) and no earnings ceiling (an earnings ceiling of £26,500 was eliminated in the 2001 budget).

From an economic efficiency point of view, the design of social welfare pensions is far from ideal. First, PRSI contributions are pure taxes for most workers. Assuming a worker will have a full contributions record over their lifetime, additional contributions do not bring additional benefits. This contrasts with a defined-contribution-funded pension scheme in which there is a strong link between contributions and ultimate benefits, or even a pay-as-you-go earnings-related system where additional earnings brings additional benefits (as well as additional contributions). Second, since current PRSI contributions fund current pensions, the national pensions system does not add to national savings. (See below, however, on the new National Pensions Reserve Fund.) Third, since non-contributory pensions are subject to an assets test, there is a direct incentive against private saving for retirement or bequests for a fraction of the population. This problem was quite severe in the past for the self-employed and farming sectors given that they were largely outside the PRSI net, and thus not eligible for contributory pensions. Finally, providing for retirement income through a state-run pay-as-you-go pension system missed an opportunity to develop domestic capital markets and to foster a broadly based savings habit.

Second Pillar: Private Sector Coverage

Absent a state earnings-related pensions system, Ireland has a relatively well-developed system of occupational pensions. Occupational coverage is regulated by the Pensions Act of 1990 and overseen by the Pensions Board. Regulation covers areas such as the preservation of benefits upon changing employment, funding standards for defined-benefit schemes, information disclosure, obligations of trustees, and the equality of treatment between men and women. The Pensions Board also advises the government on public and private pension matters.

The tax regime governing contributions to pension schemes is based on the Finance Act of 1972. Employer contributions to approved schemes are tax deductible. All contributions (employer and employee) are allowed to accumulate tax-free. Benefits are taxable as ordinary income.

Table 1 shows the assets of pension funds in most OECD economies. Irish pension assets amounted to 45% of GDP in 1996, behind only Switzerland (117%), Netherlands (87.3%), United Kingdom (74.7%), and United States (58.2%). Despite the relatively well established pensions market, research carried out by the ESRI found that only 46% workers had an occupational pension in 1995 – 83% in the public sector, 38% in the private sector, and only 27% among farmers and the self employed (OECD, 1999).

Responding to the substantially incomplete second-pillar coverage, the Pensions Board (1998) recommended that the government introduce a system of Personal Retirement Savings Accounts (PRSAs).[8] The government has promised to introduce legislation to establish these accounts. As proposed by the Pensions Board the accounts would allow employees up to age 30 to contribute 5% of earnings to tax-favored accounts. After age 30, the allowable tax-favored contribution rises by 0.5% per year, with a maximum of 30% by age 60 (O'Carroll, 1998). Other features include:

- General availability (although employers could continue to compel employees to join the firm's occupational pension scheme);
- A flexible retirement age;
- A standard minimum set of terms and conditions on applicable financial products combined with a "kitemarking" system to ensure quality among a wide range of providers;
- An option to use up to 25% of the accumulated fund as collateral for loans subject to an overall cap of £25,000.

The Pensions Board has set a goal of achieving a 70% second-pillar coverage rate, and a target replacement rate of 50% of gross earnings for the two pillars

Table 1.   Pension Fund Assets as a Share of GDP.

	1987	1990	1993	1996
Switzerland	74.7	72.5	82.2	117.1
Netherlands	45.5	78.4	83.5	87.3
United Kingdom	62.3	59.7	72.4	74.7
United States	35.7	38.1	53.4	58.2
Ireland	–	**31.5**	**40.1**	**45.0**
Canada	26.4	30.0	35.7	43.0
Japan	38.0	37.4	41.0	41.8
Finland	19.7	25.1	38.1	40.8
Sweden	33.4	31.0	27.1	32.6
Australia	–	17.6	30.1	31.6
Denmark	10.9	12.4	19.3	23.9
Luxembourg	19.5	19.7	18.7	19.7
Greece	–	6.5	8.0	12.7
Portugal	–	1.9	5.6	9.9
Norway	3.8	4.6	5.7	7.3
Germany	3.4	3.3	5.5	5.8
France	–	3.4	3.3	5.6
Belgium	2.4	2.5	2.8	4.1
Spain	–	1.5	2.1	3.8
Korea	3.2	3.1	3.4	3.3
Italy	–	–	1.7	3.0
Austria	–	–	0.6	1.2
Czech Republic	–	–	–	0.5
Hungary	–	–	–	0.2

Source: OECD (1998), *Maintaining Prosperity in an Aging Society*, adapted from Table V.1.

combined. (For the lowest-earning 30% of workers, the 50% replacement rate is assumed achievable with social welfare pensions alone; hence the 70% coverage target for the second pillar.) Interestingly, the Board argued that if the voluntary nature of the system did not lead to a substantial increase in private sector occupational coverage, a system of compulsory saving should be looked at.

Ireland's Relatively Favorable Pensions Cost Outlook

It is well known that the populations of all the industrialized countries will age significantly over the next half century. This population aging is the result of societal changes that are generally positive – notably falling mortality and greater control over fertility. Yet however welcome these trends, aging will strain government budgets, and force painful combinations of higher taxes and lower benefits. Although pension costs are set to rise as a share of the Irish economy, the good news is that Ireland is facing a much less serious problem than most of its European partners.

Table 2 shows European Commission projections of the share of those 65 and over to the working age population (here defined as the population between 20 and 64) in Ireland and in each of its EU partners. At present, Ireland has the lowest elderly dependency ratio in the EU. Although the Irish elderly dependency ratio remains below its European partners throughout the projection period, considerable population aging does occur, especially after 2020. Between 2020 and 2050 the Irish elderly dependency rate increases by roughly 20 percentage points.

In addition to the relatively delayed aging effect, the increase in the cost of public pensions is limited by the low (relative) generosity of Irish social welfare pensions. The total cost of public pensions as a share of GDP can be usefully decomposed as the product of the benefit generosity rate (defined as the ratio of the average pension benefit per elderly person to the GDP per working age person) and the elderly dependency rate.[9] Based on a recent European Commission study, I have calculated that this benefit generosity rate in the EU ranged from a low of 19.3 in the U.K. to a high of 57.8 in Austria. Ireland had the *second lowest generosity rate* in the countries studied at 23.7.

A useful way to get a sense of the costs of aging is to calculate what happens to pensions as a share of GDP *if the benefit generosity rate is held constant at its 2000 level.* The results are shown in Table 3 for the EU countries and the United States. For Ireland the share of GDP allocated to public pensions more than doubles, rising from 4.6% to 10.5%. For countries starting with more generous systems, the percentage point increases are typically much larger. Italy is the most dramatic example. The share of GDP spent on pensions rises from 14.2% of GDP in 2000 to 32.9% of GDP in 2050! Of course, future workers are unlikely to accept such a high funding burden. In a number of countries – Italy prominent among them – forward looking reforms have already been put in place that, if followed through on, would result in substantial cuts in benefit generosity rates (see McHale, 2001).

The aforementioned European Commission study projected paths for pension costs that are relatively benign compared to those shown in Table 3. These projections (shown in Table 4) take currently legislated pension policy profiles and make some optimistic assumptions about employment and output growth. Given the demographic projections, these cost projections imply huge cuts in benefit generosity rates for many countries. (These implied benefit generosity rates are shown in Table 5.) Observing the size of the implied cuts in benefits relative to incomes raises questions about the plausibility of the projections. To

Table 2. Old Age Dependency Ratio (Population 65 and over/Population under 20).

	2000	2010	2020	2030	2040	2050
Austria	25.1	28.8	32.4	43.6	54.5	55.0
Belgium	28.1	29.4	35.6	45.8	51.3	49.7
Denmark	24.1	27.2	33.7	39.2	44.5	41.9
Finland	24.5	27.5	38.9	46.9	47.4	48.1
France	27.2	28.1	35.9	44.0	50.0	50.8
Germany	28.3	31.6	35.8	41.7	51.4	58.7
Greece	28.3	31.6	35.8	41.7	51.4	58.7
Ireland	19.4	19.1	24.5	30.3	36.0	44.2
Italy	28.8	33.8	39.7	49.2	63.9	66.8
Luxembourg	23.4	26.2	31.0	39.8	45.4	41.8
Netherlands	21.9	24.6	32.6	41.5	48.1	44.9
Portugal	25.1	26.7	30.3	35.0	43.1	48.7
Spain	27.1	28.9	33.1	41.7	55.7	65.7
Sweden	29.6	31.4	37.6	42.7	46.7	46.1
United Kingdom	26.4	26.9	31.0	40.2	47.0	46.1
United States	21.1	21.4	27.4	35.5	37.0	37.3

Source: European Commission (2000), Economic Policy Report to the ECOFIN Council on the Impact of Aging Populations on Public Pension Systems. U.S. data is from the *Social Security Administration*, intermediate demographic projections.

Table 3. Implied Pension Costs Assuming Benefit Rate Constant at 2000 Level.

	2000	2010	2020	2030	2040	2050
Austria	14.5	16.6	18.7	25.2	31.5	31.8
Belgium	9.3	9.7	11.8	15.2	17.0	16.4
Denmark	10.2	11.5	14.3	16.6	18.8	17.7
Finland	11.3	12.7	17.9	21.6	21.9	22.2
France	12.1	12.5	16.0	19.6	22.2	22.6
Germany	10.3	11.5	13.0	15.2	18.7	21.4
Greece	–	–	–	–	–	–
Ireland	4.6	4.5	5.8	7.2	8.5	10.5
Italy	14.2	16.7	19.6	24.3	31.5	32.9
Luxembourg	–	–	–	–	–	–
Netherlands	7.9	8.9	11.8	15.0	17.4	16.2
Portugal	9.4	10.0	11.3	13.1	16.1	18.2
Spain	9.4	10.0	11.5	14.5	19.3	22.8
Sweden	9.0	9.5	11.4	13.0	14.2	14.0
United Kingdom	5.1	5.2	6.0	7.8	9.1	8.9
United States	4.1	4.1	5.3	6.8	7.1	7.2

Source: European Commission (2000), Economic Policy Report to the ECOFIN Council on the Impact of Aging Populations on Public Pension Systems. U.S. data is from the *Congressional Budget Office* and author's calculations.

Table 4. Cost Projections Based on Legislated Policies and Common Macro Assumptions.

	2000	2010	2020	2030	2040	2050
Austria	14.5	14.8	15.7	17.6	17.0	15.1
Belgium	9.3	9.0	10.4	12.5	13.0	12.6
Denmark	10.2	12.7	14.0	14.7	13.9	13.2
Finland	11.3	13.1	15.0	16.0	15.8	–
France	12.1	13.1	15.0	16.0	15.8	–
Germany	10.3	9.5	10.6	13.2	14.4	14.6
Greece	–	–	–	–	–	–
Ireland	4.6	5.0	6.7	7.6	8.3	9.0
Italy	14.2	14.3	14.9	15.9	15.7	13.9
Luxembourg	–	–	–	–	–	–
Netherlands	7.9	9.1	11.1	13.1	14.1	13.6
Portugal	9.4	12.0	14.4	16.0	15.8	14.2
Spain	9.4	9.3	10.2	12.9	16.3	17.7
Sweden	9.0	9.2	10.2	10.7	10.7	10.0
United Kingdom	5.1	4.7	4.4	4.7	4.4	3.9

Source: European Commission (2000). Economic Policy Report to the ECOFIN Council 0n the Impact of Aging Populations on Public Pension Systems.

Table 5. Implied Benefit Rates Based on Projected Pension Costs as a Share of GDP.

	2000	2010	2020	2030	2040	2050
Austria	57.8	51.4	48.5	40.4	31.2	27.5
Belgium	33.1	30.6	29.2	27.3	25.3	25.4
Denmark	42.3	46.7	41.5	37.5	31.2	31.5
Finland	46.1	47.6	38.6	34.1	33.3	–
France	44.5	46.6	41.8	36.4	31.6	–
Germany	36.4	30.1	29.6	31.7	28.0	24.9
Greece	–	–	–	–	–	–
Ireland	23.7	26.2	27.3	25.1	23.1	20.4
Italy	49.3	42.3	37.5	32.3	24.6	20.8
Luxembourg	–	–	–	–	–	–
Netherlands	36.1	37.0	34.0	31.6	36.7	30.3
Portugal	37.5	44.9	47.5	45.7	36.7	29.2
Spain	34.7	32.2	30.8	30.9	29.3	26.9
Sweden	30.4	29.3	27.1	25.1	22.9	21.7
United Kingdom	19.3	17.5	14.2	11.7	9.4	8.5

Source: European Commission (2000). Economic Policy Report to the ECOFIN Council on the Impact of Aging Populations on Public Pension Systems. and author's calculations.

take the Italian example once more, the European Commission estimates imply that the benefit generosity rate will fall to 21.8% – close to the rate that the rather austere United Kingdom system is at now.

From this perspective, the projections for Ireland look plausible by comparison. For Ireland to keep its pension costs to the commission's estimate of 9% of GDP by 2050, the benefit generosity rate would only have to fall from 23.7 to 20.4. This contrasts with an implied fall for Italy of almost 30 percentage points (from 50.0 to 20.8). My general point here is that the extent of the "time bomb" problem is almost certainly being underestimated for the major European economies so that, comparatively, Ireland is in a very strong position. It is all the more striking, then, that Ireland is one of the few countries putting funds aside to smooth out the aging burden.

Prefunding State Pension Liabilities: National Pensions Reserve Fund

In what is perhaps the most significant fiscal policy development in recent years, the Irish government announced plans in late summer 1999 to set up a National Pensions Reserve Fund (NPRF). The purpose of the reserve is to pre-fund a portion of state pension obligations that arise after 2025. While projections of sharply rising pension costs made the fund desirable, near-term projections of large fiscal surpluses made it politically possible.

The plan is to set aside at least 1% of GNP annually from 1999 until 2055 *regardless of the state of the economy*. Disbursements from the fund are prohibited until 2025. After that time the government can draw down funds to partly alleviate the costs of paying for pensions on a pay-as-you-go basis.

In addition the Minister for Finance set aside £3.6 billion (5.2% of 2000 GNP) of the proceeds of the privatization of the state telephone company, now called Eircom. The combined funds were initially placed in a Temporary Holding Fund pending the legislation establishing the NPRF. (This legislation was introduced in the summer of 2000).

Figure 1 shows how the fund accumulates as a share of GNP. The projections are based on assumptions of a 4% real rate of return on fund investments and zero withdrawals. The assumptions for growth of real GNP mirror those made for Ireland in European Commission (2000). However, I make the additional assumption that the growth rate of GNP equals the growth rate of GDP from 2001 onwards.[10] Under these assumptions a fund equal to 38.1% of GNP (or just over £58 billion at 2000 prices) will have accumulated by 2025, the earliest date at which withdrawals can take place.

To get a sense of the feasible withdrawal rate from the fund from 2025, note that the following schedule of *net* withdrawals exactly exhausts the fund by 2055.[11]

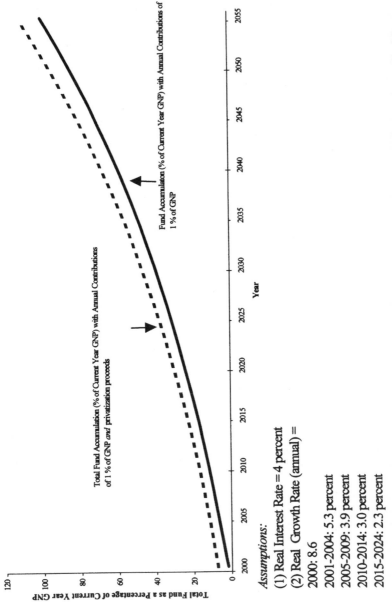

Fig. 1. National Pension Reserve Fund Accumulation with Annual Contributions of 1% of GNP and Zero Drawdowns (% of Current Year GNP).

2025 to 2029: −0.5% of GNP
2030 to 2034: +0.5% of GNP
2035 to 2039: +1.5% of GNP
2040 to 2044: +2.5% of GNP
2045 to 2055: +3.5% of GNP

Thus the fund could go a substantial way to relieving the state pension burden over this period. Of course, the pension burden does not end at 2055, the date the fund is exhausted under this illustrative scenario. Moreover, there is also the second aging-related issue of rising health care costs. It is clear from the statement of the Minister for Finance in introducing the bill that this is well understood. From a longer-term perspective, the setting up of the institutional machinery for pre-funding future obligations is more significant than the size of the initial allocations to the fund. In fact, the Minister made clear that additional contributions could be made, budgetary conditions permitting, thus signaling that the 1% contribution is a minimum number, although it is not inconceivable that legislation to lower or even eliminate the annual contribution would be introduced in hard times.

The preamble to the NPRF bill says that the fund is to "have a strictly commercial investment mandate" with the "objective of securing the optimal return over the long-term subject to prudent risk management" (NPRF Bill, 2000). To control the fund, the legislation sets out for the establishment of an independent seven-member National Pensions Reserve Commission. The Commission is supposed to have the power to appoint a "Manager" to act as its agent. In a controversial move, however, the Minister of Finance appointed the National Treasury Management Agency (NTMA), the state agency responsible for managing the national debt, as fund manager for the first 10 years. A further potential problem is that the CEO of the management organization is to be one of the seven commissioners, undermining the separation of management from the commission. (See Honahan & Lane, 2000, for a criticism of this institutional feature.)

The literature on Central Bank independence gives us some guide in evaluating this institutional arrangement. This literature points to a difficult tradeoff between protection from political interference and accountability (see, for example, Romer & Romer, 1997). Accountability demands that incompetent agents get removed. Yet the ability to remove the agents undermines political independence. The separation of the commission from active management can be seen as an attempt to balance these competing demands. If the commission retains independence from the Minister, yet is able to dismiss incompetent managers, poor managers can be removed without the process becoming politicized. With this delicate balancing act in mind, imposing a state agency – however widely respected – as the manager for 10 years, and making the manager a commission member, hardly seems like good institutional design.

Also at issue is the actual degree of political independence enjoyed by the commission itself. The Minister for Finance appoints the commissioners to five-year renewable terms.[12] The legislation states, however, that that a "commissioner may at any time for stated reasons be removed from membership of the Commission by the Minister if, in the Minister's opinion, the member has become incapable through ill-health of performing his or her functions, or has committed stated misbehaviour, or his or her removal appears to the Minister to be necessary for the effective performance by the Commission of its functions" (NPRF Bill 2000, Part II, Section 14). With the commissioners effectively serving at the pleasure of the minister, their independence could be compromised.

Turning to the investment strategy of the fund, the legislation envisions that investments are made on a purely commercial basis and prohibits the holding of national debt. This is a sensible approach. Late in 2000, Minister McCreevy added the clarification that, given the large size of the fund in relation to the size of Irish financial markets, "it is inevitable that most of the fund will be invested abroad" (Brennan, 2000).

In addition to producing a more diversified portfolio, international investment should enhance the political independence of the Commission. On the negative side, the legislation does not proscribe an active – and thus potentially costly – management approach. It is foreseeable that the managing institution will have a vested interest in a more active management approach, since passive investing involves little more than book keeping and safe keeping functions. Over long investment horizons there is considerable evidence that active management strategies under-perform passive index tracking given the cost difference and the difficulties in identifying undervalued assets in highly competitive financial markets. Even small differences in average after-cost rates of return can compound to significant differences in fund accumulation (Honahan & Lane, 2000). For example, if the cost of active management drives down the real rate of return by 50 basis points in our earlier calculations (from 4% to 3.5%), fund accumulation by 2025 falls from 38.1% 35.4% of GNP.

To sum up, the NPRF is a praiseworthy attempt to limit the cost to future generations of workers of paying for state pensions. To the extent the future workers would have been unwilling to pay those higher costs it also reduces the risks to current workers that their pensions will be cut as the population ages. The organization of the fund also has some attractive features, notably the stated intention to emphasize international investment and the separation of oversight from management. Yet there are reasons for concern. The minister has usurped the commission's discretion by appointing a state agency as manager for the first 10 years. And the CEO of the manager has a seat on the commission, raising the specter of a management-dominated commission. Furthermore, future ministers retain substantial powers to dismiss commissioners who deviate from their political objectives. Lastly, there is the concern that fund accumulation will be needlessly compromised by an overly active management strategy.[13]

3. THE ENTWINING OF FISCAL AND INCOMES POLICY

Tax Cuts, Wage Restraint, and Social Partnership

Starting in 1987, successive Irish governments have pursued a series of social partnership agreements with unions, employers, and other "social partners." The most recent agreement, the *Programme for Prosperity and Fairness* (PPF), began in early 2000 and is set to run until the end of 2002, barring a crisis of the sort that almost derailed the agreement in the latter half of 2000. Like its predecessors, the cornerstone of this agreement is the promise that the government will cut taxes in return for wage restraint.

For various reasons, past tax cuts do not appear to have put an onerous burden on the economy or the exchequer. First, Ireland had high marginal tax rates in the late 1980s. Based on the international evidence it is reasonable to assume that these high rates distorted labor supply and saving, encouraged emigration, and reduced the attractiveness of Ireland as a location for direct investment. Second, the attempt by Irish governments in the 1980s to reduce the budget deficit by raising taxes had proved recessionary. The shift to pursuing fiscal austerity via severe spending cuts – in both the current and capital budgets – coincided with substantial improvement in the growth performance. Third, but not unrelated to the first two, the shift in strategy coincided with a stunning improvement in Ireland's trend growth performance, so that tax revenues have increased even as tax rates have fallen.

The move to centralized agreements also served another function. Under industry bargaining, unions use their monopoly power to push up wages with little regard for the aggregate effects of their actions. Put differently, they ignore the externality associated with their wage setting behavior. Therefore, the economy-wide unemployment rate (and thus the pain of job loss) must be higher to keep real wage demands in line with what it is feasible for firms to pay. The result of all unions pushing for higher wages can be substantially higher equilibrium unemployment rate with limited actual real wage gains (Layard et al., 1991). (The logic of this argument is further explained in the Appendix.) Under centralized bargaining, unions can internalize the externality, allowing the economy to achieve a lower unemployment rate while maintaining stable inflation (Calmfors & Driffill, 1988). To the extent that union participation is secured by an offer of tax cuts, workers can also achieve higher after-tax real incomes. And to the extent that employment rises, the government can pay for the tax cuts through an expansion of the tax base.

This tax cutting/incomes policy worked well as long as there was slack in the economy, or for as long as the Irish Central Bank could offset any inflationary impact of an overly expansionary fiscal policy with a tighter monetary policy. Problems emerge, however, as the economy overheats. Additional tax cuts add to demand and further fuel the inflation spiral. On the other hand, raising taxes, or even withholding expected tax cuts, leads to higher real wage demands for any given level of unemployment and output.

In the Appendix, I show the problem facing the policy maker is one of having *too few instruments*. Essentially, it has one instrument – the tax rate – and two targets – an output/unemployment target and a stable inflation target.[14]

The problem can be solved if the policy maker is given a second instrument. This instrument can be another tool for controlling demand in the economy, such as control over monetary policy. Of course, this is exactly the instrument taken away under EMU.

The Appendix also shows how deferred compensation (say in the form of contributions to retirement accounts) can provide the needed second instrument. The key assumption for deferred compensation to work is that *workers value the deferred compensation, but such compensation has a limited impact on their current consumption demand.*

In a life cycle consumption model, *deferred* compensation should have the same impact on current consumption as *current* compensation with an equal present value. There are, however, two reasons to think deferred compensation has a smaller impact on current consumption.

The first is that the consumer is liquidity constrained. The consumer would like to spend more now given expectations of future income, but is unable to borrow on the strength of their future income prospects. In this case, deferred compensation – assuming it cannot be used as collateral for borrowing – has no effect on current consumption. Of course, this implies that the consumer values current compensation more than the promise of deferred compensation with an equal present value. Thus there is a tradeoff between the value of the compensation and the impact on current consumption, a relevant consideration in any social partnership negotiations.

This analysis assumes that the consumer is a rational forward-looking maximizer. There is, however, considerable evidence that people *undersave* as a result of problems of self-control in delaying gratification (see, for example, Laibson, 1997). Thaler (1990) reports evidence that the marginal propensity to consume differs between assets in ways inconsistent with the life cycle model. The marginal propensity to consume appears to be near one out of current income, near zero out of future income, and somewhere in between out of accumulated assets. This suggests that it could make a big difference to the impact on current consumption whether government compensation is given in the form of current tax cuts or is deferred in the form of contributions to illiquid retirement accounts. Moreover, although such *weakness of will* is present, consumers are often aware of their shortcomings, and take advantage of various mechanisms to commit themselves to saving more (Laibson, 1997). Given this desire for greater saving in more detached moments, it is possible that consumers will actually value the deferred compensation *more* than current compensation with an equal present value.

If deferred compensation is significantly valued by workers, the government can achieve its desired mix of wage restraint and domestic demand, and thus, in principle, both its targets.

4. A PROPOSAL FOR UNIVERSAL PERSONAL RETIREMENT ACCOUNTS

In this section, I briefly outline a plan for Universal Personal Retirement Accounts (UPRAs) as a means for implementing deferred compensation in the context of social partnership agreements. The accounts are designed with multiple objectives in mind. The (sometimes-conflicting) objectives are improved labor market incentives; increased national saving; development of domestic capital markets and the savings habit; improved provision for retirement; and, most importantly in the present context, the addition of an instrument for macroeconomic management. The accounts are meant to augment the second (occupational) pillar of the retirement income system.[15] The first pillar of flat-rate social welfare pensions is assumed to continue as before. I also assume that the accumulation of a National Pension Reserve Fund (NPRF) to pre-fund future social welfare and public sector pension obligations continues as planned.[16]

Universal Personal Retirement Accounts

- Accounts are set up for each working age adult in the state.[17]
- The government contributes to accounts according to a linear formula: a basic amount plus a fraction of earnings (possibly up to an earnings ceiling). *The*

parameters of the formula are negotiated periodically with the social part-
ners as part of the social partnership agreements.[18] Contributions to the
accounts of married individuals are split equally between each spouse's
account.

- Individuals and employers are allowed to make additional tax-deductible
  contributions.[19]
- Individuals select funds from a list of well-diversified, passively managed
  index tracker funds, or they are allocated to a well-diversified default fund
  (possibly managed by the National Treasury Management Agency in conjunc-
  tion with its management of the NPRF).[20] Fund costs and risk profiles are
  subject to regulation. No upper limit is placed on foreign content.
- Individuals can withdraw money from the fund from age 60.[21] Withdrawals
  are taxed at the individual's marginal tax rate. There is no requirement that
  funds be annuitised.[22]
- Fund balances cannot be used as collateral for loans.
- Account holders receive regular statements on their funds' absolute and
  relative performance.

An example helps to get a sense of the direct costs to the government of
contributing according to the linear formula to a quite generous plan.

Assumptions

GDP = £81 bl.
Working age population = 2.5 ml.
Labor share of income = 2/3
Base contribution = £500
Fraction of earnings contributed = 2%
No earnings ceiling applied
Total Government Contribution =

(Base Contrib. × Working Age Pop.) + (Earnings Fraction × Total Earnings)
= (£500 × 2,500,000) + (0.02 × £54,000,000,000)
= £1.25 bl. + £1.08 bl.= £2.33 bl. (≈ 2.9% of GDP).

This example considers a quite generous plan with a base contribution of £500,
an additional contribution of 2% of earnings, and no earnings ceiling. The
hypothetical base contribution is based on pre-budget proposals for a £500
pension bond. The earnings fraction is loosely based on the 2% reduction in
both the standard and top tax rates announced in last 2001 budget. With these
assumptions the total cost is £2.33 billion, or just under 3% of GDP.

One obvious concern is that government contributions to individual accounts would have a different distributional impact to a tax cutting package involving a mixture of changes in tax credits, standard bandwidth and tax rates. Nonetheless, even this simple formula provides a great deal of distributional flexibility, so that it should be possible to approximate the distributional impact of any tax-cutting package.

The possibility of reducing labor supply distortions must also be kept in mind in trading off base contributions against a higher earnings fraction. Higher base contributions could actually reduce labor supply via an income effect. A higher earnings fraction would raise labor supply via a substitution effect and lower it via an income effect. The substitution effect is what matters for economic efficiency. Given that the government has been reducing marginal tax rates to improve labor supply incentives, it is important that the deferred compensation scheme has a substantial earnings-related component if this compensation is substituting for marginal tax reductions.[23]

Issues of risk and cost have received a great deal of attention in the international literature on shifting to Chilean-style individual accounts as a means of funding retirement income. Although careful consideration would have to be given to each in the detailed plan design, I don't think that they pose insurmountable barriers to the type of plan outlined here.

On risk, the accounts are meant to supplement the existing social welfare system, which provide a defined-benefit base for retirement income. It is possible that allowing additional voluntary contributions would displace some of the current occupational coverage. To the extent that the displaced occupational coverage is in the form of defined benefit plans, this could lead to individuals facing more risk. There is, however, a worldwide trend towards replacing defined benefit plans with defined contribution plans in private pension coverage. Thus the existing structure of occupational pensions probably does not provide the appropriate benchmark. In any case, the limits on the range of plans and the emphasis on diversification should limit the risks involved.[24]

On cost, the plan envisions limiting investments to low-cost index tracker funds. It should be possible to provide the fund management services at annual costs of less than 50 basis points. Thus costly active management is eschewed.[25] Such constraints might be considered an excessive infringement on investor sovereignty for voluntary additional contributions. For the government contributions, however, such limits on fund choice are a sensible safeguard. The cost to the government of making its contributions should also be quite low. An account can be set up for everyone with a Personal Public Service Number, which can be matched to PRSI data to determine the earnings-related part of the contribution. The government's contribution could be sent directly to the individual's choice of account or to the default account if no account is chosen.

5. SOME ALTERNATIVE PENSION FUNDING REFORMS

Pension Bonds

In the run-up to the 2001 budget, a significant amount of media attention was given to a union proposal for offering pension bonds as a form of non-inflationary compensation for higher than expected inflation. Leading newspaper outlets reported that the idea was under active consideration by the government, and the idea received some support from the then finance spokesman, and later leader, of the leading opposition party, Fine Gael.

The union proposal was to provide a once off £500 pension bond to every current and former social insurance contributor in the state. This proposal has some attractive features in terms of the arguments made in the previous section. Indeed, it can be viewed as a special case of the individual account proposal in which there is no earning-related component and there is a single investment option.

First, to the extent that they are substitutes for tax cuts as a means of securing wage restraint, the bonds can serve as the needed instrument for keeping unemployment low and avoiding an inflation spiral. As with contributions to individual accounts, this presupposes that the bonds do not have a substantial impact on current consumption demand. To help ensure this, the bonds should not be cashable before retirement. Sales of bonds to third parties and the use of the bonds as collateral for loans would also need to be prohibited. Second, since very little investment machinery is needed to implement the proposal, it should be possible to put them in place quickly and at a relatively low cost. Third, since all social insurance contributors receive an asset of the same value, the proposal avoids the adverse distributional implications of other proposals.

The pension bonds proposal also has a number of considerable drawbacks. The most obvious is that it does not improve the return to work. It is thus inferior to cuts in marginal tax rates or earnings-related contributions to retirement accounts from the perspective of removing labor supply distortions.

A second drawback is that for the bonds to increase public saving by their full face value they must fully substitute for tax cuts that would otherwise have taken place. In fact, if the substitution is partial, and other private savings fall because of the increase in lifetime wealth, current consumption could increase.

A third drawback is that restricting deferred compensation to a special government bond unnecessarily limits the value of the deferred compensation to the recipient. Individual investors are prevented from investing in diversified portfolios with more attractive risk-return characteristics. Moreover, the opportunity to set up a vehicle for voluntary supplemental contributions is wasted, as is the opportunity to allow people to learn about investing in assets other than bank deposits.

Finally, a once-off (or even repeated) distribution of pension bonds in a crisis does not establish the permanent machinery for integrating deferred compensation into the social partnership framework. Although it is conceivable that pension bond distributions could be incorporated as a permanent feature of the bargaining process, permanent UPRAs with individual identification numbers should provide a more robust framework for ongoing negotiations over deferred compensation.

Tax-Based Savings Incentives

Another alternative to individual accounts is to expand tax-based saving incentives, an idea that has been strongly advocated by the Progressive Democrat party (the junior party in the government coalition). From a macroeconomic management point of view, the appeal of the idea is simple: encouraging people to defer consumption will lower aggregate demand. From a longer-term perspective, it is also hoped that such tax incentives will boost the country's saving rate.

The success of this policy in achieving its short-term and long-term goals depends, in part, on the sensitivity of saving to the after-tax rate of return. From the theoretical point of view, the response of current consumption to a change in its "price" depends on two opposing effects. A substitution effect (roughly the reduction in consumption because the "opportunity cost" in terms of future consumption foregone has increased); and an income effect (roughly the fact that a given standard of living in retirement can be attained with less saving when the after-tax rate of return is higher).

The international evidence on the impact of taxes and saving can be conveniently divided into two parts. First, there is a long-established literature that looks at the relationship between the after-tax rate of return and saving. Following a recent review of this evidence, Bernheim (1997, pp. 259–260) concluded:

> [T]here is little reason to believe that households increase their saving significantly in response to a generic increase in the after-tax rate of return. Since the evidence is quite poor, there is still considerable uncertainty on this point. However, it is difficult to identify any robust empirical pattern suggestive of a higher [interest rate] elasticity.

The lack of robustness of the findings of the more traditional studies has led researchers to look at direct evidence on the effects of particular tax-based incentives on saving behavior. These tax-favored savings vehicles do more than just alter the after-tax rate of return. In the context of the earlier discussion of not fully rational savers, these saving vehicles provide a way of making accumulated wealth less liquid and thus safe from temptation. In addition, to the extent that deposits into these accounts are made by automatic withdrawals from bank accounts or paychecks, they allow people to become regular savers without having to constantly face the decision about whether to consume or save.[26]

Individual Retirement Accounts (IRAs) and 401(k) plans in the United States have received particular attention. There is no doubt that tax incentives dramatically increase savings in the tax-favored savings vehicle. The difficult question is how much individuals increase their overall saving as distinct from simply substituting towards a tax-favored option. It is instructive to quote Bernheim (1997, p. 260) again, this time on evidence related to 401(k) plans.[27]

> [T]he available evidence on 401(k) plans allows one to conclude with moderate confidence that, all else equal, eligibility of such a plan significantly stimulates personal saving .... Although no existing study corresponds to the ideal statistical experiment, at least one sensible approach concludes that 401(k)s do not displace other saving despite the fact that its primary shortcoming probably creates a bias in the opposite direction.

Overall, then, despite the disagreement in the literature, it is reasonable to suppose that tax-based saving incentives would be effective in the Irish context. Even though such incentives might be good policy irrespective of any macroeconomic management concerns, by themselves they would be ill-designed to provide a deferred compensation instrument with the social partnership framework.

Two related drawbacks stand out. First, since it is the better off that save the most, the benefits of the saving incentives would be concentrated on the more advantaged. And second, notwithstanding that many wage earners are also savers, it is hard to imagine that unions would be willing to tradeoff wages and general income tax cuts for tax-based saving incentives. It is possible that a scheme that is concentrated on small savers would be more acceptable. It is interesting, then, that the government announced a scheme in February 2001 targeted at small savers. Unfortunately, however, the scheme is not designed to provide the crucial additional instrument to social partnership.

The Government's New Special Savings Incentive Scheme

Under fire from the European Commission and from EU finance ministers for its overly expansionary 2001 budget, the government announced a special savings scheme along with the publication of the 2001 Finance Bill. It is hoped that the scheme will take some steam out of the overheating economy by boosting private saving. Looking to the longer term, the scheme is also meant as a partial redress to the problem of under-saving for retirement and other foreseeable contingencies such as mortgage down payments, education-related bills, and periods of job loss.

Among other innovative elements, the scheme incorporates a substantial government subsidy. But the design also contains a number of flaws.

First the main elements.

- The scheme will begin on May 1, 2000, and run for five years. Accounts must be opened before April 30, 2002.
- Every resident of the state 18 or older can participate. Only one account can be opened, and Personal Public Service Numbers must be given to the investment manager. Strict controls will be applied to prevent any fraudulent opening of multiple accounts.
- Individuals can contribute up to £200 per month to the scheme. *Individual contributions receive a 25% government match.*[28]
- For the first year there is a £10 minimum on monthly contributions. No minimum applies in years 2 through 5.
- The savings accumulate tax-free. There is, however, a 23% tax on any nominal gains (total value of the fund at the end of year 5 less total contributions) to be paid at the end of the five-year period.
- A broad range of financial institutions and fund managers can manage accumulated savings, and investments can be made in a wide range of financial instruments.
- Government contributions are sent directly to the investment manager.
- Early withdrawals (for reasons other than death) are subject to the 23% tax on the entire withdrawal (contributions and gains).
- The accumulated savings cannot be used as security for a loan.

The essence of the scheme is a government offer of large saving subsidies in return for giving up liquidity.[29] Obviously, the liquidity cost is highest for the earliest contributions, since the money is being tied up for the longest period. Thus the saver must trade off subsidy against liquidity.

Is the scheme well designed to defer consumption and thus reduce demand pressures in the economy? I think there are three reasons for doubt.

(1) The savings incentives are heavily back-loaded, with the largest effective subsidies coming at the end of the five-year period. To see that the size of

the effective saving subsidy increases over the five-year period note that the equivalent (after-tax) rate of return, r^*, can be written as,

$$r^* = \sqrt[T]{(1 - 0.23)(1.25)\,[(1 + r)^T - 1] + 1.25} - 1,$$

where T is the time to maturity and r is the (pre-tax, post-management cost) rate of return on the financial investment. Figure 2 shows how this equivalent rate of return varies with the number of months to maturity assuming a 4% rate of return on investments. For ease of interpretation, I show this rate of return on an annualized rate basis, though the calculations are based on monthly compounding. In the first month of the scheme the equivalent annualized rate of return is almost 8%, roughly double even the pre-tax market rate of return. Thus even in the first period contributions receive a large effective subsidy. The equivalent rate of return, r^*, rises slowly at first, reaching almost 11% by the end of the second year. It then rises rapidly towards the end of the five-year period. In the final month (the final four months are not shown on the graph to preserve the scale) the annualized equivalent rate of return reaches almost 1400%. Since there is almost no liquidity cost to putting money into the scheme at this late stage, the incentive to participate is obviously quite high at this point. At the other extreme, the incentive to participate is weakest in the first period when the effective subsidy is the lowest and the liquidity cost is highest.[30]

How might the savings incentives have been front-loaded rather than back-loaded? Consider instead an alternative scheme in which the government adds a certain number of percentage points to the annualized return that an individual gets on their investment. For ease of comparability with the government's scheme, suppose that this alternative scheme also lasts for 5 years and all gains are taxed at 23%. The equivalent (after-tax) rate of return is now,,

$$r^{**} = \sqrt[T]{(1 - 0.23)[(1 + r + s)^T - 1] + 1} - 1,$$

where s is the subsidy measured in percentage points. To take an illustrative example, if s is set at 11 percentage points, so that the post-subsidy rate of return is 15% on an annualized basis, r^{**} is 12.2% (annualized) on contributions made in the first month. This equivalent rate of return then falls slightly over the five-year period, reaching just over 11.4% (annualized) in the last month of the scheme (see Fig. 2). The 11 percentage point subsidy is chosen so that both funds accumulate to roughly the same post-tax size – just over £16,200 – for somebody making the maximum £200 monthly

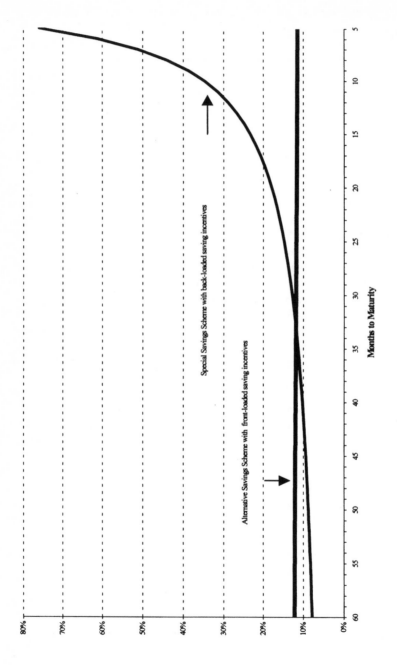

Fig. 2. Equivalent Annualized After-Tax Rate of Return Based on Month of Contribution (Month 1 to Month 56).

contribution to the scheme for the full five years. Thus, it would have been relatively easy for the government to design an equally generous scheme that provides the greatest saving incentives right at the beginning, which presumably is a desirable given the objective of taking steam out of the overheating economy.

(2) The impact on saving is theoretically ambiguous. To see this it is useful to consider three distinct groups: rational (in the sense of being forward looking life cycle consumption maximizers) large savers; rational small savers; and "irrational" savers either large or small.

- Rational large savers: These individuals already save *more* each month than the maximum monthly contribution to the saving scheme. Given the high equivalent rates of return, this group is likely to switch savings into the new savings scheme, making them better off in terms of the present value of total lifetime income. For these large savers, however, the return on marginal saving – i.e. the return on an additional pound of saving – is unlikely to increase. With an increase in income and no increase in the marginal return to saving, the standard life cycle model predicts that current consumption will *increase* for this group.

- Rational small savers: These individuals save *less* each month than the maximum monthly contribution to the savings scheme. The marginal return to saving has thus increased for this group. There is thus both an income effect (higher lifetime income allows higher consumption in every period) and a substitution effect (there is a greater reward for postponing current consumption). The income effect leads to more current consumption and the substitution effect to less, making the overall effect theoretically ambiguous.

- "Irrational" savers, large and small: The saving implications that follow from focusing on rational savers are almost certainly too pessimistic. As noted before, there is ample evidence that people are not so forward looking and calculating when making their saving decisions. Actual savings behavior appears to be affected by a number of psychological propensities such as impatience and habitual behavior. Realizing these "weaknesses," people use various devices to overcome their tendency to undersave. One device is to invest in illiquid assets such as housing, often with a commitment to build equity via monthly mortgage payments. Another device is to make automatic withdrawals from bank accounts or directly from paycheques to make deposits to investment funds. For less-than-rational savers, the proposed savings scheme – with its forced illiquidity and inertia overcoming returns – provides a powerful inducement to save more, whatever is being saved already. Moreover, since many of the participants in the scheme will be new to regular saving, participation should help to inculcate the saving habit and increase financial sophistication.

On balance, then, I think it is reasonable to suppose that the scheme will increase saving and thus take some of the heat out of the economy. Nonetheless, predicting the saving response is less straightforward than early ministerial comment allowed.

(3) The unconditional introduction of the scheme missed an opportunity to use it as a substitute for tax cuts in the re-negotiation of the PPF.

The proposed scheme, insofar as it is completely additional to the tax cuts offered in the budget and the additional wage increases offered in the pre-budget re-negotiation of the PPF, missed an opportunity to substitute less inflationary deferred compensation for current compensation. In addition, by committing to the scheme for five years, the government limited its scope to use future subsidies in future negotiations.

In the context of the chapter, I think that No. (3) is the most unfortunate flaw. Even with the back loading of the saving incentives and the ambiguity over the overall saving impact, an opportunity for adding a valuable instrument to the social partnership framework was missed. While a system of UPRAs with negotiated government contributions provides the most flexible (and yet enduring) way to add the needed second instrument to social partnership, putting the saving scheme on the table in the negotiations with the social partners before the budget would have been a reasonable substitute. The scheme – though probably under consideration for some time – had the look of a hurried face-saving response in the aftermath of an embarrassing recommendation from Ireland's European partners to take steps to cool the economy.

6. CONCLUDING COMMENT

To borrow from the title for this conference, Ireland has indeed been "open for business" – especially American business – in recent decades. Just as importantly, Ireland's disproportionate share of multinational investment indicates that it has been an attractive place to do business. Many factors lie behind this success – a relatively well-educated workforce, location, language, an attractive tax regime, the large Irish Diaspora, among others – but the move to a more consensual, nationally focused system of industrial relations under the sequence of social partnership agreements has played an important role. With the economy overheating and macroeconomic policy constrained under EMU, the social partnership framework is in danger of collapsing if it doesn't adapt. I have argued that the addition of an instrument for negotiating deferred compensation would be one useful adaptation.

The Irish economy would also benefit from an increase in the national saving rate. The country has relied to its great advantage on foreign direct investment to catapult itself among the world's most productive nations. The large and growing gap between Irish GDP and GNP is a warning, however, that the economy might now be overly reliant on labor income from potentially mobile multinationals. This does not mean that Ireland should become any less friendly to overseas investors. But Irish citizens must save and (internationally) invest more themselves. One important way to increase savings is to continue to develop mechanisms for collective and individual pre-funding of retirement income needs.

NOTES

1. It was Ireland's perceived breach of Broad Economic Policy Guidelines agreed to by the government that brought the rebuke. But given their broad coverage, these guidelines were often contradictory. The guidelines do tell the Irish government to "use budgetary policy to ensure economic stability given the extent of overheating in the economy" and to "gear the 2001 budget to this objective" (European Commission, 2000, p. 35). However the guidelines also recommend "that the objectives of the national development plan be given high priority" and that "a comprehensive strategy to increase the participation of women in the labour market, including the removal of tax-benefit disincentives" should be pursued. The government can reasonably argue that it was meeting these guidelines with the spending rises and tax cuts it pursued in the budget. The guidelines also tell the government to give priority to "monitoring wage developments so as to ensure they are consistent with the wage moderation needed for employment growth." Given that the union leadership reserved its final decision on whether to accept the re-negotiation of the social partnership agreement until it heard the Minister's budget speech, a plausible case can be made that the giveaway budget was required to prevent a collapse of the social partnership.

2. The inflation rate subsequently fell back in December and January, as oil prices stabilized and the euro staged a modest recovery. Other causes of the inflation rate decline were the falling out of index rise of the cigarette tax increase announced in the 2000 budget, the one percentage point decline in VAT announced in the 2001 budget, and the winter sales.

3. I should add that this tradeoff story oversimplifies the considerations facing the government in devising the budget. One important fact is that the Minister for Finance expressed public doubt that the Irish inflation problem was seriously affected by domestic demand conditions. Instead, he pointed to the impact of rising oil prices, a weakening euro, higher mortgage costs following ECB interest rate increases, and once off effects of excise tax increases from his 2000 budget. The government also seemed to be on extreme guard against alienating any section of the electorate, following a series of politically damaging controversies and with an eye to a possible election in 2001.

4. Non-contributory means-tested old age pensions were first introduced in Britain and Ireland during the wave of liberal reforms (1906–1914). After independence, Ireland continued with the British System, paying a means-tested pension to people aged 70 and over (an eligibility age that remained in effect until 1973) (Johnson, 1999).

5. It is interesting to note that SERPs have been substantially scaled back through a sequence of reforms in the 1980s and 1990s, and there are plans to phase out the scheme altogether.

6. Irish governments appear to value the credit they get for raising pensions at budget time.

7. A major change in the 2001 budget was the removal of the ceiling on employer PSRI contributions. Making the standard assumption that the incidence of labor income taxes is predominantly on workers, this change implies a large increase in the marginal tax rates applying to labor income for high earners. This effect will swamp the 2 percentage point reduction in the top rate of income tax (42% to 40%), and was a surprising move given the government's stated goal of improving work incentives.

8. The other main recommendations of the board were that the government intro-duce a mechanism to pre-fund future pension obligations, and that the social welfare pensions be raised to a minimum of 34% of average earnings over a period of 10 years (from 28.5% in 1998). The government adopted the pre-funding proposal (see Section below). The more than 10% increases in the value of social welfare pensions in the 2001 budget is some evidence of the government's commitment to raising the relative value of pensions. It is worth pointing out, however, that these rather generous increases occurred in the context of a high inflation rate (reaching 7% year-on-year in November 2000), rapid increases in wages, and a budget surplus of over 4% of GDP that made generosity rather easy. There is no guarantee that social welfare pensions will rise, or even hold their own, as a share of average income in the years ahead.

9. The decomposition is given by,

$$\frac{B}{Y} = \frac{\dfrac{B}{PE}}{\dfrac{Y}{PWE}} \times \frac{PE}{PWA} = \text{Benefit Generosity Rate} \times \text{Elderly Dependency Rate}$$

where,

B = total pension benefits; Y = GDP; PE = population 65 and over; PWA = working age population (20 to 64).

10. In recent years, the growth in real GDP has been outpacing the growth in real GNP, indicating a possible downward bias in the size of the Fund. On the other hand, the European Commission estimates for real GDP growth appear conservative, indicating an upward bias.

11. The figures are the net impact of the 1% of GNP that continues to be added to the fund and the sequence of gross withdrawals assumed here for illustration purposes.

12. Commissioners, other than the CEO of the "Manager," cannot serve more than two consecutive terms.

13. From an efficiency perspective, using a state fund as a vehicle for pre-funding is also less than ideal. The efficiency issues here closely parallel the efficiency issues with

the flat-rate social welfare pensions discussed above. The additional income (and other) taxes used to pay for the pre-funding will appear as pure taxes to those who pay them, since there isn't a direct linkage between those taxes and later benefits. Thus, those taxes add to labor supply distortions. In terms of national saving, the fund should lead to higher saving provided that the contributions to the fund would otherwise have been dissipated in additional tax cuts and spending rises. Without this dissipation, the result would be a smaller national debt, implying that there is no net impact on national saving from the pre-funding effort. Lastly, since asset management is centralized, and mostly invested abroad, the fund does little to develop domestic capital markets or domestic savings habits.

14. Here I assume that there is little scope to use government spending as an instrument for fiscal demand management. Spending on such areas as health and education cannot be easily adjusted upwards and downwards to fine tune the economy and it is probably unwise to delay needed infrastructure projects. In contrast, governments have more latitude in deciding on the timing of tax cuts. Moreover, to the extent that spending commitments also comprise part of social partnership deal, government spending is not available as a free instrument for demand management purposes.

15. See McHale (2001) for an overview of the two pillars of Ireland's pensions system.

16. See McHale (2001) for an overview of the institutional machinery of NPRF, and for estimates of likely fund accumulation as a share of GNP.

17. To help inculcate the savings habit, the system could also be extended to children. In principle, the system could also be extended to the current elderly, although increases in the flat rate pensions would probably be a more efficient way to target additional support on this group.

18. The negotiations could be limited to the share of earnings parameter, with the base amount remaining constant over time.

19. This is not essential to plan. Yet with the low level of occupational pension coverage, it is desirable that there is universal access to a tax-favored pensions plan. This element could be dropped if the government goes ahead with its plans for separate Personal Retirement Saving Accounts, though it might be better integrate the UPRA and PRSA plans to avoid a multiplicity of retirement saving vehicles. The government and social partners would need to stress that future government contributions are not guaranteed, so that individuals would have to make adequate provision for their retirement needs unconditional on the government's contributions.

20. The existence of this default account raises issues of possible government interference in the fund's management. This potential politicisation problem could be minimized by a requirement that all investments are in non-Irish assets.

21. Controls might need to be put in place to prevent people from drawing down their funds at an early date in order to qualify for asset-tested non-contributory pensions. One possible control is to include accumulated assets at age 60 in the assets test.

22. I have not included an annuitization requirement given that the first pillar of social welfare pensions continues to provide a basic annuity. Such a requirement might be considered, however, to overcome the well-known adverse selection problem in the annuities market – the people most likely to buy annuities are those who expect to live the longest.

23. From a political point of view, making larger contributions for higher earners will be a hard sell. It is thus important that the government emphasize that the deferred compensation is substituting for tax cuts, and to the extent that those cuts would have included rate cuts, higher earners would have disproportionately received the benefits.

24. If the remaining risk is considered unacceptable, the government could provide a lower-bound guarantee on fund returns. This involves the government adopting a potentially expensive contingent liability, however.

25. Over a 30-year investment horizon a 50 basis point annual management cost on accumulated assets growing at a pre-cost rate of 4% per annum is equivalent to a roughly 13% front-end charge on money invested (with no charges thereafter). If the annual management charge is 100 basis points, the equivalent front-end charge rises to roughly 25%. If it is 200 basis points – not unusual for an actively managed fund – the equivalent front-end charge is 44%. Thus, what seem like small differences in management costs compound over time to dramatically lower the value of investments.

26. Of course, automatic withdrawals into investment funds can take place outside of these tax-favored savings plans. Individuals might be less likely to set up these automatic withdrawals and deposits without the lure of tax incentives, however.

27. The study referred to in the quote below is Poterba, Venti and Wise (1995). For a critique of the Poterba et al. approach, see Engen, Gale and Scholz (1994).

28. This is equivalent to making the total contribution tax deductible at the 20% standard rate of income tax. For example, if someone on the standard rate of income tax contributes £80 out of after-tax income, the total contribution (including the 25% government match) is £100, which is equivalent to allowing the individual to contribute 100 pre-tax pounds.

29. Making the full amount of any early withdrawals subject to the full 23% tax imposes a large penalty for early liquidation.

30. An effect that could work in the opposite direction is present if there is a fixed cost of joining the scheme. Early (and sustained) participation allows the saver to spread the fixed cost over a longer period. In contrast, joining the scheme close to the end allows little time to spread out the fixed cost. Assuming, however, that the fixed cost is zero or has already been paid, the incentive to make a contribution rises strongly with closeness to the end of the scheme.

31. This simple model excludes the possibility that price level increases reduce the real money supply. In other words, it assumes that the aggregate demand curve for the economy is vertical. If price level increases cause a decline in aggregate demand, then the economy has a natural adjustment mechanism for responding to money supply shocks, at least over the long term, and a second instrument is not needed to attain both targets. One complication is that as a wage-price spiral takes hold, aggregate demand could overshoot the output target, so that the deferred compensation instrument continues to have value.

32. I have concentrated on the case where since this is when the policy maker faces a dilemma in responding to an exogenous increase in the money supply. In contrast, if the no-wage-spiral schedule is downward sloping. An exogenous increase in the money supply now requires a tax cut to eliminate the wage-price spiral, causing output to go above the target.

ACKNOWLEDGMENTS

I thank Martin Feldstein, Janos Kornai, Danny McCoy, and Vincent Munley for helpful discussions and comments. All remaining errors and deficiencies are of course my own. The financial support of Harvard University and the Lehigh

University Martindale Center is gratefully acknowledged. This chapter was completed while I was an associate professor at Harvard University.

REFERENCES

Bernheim, D. (1997). Rethinking saving incentives. In: A. Auerbach (Ed.), *Fiscal Policy: Lessons from Economic Research* (pp. 259–311). Cambridge: MIT Press.

Brennan, C. (2000). Bulk of pension fund will be invested abroad. *The Irish Times*, (November 24).

Calmfors L., & Driffill, J. (1988). Bargaining structure, corporatism, and macroeconomic performance. *Economic Policy*, (6), 13–61.

Department of Finance (2000). National Pensions Reserve Bill, 2000. Available at: http://www.irlgov.ie/finance

Engen, E. M., Gale, W. G., & Scholz, J. K. (1994). Do savings incentives work? *Brookings Papers on Economic Activity, 1*, 85–155.

European Commission (2000a). European Economy Public Finances in EMU, 2000. *European Economy*, Brussels, Directorate-General for Economic and Financial Affairs.

European Commission (2000b). Economic Policy Committee Report to the ECOFIN Council on the Impact of Ageing Populations on Pension Systems.

Franco, D., & Munzi, T. (1996). Public pension expenditure prospects in the European union: a survey of national projections. *European Economy*, (3).

Johnson, R. (1999). The effect of social security on male retirement: evidence from historical cross-country data. Harvard University mimeo.

Laibson, D. (1997). Golden eggs and hyperbolic discounting. *Quarterly Journal of Economics*, *CXII*(2), 443–477.

Lane, P. (2001). On the provision of incentives to save. Trinity College Dublin mimeo.

Lane, P., & Honahan, P. (2000). Where the pensions bill falls down, *The Irish Times*, (October 11).

Layard, R., Nickell, S., & Jackman, R. (1991). *Unemployment: Macroeconomic Performance and the Labour Market*. Oxford: Oxford University Press.

McHale, J. (2000). Time for creative policies on pensions. *The Irish Times*, (January 21).

McHale, J. (2000). Options for inflation control in the Irish economy. *Quarterly Economic Commentary*, (September).

McHale, J. (2001). The risk of social security benefit rule changes: Some international evidence. In: J. Campbell & M. Feldstein (Eds), *Risk Aspects of Investment-Based Social Security Reform*. Chicago: University of Chicago Press.

O'Carroll, G. (1998). National pensions policy initiative. *The Irish Banking Review*.

OECD (1998). *Maintaining prosperity in an ageing society*. Paris: OECD.

OECD (1999). Economic surveys: Ireland, Paris: OECD.

OECD (2000). *Economic Outlook*, (December). Paris: OECD.

Poterba, J. M., Venti, S. F., & Wise, D. A. (1995). Do 401(k) contributions crowd out other personal saving? *Journal of Public Economics, 58*, 1–32.

Romer, C., & Romer, D. (1997). Institutions for monetary stability. In: C. Romer & D. Romer (Eds), *Reducing Inflation: Motivation and Strategy*. Chicago: University of Chicago Press.

Thaler, R. (1990). Savings, fungibility, and mental accounts. *Journal of Economic Perspectives*, *IV*, 193–205.

APPENDIX: A SIMPLE TARGETS AND INSTRUMENTS MODEL

I argued in the text that Irish policy makers face the problem of having too few instruments to achieve their policy targets. Policy makers wish to use tax policy to buy wage restraint and thus raise the potential output of the economy (or equivalently to lower the non-accelerating inflation rate of unemployment or NAIRU), but they also wish to use tax policy to as a demand management tool for stabilizing inflation.

In this Appendix, I develop a very simple model in which the policy maker has two targets (an output level and stable inflation), and a single instrument (the tax rate). Starting from a situation in which both targets are met, the economy experiences a positive demand shock that sets off an inflation spiral. As the government attempts to slow demand by raising taxes, workers push for higher real wages for any given output level in order to protect their after tax incomes. Following the demand shock, I show that under certain conditions it is impossible to attain both the output and stable inflation targets. I also show how giving the government an additional instrument can solve the problem. The instrument can either be control over a variable that lowers real wage demands but has limited impact on output demand (e.g. deferred compensation), or control over a variable that lowers output demand but has limited impact on real wage demands (e.g. control over the real money supply).

The model is described by four equations (a superscript e denotes an expected value of the variable):

$$w - p^e - t = \alpha + \beta y \qquad \text{(after-tax real wage target)} \quad (1)$$

$$p - w = \theta \qquad \text{(price mark-up)} \quad (2)$$

$$\pi^e = p^e - p_{-1} = p_{-1} - p_{-2} = \pi_{-1}$$
$$\Rightarrow p^e - p = \pi - \pi_{-1} = \Delta\pi \qquad \text{(expectations formation)} \quad (3)$$

$$y = m - \phi t \qquad \text{(output demand)} \quad (4)$$

where,

w = logarithm of nominal wage
p = logarithm of price level
y = logarithm of output
t = tax rate
π = inflation rate
m = logarithm of the money supply

Equation (1) defines the after tax real wage target of wage setters. In a union wage setting framework, this equation records how unions push for a higher after-tax real wage the higher is output (or the lower is unemployment) in the economy. When economic conditions are buoyant workers are emboldened to push for higher after-tax wages, with the link between wage demands and economic conditions given by the size of the coefficient, β. The equation assumes "real wage resistance," in that after-tax real wage demands at any given level of output are invariant to the tax rate. Equation (2) describes price setting in the economy. I assume that one unit of output requires one unit of labor, and prices are set as a constant mark-up over unit labor costs. Equation (3) imposes a crude form of backward looking expectations formation, with expected inflation equal to last period's actual inflation. Under this assumption the price surprise, $p - p^e$, is equal to the change in the inflation rate. Finally, Eq. (4) describes aggregate demand in the economy, with demand (and thus real output) positively related to the real money supply and negatively related to the tax rate. For simplicity, I assume that aggregate demand does not depend on the price level in the standard way.

Equations (1), (2), and (3) can be combined to produce a standard Phillip curve-type relationship.

$$\Delta\pi = \beta\,(y - y^*) \qquad \text{where,} \quad y^* = \frac{\theta - \alpha - t}{\beta} \tag{5}$$

When real output is greater than the economy's non-inflationary potential, y^*, a wage-price spiral develops and the inflation rate increases. Moreover, because of the impact of taxes on wage setting, potential output is negatively related to the tax rate.

I now assume that the government is pursuing two targets: a stable inflation or no-wage-price spiral target ($\Delta\pi = 0$), and an output target ($y = \bar{y}$). Initially, I assume that the policy has control over two instruments, the real money supply (m) and the tax rate (t). Substituting Eq. (4) into Eq. (5) determines the set of combinations of the two instruments that can achieve the stable inflation target.

$$t = \frac{\alpha - \theta}{\beta\phi - 1} + \left(\frac{1}{\phi - (1/\beta)}\right) m \tag{6}$$

In Fig. A.1, I graph this schedule as upward sloping in tax rate/real money space. The condition for the schedule to be upward sloping is that $\beta\phi > 1$. Since this is the interesting case, I concentrate on it in what follows.

Imposing the restriction that output equals its target value in Eq. (4) yields a schedule showing the tax rate/money supply combinations that meet this target.

This schedule, also graphed in Fig. A.1, is upward sloping and has a flatter slope than the stable inflation schedule (where I continue to assume that).

$$t = \frac{1}{\theta}m - \frac{1}{\theta}\bar{y} \qquad (4')$$

When the policy maker has control over both instruments it can select the tax rate/money supply combination (t_0, m_0) that achieves both targets (point A).

Now assume that the policy maker loses its power to control the real money supply. Furthermore, assume that the real money supply increases to m_1. With just one instrument the policy maker is now unable to achieve both targets simultaneously. Assuming the no-inflation-spiral target has precedence, real output must fall below its target level (point C).

The intuition behind this result is more easily seen with the help of Fig. A.2, which graphs the expectations augmented Phillips curve (Eq. (5)). Starting at point A (where both targets are achieved), an increase in the real money supply shifts the economy to point B. Real output is now above target, but there is an inflation spiral. As the policy maker tries to slow the economy by raising the tax rate the expectations-augmented Phillips curves shifts upwards (or, equivalently, the non-inflationary potential output of the economy falls). The reason for this deterioration is that unions push for higher real wages at any output level to protect after tax incomes. Stable inflation is only restored at point C. At this point, however, real output is below target.[31]

The problem facing the policy maker is that the attempt to slow aggregate demand by raising taxes has undermined wage restraint. Unable to control aggregate demand using fiscal policy, the policy maker needs another instrument for controlling wage setting. One possibility is that the government can affect wage demands through a policy of making deferred contributions to retirement accounts. With the additional instrument we can rewrite Eq. (1) as

$$w - p^e - t + \delta c = \alpha + \beta y \qquad (1')$$

where c is the contribution rate (measured in levels) to the retirement accounts, and δ is a parameter that captures the relative value to workers of tax cuts and retirement account contributions. The stable inflation schedule is now given by

$$t = \frac{\alpha - \theta - \partial c}{\beta\phi - 1} + \left(\frac{1}{\phi - (1/\beta)}\right)m \qquad (6')$$

If we make the further simplifying assumption that contributions to the retirement accounts do not affect demand (say because consumers are liquidity constrained), then the policy maker has an instrument that can shift the stable inflation schedule in Fig. A.1. With the aid of this second instrument, the government is able to attain both targets (point D) by a combination of a tax rate increase and appropriate contributions to retirement accounts.[32]

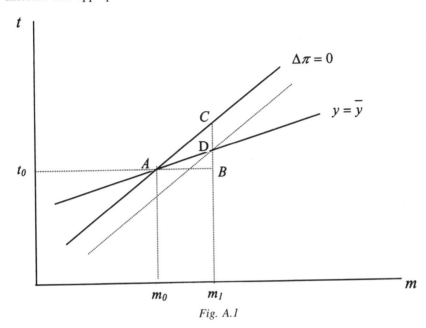

Fig. A.1

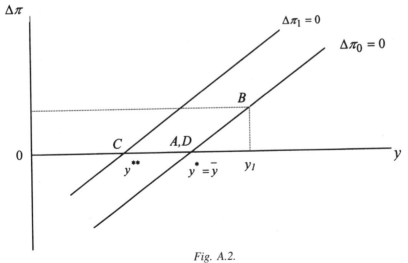

Fig. A.2.

7. PRIVATIZATION OF ELECTRICITY AND TELECOMMUNICATIONS IN IRELAND

L33

L94 L96 L98

Moore McDowell

1. INTRODUCTION: THE POLICY BACKGROUND TO PRIVATIZATION

Privatization in Ireland is a much more recent development than in other EU states, and especially the United Kingdom. In political terms, this has reflected a long-standing and widely accepted involvement of the state in economic activity. This has taken two main forms. One is direct involvement through state ownership. The second is the panoply of measures developed over nearly fifty years to encourage industrial development. There has been little ideological support for reducing the role of the state. Politically, an important element in sustaining a large state sector has been the large number, and local concentrations, of public sector employees.

The consensus supporting state enterprise as a continuing feature of the Irish economy began to unravel during the 1980s, however. In part this was a result of the fiscal crisis which followed the unsustainable deficits which characterised Irish fiscal policy from 1977 to 1982. Not only did these result in the need for a substantial increase in taxation as a proportion of GNP during the 1980s, but a considerable part of the cumulative deficit was a consequence of current subsidies to, and capitalisation of, previous losses in the state sector. At the same time it was becoming increasingly apparent that the efficiency of the state

The Irish Economy in Transition: Successes, Problems, and Prospects, Volume 85, pages 143–177.

sector was far below efficiency levels in comparable state and private sector operations in other countries. By the end of the decade, decision makers were faced with political demands for tax reductions and retrenchment in public spending, influenced by the policies being implemented by the Thatcher administration in Great Britain.

At the beginning of the 1990s state ownership was present across many economic sectors. In addition to the railways, the state had an effective legal monopoly on scheduled road passenger services. Until the late 1980s it had owned the only Irish airline, a licensed monopoly. The largest domestic airline was still in state ownership. It also owned a freight and passenger shipping line on the Irish Sea. In the energy and utilities sector the state owned an oil refinery. Electricity generation and distribution was a state monopoly. The same applied to natural gas distribution. The telephone system was another state monopoly, as was the postal service. In manufacturing, the state owned a large food processing and sugar manufacturing operation. It owned a fertiliser manufacturing operation. It owned a bulk chemical manufacturing operation. It owned the country's commercial peat exploitation business. And it owned a clapped out steel mill on an in-shore island near Cork which relied on scrap iron and steel for its raw material. In the financial sector the state owned two small industrial banks and had ownership rights over a third, somewhat larger retail banking operation which operated on a mutual basis. Through the Post Office it operated a nation-wide savings bank which enjoyed a fiscally privileged position. It had recently taken a failed commercial insurer into state ownership, and operated the country's only licensed supplier of health insurance. The country's largest life assurance operation was also *de facto* in public ownership. Broadcasting had only just ceased being a state monopoly, but the state retained the right to limit by licence entry into broadcasting; and it protected (and continues to protect) the state-owned dominant broadcaster by a compulsory annual licence fee payable by any household owning a TV which goes to the state broadcaster.

Ten years later, however, the landscape had changed dramatically. The steel mill was sold for £1 in 1999. The chemical company was disposed of to a multinational. The fertiliser business went the same way. So did the oil refinery and the cross channel ferry company. The two state-owned banks were up for sale. The mutual bank had been sold. The life assurer had been privatized and has become, through acquisition of a building society (S&L), a mainstream banking firm. The commercial insurer was back in the private sector. The food processor had been privatized and floated off on the stock exchange as was the telecommunications company. The same was under consideration for the state airline and many of the other concerns. The government was considering how to deal with the question of privatization of generation and distribution in the electricity sector.

As we shall see, however, the privatization process has not been a smooth one, particularly in the sectors being examined in this chapter. The consequence has been that the concerns involved remain less than fully competitive by international standards, a factor which has consequences for the business environment in Ireland. Part of the reason for this lies in a lack of clarity as to why privatization was being implemented. In addition to the change in the prevailing intellectual climate, there were several pressures which either forced or justified the privatization process. These included, not in any order of importance, the following:

- the requirements of the Maastricht Treaty and adherence to the single currency that the debt-to-GDP ratio should be improved dramatically relative to the position at the turn of the decade;
- increasing difficulty in providing capital to state sector firms in the context of tightening restrictions on state aid to industry under EU rules on competition;
- the prospect of liberalisation of the domestic markets in which many state sector firms operated, which implied entry and competition from private sector firms with access to capital markets;
- the move by private sector financial institutions in Ireland and in the U.K. away from mutual status to corporate status;
- the need to enable state sector firms to enter into joint ventures, alliances, or outright mergers with other providers in order to achieve scale economies;
- a growing awareness that solving the problems of the chronic loss makers in the public sector would be difficult, if not impossible, as long as they remained in state ownership.

All of these were undoubtedly good, practical reasons for an unprincipled but expedient decision to move decisively away from the model of state ownership in the wide range of sectors in which there was substantial presence of state sector firms. In most cases, the reasons were consonant with the theoretical and empirical economic analysis which had emerged over the previous twenty years supporting a shift from state to private ownership. But the move did not, at least formally, involve an acceptance of the conclusions of that analysis. Rather, it represented an ad hoc response to immediate political problems.

As a result, there has been no real policy decision on the issue of state as opposed to private sector production of goods and services in terms of the social and economic efficiency of the alternative modes of economic organisation.

Unfortunately, a failure to confront the conclusions of the economic analysis means that there is no conscious, consistent, long-term policy on the issue of ownership of productive resources. It has also led to some muddled thinking and practice where the process of privatization has been concerned. A further consequence of the absence of a willingness to confront the economic analysis has been that there has been little by way of debate about the mechanics of privatizing. How you do it matters.[1]

A simple example will help explain how lack of clear thinking led to conflicts in terms of the objectives and processes of privatization. One dominating concern until relatively recently was the contribution that privatization could make to the Exchequer finances and to the debt/GDP ratio. Under the Maastricht Treaty, which provided the framework for the process of monetary unification within the EU, a maximum ratio of public debt to GDP was laid down, which was less than that which obtained in Ireland in the middle 1990s. Candidate states, to be accepted into the proposed currency union, had to observe certain fiscal guidelines. Two of these were related to the budget deficit and the debt-to-GDP ratio. Hence, there was a policy imperative to get the ratio of government debt outstanding to GDP moving downwards. That obviously constrained borrowing. Given the prevailing real growth rates in the early to middle 1990s, a sufficient movement in the ratio implied moving towards a budget surplus unless some other mechanism could be found. Privatization provided such a mechanism, even if from an accruals-based approach to the Government's balance sheet it did not mean changing the net worth of the Exchequer commensurately with the change in its gross liabilities.

This objective implied an immediate potential conflict between the duty of the state as a guardian of the public interest in improving economic efficiency and its interest as a cash flow maximiser. This is nothing new: the same issues arose in the U.K. over the previous decade. Liberalisation of the markets in which state firms were to be privatized meant a reduction in the potential flow of funds to the Exchequer from the sale of those firms. Without full liberalisation, however, the efficiency gains from privatization in terms of economic efficiency would be reduced substantially.

2. PRIVATIZATION IN ENERGY AND TELECOMMUNICATIONS

The privatization process to date in Ireland may be conveniently classified into three categories. In the first, the state moved to divest itself of commercial entities which were already operating in commercial markets. These included the major life insurer, the food sector operation, the chemical company and similar enterprises. The decision having been taken, the process was relatively simple, industrial relations problems apart. One of two roads was taken: the company was floated on the stock exchange (e.g. Irish Life, Greencore) or disposed of by sale to existing firms in the same or connected businesses (e.g. Irish Fertiliser Industries). The second concerned chronic loss-making state sector firms. Here privatization (where it happened) consisted for all practical purposes in seeking a lowest price tender to take the concern off the state's hands. Irish Steel is the *locus classicus* to date, but a similar exercise looks likely in terms of urban public transport. In the Irish Steel case, the concern was nominally sold to an Indian steel producer, ISPAT, for £1. However, the real price paid by ISPAT was in the form of commitments to maintaining agreed production and employment levels into the future.

The third category, and the one which is of most importance in this chapter, contained the state-owned monopolies or highly protected producers. The difficulty here is that with such concerns there is the very real concern that "privatization of a firm that enjoys substantial market power will tend to improve internal efficiency, but at the risk of worsening allocative efficiency unless profit-seeking behaviour is held in check by an appropriate framework of competition and regulation" (Vickers & Yarrow, 1988, p. 35).

The improvement in internal efficiency is predicted to flow from the change in the allocation of property rights in the residual income of the firm and the changed incentives for decision makers and employees that result from this. At its simplest, the firm will economise on scarce resources because it pays people to do so. The worsening of allocative efficiency flows from the incentive to reduce output in many cases. Higher output is frequently associated with monopolised public ownership as a result of the operation of the kind of forces identified by Niskanen (1977) in the case of what he terms "bureaucratic production" as a result of the presumed incentive to maximize firm spending subject to a budget constraint.

In this sector, then, privatization will necessarily be accompanied by the introduction of regulatory structures. In the context of the EU this is complicated by the fact that the EU itself imposes parameters on the regulatory process in order to reduce the risk of regulatory distortion of the internal market of the union. For example, in Ireland, as elsewhere, the privatized telecom firm was required to observe a universal service obligation (USO), a common feature of telecommunications regulatory regimes. However, the precise nature of what is covered by the concept of the USO is not something on which the Irish regulator has a free hand. Instead, the EU directive lays down parameters for USO provision. For example, provision of on-street pay phones is a mandatory element in the USO. Hence, the regime requires the incumbent telecom, *eircom,* to offer "universal" geographical coverage and open access[2] in pay phone services while not imposing the same requirement on other service suppliers, virtual or actual.

The Structural Approaches

Initially there was a broad similarity in the approaches taken by the government in commencing the privatization process. The common feature of the approach to change in both sectors was the decision to commercialise first, then liberalise, then consider a change in ownership structures. The starting points were different in the two sectors, however. In the case of energy, the state's involvement was entirely by means of state-owned commercial entities. These were the Electricity Supply Board (ESB), established in 1927 to generate and distribute electricity based mainly on the hydroelectric schemes which started with the Shannon; Bord Gáis Eireann (BGE, Irish Gas Board), established to distribute gas from the Kinsale Head, discovered and exploited by Marathon Oil; and Bord na Móna (BnM, Peat Board) established in 1936 to develop the country's large turf (peat) deposits. These statutory companies operated according to something close to commercial standards. Subject to some political intervention over the years affecting generating and distribution policy, and, latterly, affecting employment decisions, the basic structures of electricity supply had been market orientated from the inception of the ESB. In the case of electricity, therefore, commercialisation did not involve changes in structures, but consisted in encouraging the ESB, positively and negatively, to concentrate on more conventional commercial considerations at the expense of social objectives, although this was far from being a smooth transition in terms of political guidelines to the ESB.

Even after the move towards commercialisation, the ESB, as the state monopoly supplier, still retained some universal service obligations. USO features of pricing policies continued to be a significant constraint on commercialisation.

In the case of telecommunications, the provision of services was originally the responsibility of a line department of the main civil service administration, the Department of Posts and Telegraphs (P + T). This structure was inherited from the U.K. in 1922. It operated according to civil service procedures, under civil service staffing, and was headed by a minister who was a member of the cabinet. As a telecommunications operation, P + T was a by-word for inefficiency, bureaucratic delays, over-manning and technical incompetence, all of which were compounded by the constant complications of political intervention affecting service to the public and input usage.

In 1983 the Government started the process of liberalizing the telecommunications market by winding up P + T as a service supplier and transferring the telecommunications service supply function from the core civil service to a newly established, state-owned corporation, Bord Telecom Eireann (BTE) generally better known as Telecom Eireann, TE. The new state-owned company commenced operations in January 1984. The express purpose of this move was to commercialise the provision of telecommunications services, while maintaining such existing features as the universal service obligation. The government retained a regulatory function related to pricing and also, curiously, to some aspects of phone number allocation. At the same time the country's postal services were hived off to a new state owned entity, An Post (lit., The Post, AP). It, too, was established as a commercial entity. Both TE and AP were saddled with significant universal service obligations.

The change in structures in postal services and communications marked the formal implementation of a policy of withdrawal of the state from direct service provision subject to political control and the adoption of a principle of commercial provision while retaining state ownership, and explicit state funding of commercially non-viable services or explicit cross subsidisation via price regulation. It applied right across the state sector.

The EU Dimension

From the middle 1980s onwards, EU policy as framed in a series of directives, sought to open and liberalise the utilities markets across the Community. This was inspired by three complementary motives. The first was the need to "complete the internal market." This meant permitting free trade in services, including the services provided by utilities. The second was concerned with distortions on the supply side, particularly those arising from state aids, whether direct (as in subsidies) or indirect (as in granting protection from competition in the home country). The third was a recognition that, in an integrated market where economies of scale and scope were to be expected, in the utilities sector it was necessary to create structures which would permit the emergence of market players which, in number, identity and size, would reflect the requirements of commercial sustainability rather than the demands of political interest groups.

The key initial element was the commitment to opening markets on the basis of freedom to compete subject to hard budget constraints. Combined with this, however, was a recognition that the requirements of social policy would have to be met, including such features as universal service obligations. This implied creating a common regulatory framework to determine the modalities of competition. Hence, the directives which called for liberalisation did not call for a neo-classical competitive market across the community, but for the establishment of regulated markets open to entry from players prepared to operate and compete subject to the common regulatory framework.

The Regulatory Environment

Liberalisation is frequently coupled with the concept of deregulation in the public mind, and the terms are often, if incorrectly, used interchangeably by commentators. In fact, where many, even most, sectors are concerned, liberalisation requires re-regulation, and the new regulatory regime frequently exceeds in complexity that which it replaces. The reason is simple. Insofar as the rationale for a restricted competition regime lies in the existence of one or more of the usual aspects of market failure, permitting competition implies creating regulatory instruments to counter the instances of market failure if the liberalised market is to avoid the inherent problems. This will in particular be the case where liberalisation affects sectors characterised by the problems associated with network economies. Where liberalisation is concerned, the experience of regulators elsewhere suggests that Ireland shared in the well known second mover advantage: the evolution of regulatory intervention in other countries has permitted latecomers to proceed more effectively in replacing state control by regulated competition. In the English speaking world the U.K. experience provides a sort of laboratory experiment the observation of which has yielded useful lessons.

Commenting on the first decade of liberalisation of telecommunications in Britain, Beesley and Laidlaw (1995, p. 316) have observed: "Although regulatory reform was not central to the privatization policy, it quickly became the focus of debate." The context, of course, was the overwhelming dominance of the market by British Telecom, (BT), and the authors pointed out that the natural response to the problem was to look to the U.S. for lessons to be drawn from the long-standing regulatory regime affecting the Bell System and the regulatory reforms attending the break-up of the system. The most important lesson to be drawn from the study is that in Britain the regulatory system had to develop from an initial set of structures and policies as the implications of deregulation and the requirements of supra-national obligations became clear.

The second mover advantage has been experienced in other countries, as well, especially in smaller countries. Australia drew on New Zealand's experience; and Guatemala learned from Australia, New Zealand and Chile (Spiller & Cardilli, 1997). It is hard to believe that all these did not learn from the U.K. Consequently, when the Irish government commenced liberalisation and privatization in the middle 1990s, it had a wealth of experience to draw from. This suggests that any failure in the regulatory structures established cannot be excused on the basis of incomplete information.

The two regulators established were the Office of the Director of Telecommunications Regulation (ODTR) and the Commission for Electricity Regulation (CER). In addition to these, of course, it has to be recognised that the EU Commission has a major role to play in the implementation of regulation by virtue of its powers to lay down mandatory guidelines not only for service suppliers but also for the regulators.[3]

3. TELECOMMUNICATIONS

The Privatization Process

When the Government transferred the telecommunications business of the Department of Posts and Telegraphs to the new state enterprise, Bord Telecom Eireann, later Telecom Eireann, it transferred the bulk of its assets and most of the related liabilities. Included in the assets were the work force. Not included were adequate funds to meet defined benefit pension commitments. Included in liabilities were loans raised to finance infrastructure investment during the 1970s and early 1980s. The balance sheet and cost base of the new entity were seriously compromised by these decisions. This was a partial explanation of the poor financial performance of the new company in its first few years (see Table 1 below).

Table 1. Operational Data for TE and Eircom.

	Turnover	Profit	Employment	Lines	New	Growth	Backlog
1984–1985	£389 m	–17%	17,300	664 k	93 k	66 k	40 k
1985–1986	£467 m	–5%	15,800	695 k	72 k	31 k	30 k
1986–1987	£516 m	–1.5%	15,100	746 k	75 k	51 k	22 k
1987–1988	£553 m	3%	14,600	789 k	78 k	43 k	16 k
1988–1989	£621 m	8%	14,300	834 k	91 k	45 k	8 k
1989–1990	£704 m	11%	14,200	916 k	105 k	82 k	6 k
1990–1991	£782 m	12%	13,500	983 k	118 k	67 k	2 k
1999–2000	£1580 m*	–11%*	11,300*	1.59 m	220 k	9 k	NA

* These figures are related to the fixed line business alone and should be treated with caution, given problems of assigning costs and revenues as between fixed line and other business operations.
Source: Annual accounts, TE and *eircom*.

This illustrates one of the problems in using privatization as a means of securing enhanced economic efficiency. It assumes (correctly) that the privatized/liberalised entity, now faced with a hard budget constraint, has a strong, even compelling, incentive to take steps to eliminate inefficiencies which were absent under state ownership and a soft budget constraint. An incentive may be a necessary element in a desired outcome, but it is far from a sufficient condition for its achievement. Despite the shift to a commercial entity, and despite the fact that under EU rules the market was going to be opened to competition, little was in fact done to deal with either the cost base or the unfunded liabilities. On the eve of privatization the work force was still about 90% of what it had been when the operations were vested in TE. With over 11,000 employees it had 50% more employees per telephone line than the OECD average. Much of its subsequent difficulties can be traced to the fact that the government did not try to reduce inefficiencies before setting the entity into a market environment in 1984. Consequently, the newly commercialised entity started life with at least 200% of what would have been a cost effective staffing level, and spent the next 15 years getting this down to a mere 150%. The excess costs meant higher prices in a non-competitive environment which hampered its growth. The inability to get its cost base down to an appropriate level by the time of privatization meant that new entrants could be confident that TE/*eircom* would be severely constrained in terms of a price response to entry, given that it would be held to be a dominant firm and could be open to a charge of predatory response if it cut prices sharply.

This goes back to the issue of lack of clarity as to the rationale behind privatization. While it was true that exposing the state-owned firm to competition and later privatizing it could be expected to move its decision making in the direction of increased economic efficiency, its commercial viability in a competitive environment would be compromised by being obliged to undertake most of this transformation after rather than before the change of ownership and market environment. A predictable consequence of this is a reluctance to see serious competition at an early date. This is borne out by the attitude of the government to EU-mandated liberalisation programmes. Broadly speaking, the government's position was to stall, to seek derogations, and to opt for the longest transition period possible.

This lack of consistency also affected the question of the process of privatization. There was an inherent conflict between liberalisation and profitability. Hence, if the government was to achieve a high price for the assets of the state firm on privatisation, a less competitive regime was preferable; but this implied slower progress towards economic efficiency and lower end user prices. The tale of the flotation of *eircom* in 1999 is an unhappy one, largely because the government, wanting a high price to maximize the return to the Exchequer, had to try to sell shares in an entity which had an inherited high cost base and which faced the prospect of increased competition for as much as they could get. That involved talking up the share price, which is precisely what happened.

In July 1999, the privatization of telecommunications was completed by an IPO through which 50% of the shares in the company, now renamed as *eircom*, were offered for sale. The offer was in the main aimed at small investors rather than institutions. This was part of a conscious political decision to which there were two elements. In the first place, following the policy adopted by the British government a decade earlier, the government favoured extending share owner-ship in a population where fewer than 7% of households were estimated to own shares directly. The second reason lay in creating and sustaining public support for privatizing entities which had been in the public sector primarily because of fears of exploitation of market power.

Two years earlier, and consonant with the argument that privatization was a necessary condition for the development of the national telecom as a viable commercial entity, Telecom Eireann had, with government encouragement, sold 35% of its shares to two overseas telecoms, KPN and Telia. At the same time, underscoring the socio-political dimension to the process of privatization, TE had agreed to grant shares on advantageous terms to its work force. In part this consisted in a free share offer to employees (5%). The balance, just under 10%, was sold to the unions representing staff, again on advantageous terms.

The public was invited to subscribe for shares at a price of £3.07 (€3.90). The issue was wildly over-subscribed, in part at least as a consequence of govern-ment pronouncements aimed at encouraging the take up of shares. The offer was structured in such a way as to bias allocations towards smaller bidders, and the general opinion was that this virtually guaranteed a substantial profit, since the institutions were predicted (accurately enough, as it turned out) to be anxious to buy in the secondary market. Within a couple of weeks the shares had gone to a large premium, peaking at close to £3.80. After that, and more or less steadily, the shares lost value, while the majority of small shareholders held onto their stock, in part because they were promised a 5% share bonus if they held on for two years and in part through inexperience.[4] By the end of 2000 *eircom* shares were trading at a 30% discount on the issue price. Since then, they have recovered somewhat on the basis of further developments to be described shortly. However, anyone who bought shares at the issue price and held onto them has suffered a significant capital loss, a matter which has serious implications for any ideas the government may have about public flotation as a vehicle for a future essay in privatization.

In fact, the whole question of valuation was central to the question of the privatization process where *eircom* was concerned. When the government sold 35% of the shares in TE to the "strategic partners," they received about £700 m (much of which was reinvested in TE in the form of funding pensions). That valued the business at £2,000 m. A year later, they transferred 14.9% of the shares to the workforce and the unions on terms which suggested a market valuation of £3,500 m. Eighteen months later 50% of the shares were offered to the public at a price which valued the business at about £5,000 m. Even allowing for the rise in telecommunications stock prices over this time, we are left with an unavoidable conclusion that either the first tranche was sold too cheaply or people paid too much for the last 50%. *Eircom* stock prices have fallen faster than comparable telecoms since the beginning of 2000, which suggests that the second conclusion is correct. Of course, the first could be correct, too.

Since flotation, the public has been treated to the spectacle of the Minister responsible for the flotation attempting to defend the selling price on the basis that (as of mid-2000) the price had been in excess of the issue price for well over half the period since flotation, while the chief executive of the company said publicly that the issue price which the government had decided had been too high (which, since he was CEO at the time of flotation, raises interesting questions about corporate governance and responsibility). The Minister argued that the price was a compromise between the higher and lower valuations suggested to her by the financial advisers to the flotation, but was closer to the higher bound.

All this notwithstanding, the two-stage reformation of the telecommunications system did yield an efficiency dividend. At the end of its first year of operations, in which it recorded a loss equivalent to 17% of turnover, TE had 664,000 lines installed to customers. It installed a gross 93,000 lines in that year, with a net increase in the number of lines of 66,000. However, at the end of the year it had a backlog of 40,000 lines ordered but not installed. By the early 1990s it had nearly a million lines installed, added a gross 118,000 in a year for a net growth of 67,000, and the backlog was effectively zero (2,000 would represent a one week wait). Between 1994 and 1991 the total labour force employed fell from 17,500 to 13,500. A loss of 17% of turnover was turned to a profit of 11% of turnover.

There can be no question of the importance of the change in organisational form, from state service to commercial entity. During this time, however, there was little by way of a change in the competitive environment. In fact, far from facing an increased threat of competition, TE actually succeeded (with government connivance) in temporarily foreclosing the market in its most important commercial area, Greater Dublin. The city's largest CATV operation, covering about 40% of the houses and passing about 60%, had been acquired by the state broadcaster, RTE. RTE at the end of this period divested itself of its 75% shareholding in the CATV operation, Cablelink, and sold it to TE. This was at a time when it was becoming increasingly obvious that CATV lines offered the possibility of providing a major element in a competing telephone system which could also offer broad-band signal service, a clear threat to the market position of the incumbent telecom.

The Regulatory Environment

The privatized and liberalised telecommunications sector is directly regulated by the Office of the Director of Telecommunications Regulation (ODTR). This has been operational since 1996. Its functions are as laid down by statute, but also reflect the over-arching EU regulatory framework. In effect, the ODTR must implement regulatory guidelines which are consistent with (but may exceed) those established by the EU. The EU framework is contained in a series of Commission and European Parliament/Council of Ministers Directives issued over the past ten or more years. Many of these contain purely technical requirements affecting some particular aspect of the telecommunications markets. Some, however, lay down general principles and operational guidelines for the regulatory supervision of markets and for the behaviour of firms in those markets.

The starting points here are the Commission Directives 90/387/EC and 90/388/EC. These documents established the general framework for competition within national markets and the conditions to be introduced to ensure the establishment of the EU's internal market through open network provisions. In 1996 two directives were issued, the first of which, 92/2/EC, dealt with mobile (cell) telephone services and personal communications, and laid down the necessary conditions for the opening of national markets to competition in this area. The second, 96/19/EC, advanced the position laid down in the first two directives by laying down a timetable and operational procedures to provide for full competition in telecommunications. The structural requirements for competition and the removal of barriers to entry were the subject of a Commission Directive, 1999/64/EC, which required the separation of effective control of CATV service provision from existing telephony services.

Within Ireland, the ODTR has been involved in several aspects of regulatory control. A rolling price cap procedure along the U.K. lines of RPI – X[5] has been imposed on *eircom* as the dominant incumbent for fixed line services and a major provider of mobile telephony services. Access to the existing fixed line network has been opened by a series of measures designed to "unbundle the local loop." In addition, the ODTR has been involved in the allocation of new licences to supply services in the mobile telephony sector. This has not been without controversy, and in the most recent case disappointed bidders succeeded in having the courts overthrow the procedures adopted by the ODTR, following which a compromise was reached between the franchise bid winner and the plaintiff.

In contrast to the approach taken in Britain after privatization, the regulatory environment in Ireland was significantly more liberal. The British regime opted for limiting the number of licensed infrastructure suppliers to two, BT and Mercury, for several years after the initial privatization. In Ireland, the ODTR has been willing to grant licences on a more liberal basis. The British approach has been the subject of some criticism. As early as 1988 it was argued (Vickers & Yarrow, p. 231) that as a result of the restrictions on entry, while "initial rounds of price competition between BT and Mercury give evidence of some rivalry between the two firms, . . . the prospects for competition in the longer run are not so rosy . . . . [C]onditions in the regulated duopoly are very favourable to peaceful coexistence." We seem to have learned something from the U.K. experience.

The Impact of Privatization and Liberalisation

The ODTR (1998, 1999, 2000) has issued a series of reports on the performance of the telecommunications sector in Ireland. These show a steady improvement in the absolute efficiency of service provision over the last four to five years. They also show a relative improvement, especially earlier on. If the relative improvement has appeared to slow down recently, this is to a considerable degree due to the impact of liberalisation and privatization in other OECD markets.

Recent Developments

Since privatization, the history of *eircom* has not been a happy one. Its poor financial performance has been compounded by the downwards shift in telecom stocks across the world. The latter in part explains the very disappointing record of the share price. However, there are fundamental factors at work which would, in my opinion, have caused the share price to be weak in the first place. These are:

(1) the opening of the fixed line telecommunications sector to competition in value added services;

(2) technical developments which have made limited entry into fixed line infrastructure provision commercially viable;
(3) given this last, the regulatory cost of the position of *eircom* as a designated operator with "significant market power";
(4) the emergence of the "seamless service dimension" to telecommunications, which has introduced competition for standard voice and non-voice services offered by conventional telecoms;
(5) the growing intensity of competition in mobile (cellular) telephony, which has simultaneously increased pressure on the fixed line business of telecoms and destroyed the profitability of their own mobile arms.

By the middle of 2000 the financial press was speculating loudly about the poor prospects of *eircom* as it stood. The wave of telecoms consolidations had not included any serious interest in the acquisition of *eircom*, for the most part because of its continuing exposure to the consequences of a bloated cost base. It also reflected the fact that from the point of view of a potential purchaser, even if *eircom*'s cost base problems were solved, it was not obvious where synergies with other operators were to be derived by acquiring a small scale telecom confined to the Republic of Ireland. It would not bring much to any possible party.

Things were not helped by quarrels between the two strategic partners and the announced decision of one (and a refusal by the other to indicate its intentions) to liquidate its holding in *eircom* in the near future. Even at the depressed market price for shares, they stood to make a substantial gain, given the prices they had paid a few years earlier. It became widely accepted that the sum of the values of the parts of *eircom* now exceeded the value of the whole. This reflected the fact that *eircom*'s mobile subsidiary was an attractive proposition where a potential consolidatory acquisition was concerned. It had a strong market share, a low cost base, and could be merged into the operations of a larger multinational service supplier. When BT made a successful bid for the second mobile operator, East Digiphone, in mid-2000, the game was up. At the end of 2000, Vodaphone reached an agreement for a share swap purchase of *eircell*.

Late in 2001, an investment consortium, Valentia Ltd., headed by Sir Anthony O'Reilly (who had been CEO of the Heinz Corporation, and is now the executive chairman of Independent News and Media plc) and including an investment vehicle of George Soros, successfully bid for and acquired the share capital of *eircom*, and took the company private.

Business Perspective

Ireland is not as yet a relatively competitive market for telecommunications services in terms of prices, as is made clear from the most recent comparative data produced by the ODTR (December, 2000; see Appendix graphs). However, there are two redeeming features of the position which emerge from this data. The first is that in crucial business sectors the technical availability of high quality service is no longer a problem. The second is that not only is the cost position of service supply much better to the business sector than to the household sector, but that in the business sector the relative position has been improving despite improvements in the absolute cost levels in other European markets. Finally, all the indications are that over the next year this position is going to improve substantially in both sectors as a result of new entry in service and infrastructure supply as well as the roll out of integrated voice telephony and data transfer services using broadband infrastructure.

4. ELECTRICITY

Liberalisation and Privatization

As with telecommunications, the objectives of reform to the supply side of generation and distribution can be examined under the two headings of liberalisation and privatization. They share as a goal improved economic efficiency. Measuring efficiency in a non-profit firm is always difficult; but on the basis of simple indices, the ESB had actually been showing substantial efficiency gains in terms of physical labour productivity for some time before the privatization issue became a serious consideration. Higher electricity prices and poor productivity indicators in earlier years were to some degree a result of the fact that Irish public sector firms were expressly obliged to treat high employment levels as arguments in their objective functions. During the 1990s, however, a successful effort to improve efficiency resulted in a reduction of 40% in manpower usage at a time when output measured by units delivered increased by nearly 60%. This was achieved in the main by a combination of reduced manning levels in generation and reduced central staff usage. The former reflected the replacement of older, smaller power stations by larger, more modern technology stations. The latter reflected a successful campaign to restore management authority in an organisation which had been treated to a considerable degree as a sort of labour-managed enterprise. In principle, that suggests that the standard, cost-based gains from privatization were likely to be limited. Liberalisation of the market was likely to be of greater importance.

It may not be surprising, then, that in contrast to telecommunications, so far the incumbent supplier, the ESB, has not been privatized, although preparations have been made in order to facilitate a transfer of some or all the assets of the ESB to private ownership. Instead, while the incumbent remains within the state

Table 2. Growth of the ESB, 1930–1999.

Year	Units Generated and Purchased	Customers	Permanent staff (approx)
	(Millions)		
1929/1930	60.9	48,606	
1939/1940	407	172,545	
1949/1950	784.8	310,639	
19591960	2,096.00	610,946	
1969/1970	5,245.70	786,500	
1979/1980	10,213.60	1,043,428	
1985/1986	11,465.10	1,194,765	13,500
1990	13,895.40	1,278,870	
1991	14,634.60	1,302,061	
1992	15,470.60	1,326,547	
1993	15,831.40	1,348,196	
1994	16,485.70	1,375,975	
1995	17,237.80	1,407,772	
1996	18,435.00	1,442,416	9,500
1997	19,365.00	1,483,740	
1998	20,544.00	1,528,359	
1999	21,676.00	1,577,162	7,500

Source: ESB annual reports.

sector for the time being, the market has been partially opened to private sector suppliers. There are two key determinants of the shape of the sector as it is emerging. In the first place, the original impetus for structural change came from mandatory requirements for change laid down by the EU, which has been determined for nearly a decade to force open the energy markets of the member states of the EU.

The main development here was a Directive issued by the EU Parliament and Council of Ministers in 1996 (96/92/EC). That document required the member states progressively to open their markets to competitive supply. In the first phase of the programme, the requirement was for the opening of the section of the market consisting of the largest (and, therefore, commercial) electricity users. In the initial phase, this was set at an annual demand of 40GWH. In the Irish case this implied about 30% of total demand, covering about 300 users. In the second phase, this was to be extended to a further tranche of users. Full liberalisation of commercial users was to be introduced within six years, although Ireland was one of a number of countries permitted to delay this. As it turned out, the government chose not to avail of this permission to seek temporary derogation. Final and full liberalisation would await a third phase.

Initially it was envisaged that member states could proceed relatively slowly, but in Ireland's case the government decided that it would accelerate the process and introduce partial liberalisation earlier rather than later.

Unlike those of member states on the mainland of Europe, the Irish generation system was largely self-contained because the country is part of an island off an island off the mainland.[6] The generating capacity was by legislation the preserve of the incumbent monopoly. There was, therefore, a monolithic vertically integrated entity generating, transmitting, and retailing electricity. Private generation of power for sale to end users was prohibited. It was legally possible to produce power as a by-product or (on a very small scale) using dedicated generating capacity, but such power could be sold only to the ESB. The position was further complicated by the fact that as part of the government's policy of promoting the development of domestic primary energy resources, the ESB was obliged to establish generation capacity to use the output of turf (peat) from the state-owned BnM. Further, for regional employment reasons, the ESB was obliged to locate a large number of relatively small stations close to the peat bogs. This increased transmission costs for high voltage supply to load centres and committed the ESB to using stations which, with the passage of time, were becoming less and less efficient in terms of scale economies. Finally, until relatively recently, the ESB had to place such stations at an unwarranted high position in the load merit ranking, while being obliged to pay a price for the turf which was sufficient to cover BnM's costs of production.

The policy of encouraging domestic primary energy supply was later extended to offering higher than commercially warranted prices to BGE for natural gas from the Kinsale head field. Privatizing such a system was bound to be extremely difficult both technically and politically. As a result the initial phase of liberalisation has as yet seen no moves to privatise the existing generating or transmission. Given that the process of liberalisation and (partial, if at all) privatization in Ireland has been relatively recent, it may be useful to consider what has happened in Ireland against the background of the privatization programme for electricity in Britain. When the British system was re-structured for privatisation, twelve separate regional distribution companies were set up in England and Wales (Scotland was dealt with separately). The entire Irish market was smaller in terms of numbers of customers and load than the smallest regional catchment area in England and Wales, while it was larger in geographical spread than any of them. Transmission and distribution were functionally separated from generation in Britain. The scope for doing something similar in Ireland was limited by the small scale of the Irish market.

The British privatization structure involved the vertical separation of generation (three companies, initially, but with no barrier to entry by further privately owned generating capacity) from transmission and distribution.[7] It provided for horizontal separation of generation, and maintained the regional horizontal separation of distribution. Transmission was transferred to a separate operator (National Grid) which was jointly owned by the regional distribution companies. The latter were simply a reincarnation of the old CEGB regional distribution boards under private ownership. The retail market was divided into "franchised" (smaller customers) and "non-franchised" (larger customers) markets. The franchised market was reserved to the local distribution company, while the non-franchised market was open to any supplier with what was described as a "second tier licence." The cut-off point was a minimum load demand of one megawatt. Customers with a maximum demand of one or more megawatts could seek supply from any licensed supplier, who could be a generator or a "virtual" generator (any company that had contracted to purchase bulk electricity for sale onwards, including distribution companies).

In the Irish case, privatization/liberalisation, which took place a decade after the U.K. privatization, has taken a somewhat different structural form. The incumbent generator, the ESB, has not been horizontally dismantled. It retains all its existing generating capacity. For the moment it remains within the public sector. Internally, however, it has been vertically separated into three entities, with full operational and pricing separation between them. The transmission and distribution system has been separated from the generating system to form two separate entities. In addition a separate supply entity has been set up. This reflects the separation of the market along U.K. lines into the franchise and non-franchise sectors. In the franchise sector the current single supplier is ESB PES (public electricity supply). It supplies smaller customers over the transmission and distribution assets of ESB Distribution, and owns the generating capacity. In the non-franchise sector of the market, a separate ESB-owned entity, ESBIE (ESB Independent Energy), operates, competing with ESB PES and non-ESB licensed suppliers, of whom there are two at present. "Chinese walls" within the ESB are in place designed to separate ESB PES commercially from ESBIE.

As of early 2001, the two independent non-franchise suppliers are "virtual" suppliers, described as VIPPs (virtual independent power suppliers). They do not generate power to meet their supply contract obligations to large customers, but purchase bulk power from ESB PES. This is supplied to them at prices which emerged from a bidding process in 2000, when ESB PES put up for auction a proportion of its power capacity. In this auction there were quota restrictions on maximum bids in place to ensure that the three bidders would have adequate supplies to operate as credible downstream suppliers. No supplier could bid for more than 40% of the available supply. There are, therefore, four suppliers competing in the non-franchise market: ESB PES, ESBIE, and the two VIPPs, ePower (domestically owned with some foreign investment) and Energia (connected to the Northern Ireland supplier). Each of the two VIPPs is in the process of constructing separate generating capacity, while a further development of independent capacity will emerge in all probability from a joint venture between ESB and the Norwegian energy corporation, Statoil.

Load management and provisions for "top up" and "spillover" supply flows are the subject of a regulated pseudo-market operated by ESB Distribution. The regulator is the Commission for Energy Regulation established in 1999. The regulator has the power to determine trading conditions, including market compartmentalisation, transmission and distribution access, provisions for top-up and spillover, and pricing structures including capacity and supply elements of prices. The structural features of the system as it obtains at present can be seen as being a reflection of the requirements of 96/92/EC. This laid down the parameters for the operations of a liberalised system in terms of the creation of institutions designed to provide ease of entry for suppliers, ease of access by end-users to suppliers, and cost-based access to the transmission and distribution systems to enable the market to operate competitively. These provisions provide the framework for both ownership structures and the regulatory environment in the open market for energy supplies which is being implemented.

The Irish market as it stands, therefore, is far less competitive in terms of formal structures and numbers of operators than the U.K. market.[8] In addition, in legal terms, as long as the generating, transmission and distribution assets remain in the beneficial ownership of ESB, the extent of "privatization" really only applies to the operations of the two current VIPPs. In principle, the Government is committed to some form of privatization of the assets of the ESB, but it is a fair bet that: (a) any such change will be limited to the generating capacity; and that (b) this will be delayed because there are problems within the existing ESB generating capacity which will give rise to serious headaches if a transfer to the private sector is implemented. In the main this reflects the consequences of decisions made over the decades concerning the basis for power generation and the transmission system which resulted from it.

In one respect, the privatization of electricity in Ireland faces a difficulty comparable in principle, if not in magnitude, to that which faced the U.K. authorities. In the latter case the problem arose from the existence of a small but significant nuclear generating capacity. Given the potential cost implications of changing environmental requirements originating in Britain and/or being imposed on an EU basis, and growing concerns about the costs of de-commissioning existing capacity and political resistance to replacing, let alone expanding, nuclear generation plants were seen as financial black holes. The British Government had to choose between obliging the two other successors to the CEGB to shoulder the cost by allocating nuclear plant to them, or retaining it in state ownership for its remaining life. The latter was chosen and, I believe, correctly. To have opted for the former would have been to impose unquantifiable commercial risk exposure on commercial operators and to put the first movers at a disadvantage compared with any subsequent entrant into power generation.

In the Irish case, the comparable problem lies in the peat-powered capacity. This has two elements: plant installed in the period 1945 to 1970, and a new 200 MW generating pant being commissioned at the moment. The older plant is technologically obsolete and operates at hopelessly low scale. The cost of peat is determined by the need to keep BnM solvent. Simple commercial considerations would dictate rapid closure, with the capacity being replaced by alternative, modern CCGT systems, located nearer to load centres. Political pressures to keep the stations open arise not just from union pressure to maintain power station employment, but from the fact that closure would have severe regional unemployment consequences among less skilled labour employed by BnM. EU-based environmental pressure has resulted in the decision to seek tenders for the construction of the new peat station (illogical as it may seem, this is treated as being more "sustainable" than oil or gas). The ESB "won" the tender (BnM would have nothing to do with it!) and now has to shoulder the cost. In the long run this won't matter; but added to the older turf capacity, it creates a serious problem for any attempt to transfer ownership to a private sector operator in the near future.

The Business Perspective

The changes in the electricity sector which are now under way have major implications for energy costs and overall competitiveness. Costs in the "eligible" sector of the market (that which is open to competitive supply from VIPPs) are not easily obtained, since supply contract terms reflect the outcome of competitive offers and are a matter of commercial secrecy rather than being a matter of public information. Supply prices in the remainder of the market, however, provide a basis on which to arrive at some judgement as to where costs in the eligible sector lie.

Bulk supply is available to the VIPPs at a discount of up to 10% on base load tariffs. It is reasonable to conclude, therefore, that supply costs in the eligible sector are at a similar discount to the supply costs in the rest of the market. The absolute and relative level of these charges to industrial/commercial users may be judged by looking at three typical load basis charges, as contained in the Appendix graphs. While Irish electricity costs for business users are far from being the lowest in the EU, the fact is that they compare favourably with most countries, including some of the larger states in the union.

NOTES

1. I provided a longer analysis of the confused thinking behind the privatization programme in a paper delivered to the Statistical and Social Inquiry Society of Ireland in January 2000. See references.

2. Open access means that any service supplier's pre-paid cards may be used in *eircom* phones, while other suppliers may refuse to take *eircom* pre-paid cards.

3. For example, the universal service obligation laid down for telecoms includes the provision of on-street pay-phones as a result of a decision of the Commission.

4. The newspapers were full of reports of small shareholders who were reluctant to sell their shares after the price fell below the issue price because this would involve realising a loss.

5. This pricing regulation requires the utility to observe a ceiling on price increases set at a discount to the inflation rate as measured by the U.K. Retail Price Index. Its objective is to encourage the entity to realise potential efficiency gains and to pass some of these on to its customers. While it has its drawbacks, it is widely held to be superior to rate of return regulation which is notoriously prone to the so-called "Averch-Johnson" effect, whereby a regulated utility overinvests in capacity in order to retain profits.

6. On the mainland of Europe there is substantial inter-connector capacity between the national grids. This has been in place for a considerable time. In Ireland an inter-connector between the Republic and Northern Ireland was constructed over thirty years ago, as a device to improve system security, north and south. The capacity of the inter-connector was quite limited, reflecting the overall capacity in both systems and the purpose for which it was built, which was to provide the equivalent of an element of spinning reserve to each system. In any case, from the middle 1970s the IRA, for reasons which are not entirely obvious, sought to promote unification of the island by a series of attacks on the inter-connector, which was subsequently de-commissioned.

7. The interested reader who wishes to obtain a condensed but readable account of the implementation of privatization of the electricity market in the U.K. is referred to Yarrow (1994).

8. Since the time of writing this position has further deteriorated, as one of the VIPPs has signalled its intention to withdraw from the market.

REFERENCES

Beesley, M., & Laidlaw, B. (1995). The development of telecommunications policy in the U.K. 1981–1991. In: M. Bishop, J. Kay & C. Mayer (Eds), *The Regulatory Challenge* (Ch. 13). Oxford: OUP.

European Union (Telecommunications): Council Directive on the Establishment of the Internal Market for Telecommunications Services through the Implementation of Open-network Provisions, 90/387/EC; Commission Directive on Competition in the Markets for Telecommunications Services, 90/388/EC; Commission Directive on Mobile Telephony and

Personal Communications Services, 96/2/EC ; Commission Directive on the Introduction of Full Competition in Telecommunications, 96/19/EC; Commission Directive on the Separation of Ownership of Cable TV and Telephony Services, 1999/64/EC.

European Union (Electricity): Directive of the European Parliament and the Council of Ministers on the Establishment of the Internal Market in Electricity, 96/92/EC.

McDowell, M. (forthcoming). The rationale and scope for privatization in Ireland. *Journal of the Statistical and Social Inquiry Society of Ireland.*

Office of the Director of Telecommunications Regulation (December 2000). The Irish telecommunications market two years after liberalisation. *ODTR Quarterly Review.*

Spiller, P., & Cardilli, C. (1997). The frontier of telecommunications deregulation: small countries leading the pack. *Journal of Economic Perspectives, 11*(4), 127–138.

Vickers, J., & Yarrow G. (1998). *Privatization: an Economic Analysis.* Cambridge, Mass. and London: MIT Press.

Waverman, L., & Sirel, E. (1997). European telecommunications markets on the verge of full liberalisation. *Journal of Economic Perspectives, 11*(4), 94–126.

Yarrow, G. (1994). Privatization, Restructuring and regulatory reform in electricity supply. In: M. Bishop, J. Kay & C. Mayer (Eds), *Privatization and Economic Performance* (Ch. 3). Oxford: OUP.

APPENDIX

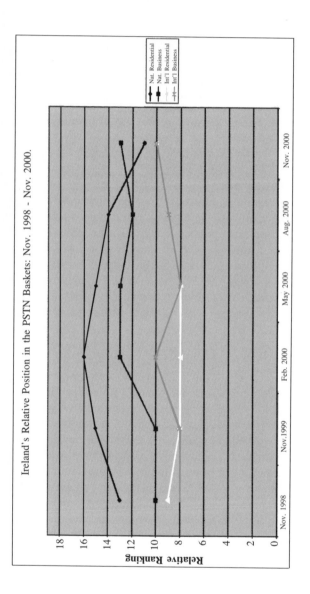

Graph 1.

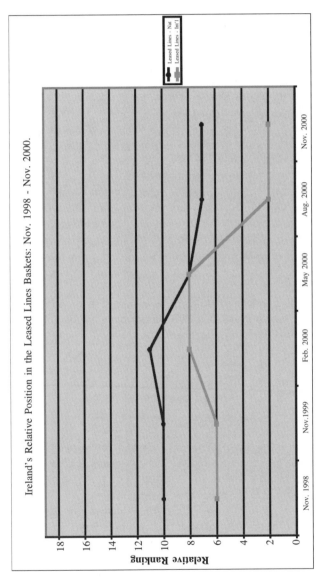

Graph 2.

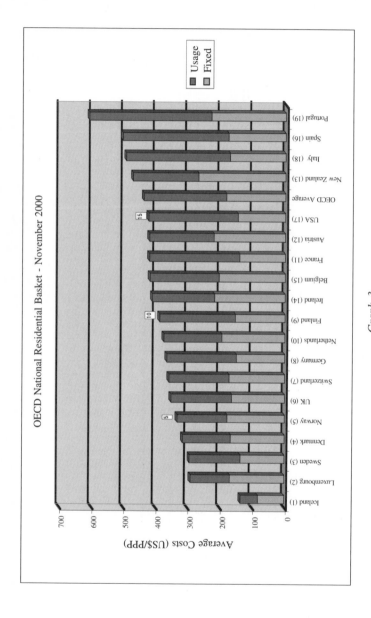

Graph 3.

Note: Figures in parentheses refer to the respective countries' ranking in the previous survey.

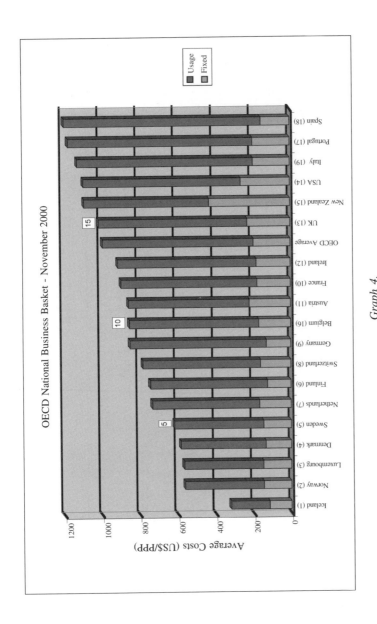

Graph 4.

Note: Figures in parentheses refer to the respective countries' ranking in the previous survey.

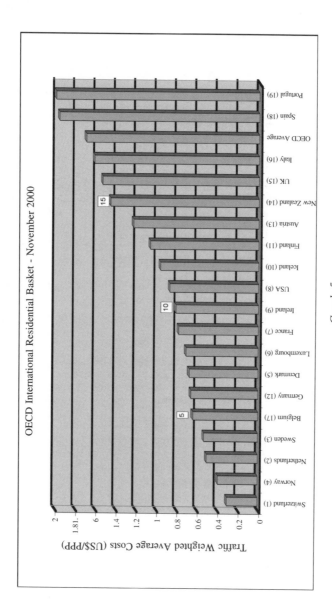

Graph 5.

Note: Figures in parentheses refer to the respective countries' ranking in the previous survey.

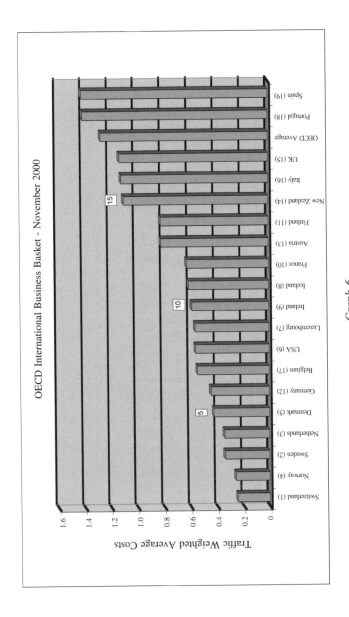

Graph 6.

Note: Figures in parentheses refer to the respective countries' ranking in the previous survey.

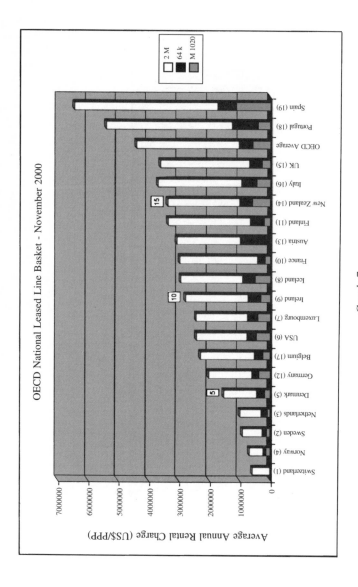

Graph 7.

Note: Figures in parentheses refer to the respective countries' ranking in the previous survey.

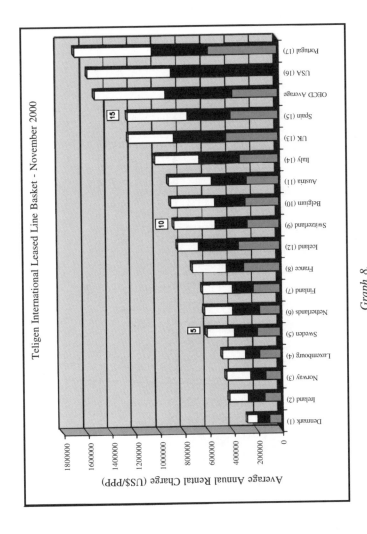

Graph 8.

Note: Figures in parentheses refer to the respective countries' ranking in the previous survey.

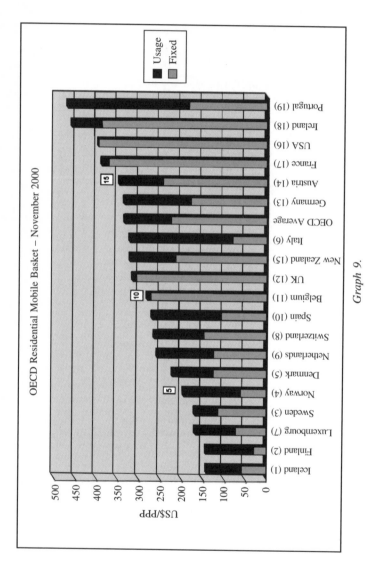

Graph 9.

Note: Figures in parentheses refer to the respective countries' ranking in the previous survey.

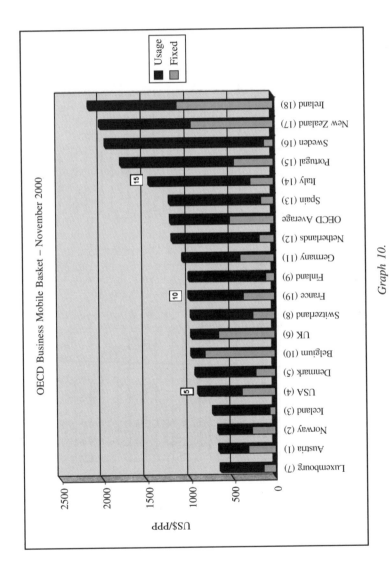

Graph 10.

Note: Figures in parentheses refer to the respective countries' ranking in the previous survey.

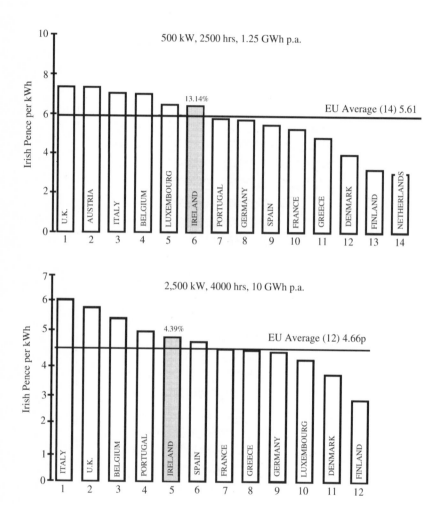

Graph 11.

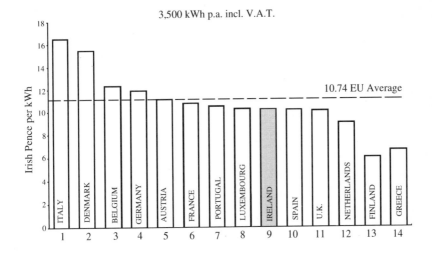

Graph 12.

8. HAS IRELAND OUTGROWN ITS CLOTHES? INFRASTRUCTURAL AND ENVIRONMENTAL CONSTRAINTS IN IRELAND

John Fitz Gerald

E66 J11
R21 R38
H54

1. INTRODUCTION

The Irish economy has performed very well over the second half of the 1990s with very rapid growth and a very large reduction in unemployment. This success story is, by now, well known. However, success brings new problems and challenges. In particular, the economy has outgrown its clothes! The infrastructure that was appropriate for a relatively poor EU economy in the 1980s is wholly inadequate to deal with the needs of the present. In addition, rapid growth is putting the quality of the environment under pressure.

This paper considers the infrastructural and environmental constraints facing the Irish economy over the next decade. In Section 2 the economic background to these challenges is first discussed. Section 3 briefly considers how the objectives of economic policy have changed. The existing endowment of infrastructure is discussed in Section 4 and Section 5 considers the role of public investment in a modern economy. In the light of this discussion, priorities for investment in Ireland over the next decade are discussed in Section 6. Section 7 analyses the

The Irish Economy in Transition: Successes, Problems, and Prospects, Volume 85, pages 179–203.

environmental constraints facing the economy and Section 8 sets out a series of supplementary policy measures that are needed if future investment is to be fully productive. Finally, in Section 9, we draw some brief conclusions.

2. ECONOMIC BACKGROUND

In the late 1970s the then Irish government pursued a "dash for growth" policy which involved a huge fiscal injection. Even at the time economists warned that this was unsustainable (Geary, 1979), and, in the early 1980s, when the storm of world recession hit, it almost wrecked the Irish economy. The result was a period of almost 10 years of fiscal retrenchment in the 1980s as successive governments tried to put the economy together again. The process was extremely painful, involving both major increases in taxation and a massive cutback in state expenditure. Most investment in infrastructure, such as in roads and social housing, was halted.

Figure 1 shows the growth rate for GNP for each of the five-year periods from 1970 to 2000. With the exception of the first half of the 1980s, when the fiscal retrenchment knocked the economy way off course, between 1960 and 1990 there was relatively little deviation from an apparent trend growth of 4% a year. For the 1990s the growth rate picked up, so that the economy is currently growing at a rate well above its past trend. However, as the growth in labour supply slows, the capacity growth rate of the economy will also slow.[1]

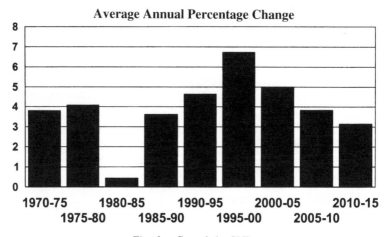

Fig. 1. Growth in GNP.

Source: Duffy, Fitz Gerald, Kearney and Smyth, 1999.

Probably more remarkable than the apparent pick-up in the trend growth rate is the experience on employment growth (Fig. 2). By contrast with a dismal performance in the 1980s, employment has grown at an unprecedented rate in the 1990s. The bulk of this employment growth is occurring in the private sector. However, as with growth in GNP, slower growth in labour supply will also see a slowdown in employment growth over the course of the current decade.

The reduction in unemployment is equally remarkable, falling from a peak of over 15% of the labour force in 1993 to just under 4% today, the lowest level seen since the early 1970s.

Because of the successful fiscal retrenchment in the 1980s, Ireland began the 1990s with the public finances showing steady improvement, in spite of a high debt. Since then the exceptional rate of growth in the economy and the very favourable demography have meant that the government deficit of the 1980s has been turned into a very large surplus today (Fig. 3).

The result of the period of rapid growth is that Ireland, which in 1990 had a GDP per head of around 74% of the EU average, already exceeds the EU average. A more appropriate measure is GNP per head (which excludes profit repatriations by foreign multinationals). On this measure Ireland can also be seen to have narrowed the gap in living standards, with output per head compared to the EU as a whole rising from 66% in 1990 to around 100% over the next few years (Fig. 4).

Average Annual Percentage Change

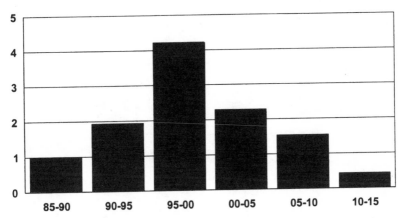

Fig. 2. Growth in Employment.

Source: Duffy, Fitz Gerald, Kearney and Smyth, 1999.

As Percent of GNP

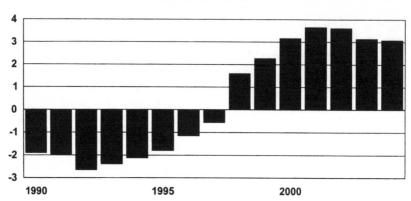

Fig. 3.   Government Surplus.

Source: Duffy, Fitz Gerald, Kearney and Smyth, 1999.

Irish GNP Relative to EU

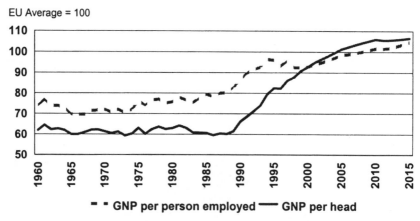

Fig. 4.   Relative Standard of Living.

Source: Duffy, Fitz Gerald, Kearney and Smyth, 1999.

Even with the benefit of a big increase in the EU structural fund payments from 1989 onwards, the volume of public investment grew relatively slowly. The effect of the low level of public investment in infrastructure over a 13-year

Table 1. Government Investment as a Share of GDP.

	France	Ireland	USA
1985	3.4	3.9	3.8
1990	3.6	2.1	3.8
1995	3.4	2.3	3.2
2000	3.1	3.9	3.5

Source: OECD National Accounts.

period, roughly from 1980 to 1993, has been that the economy in the late 1990s was unprepared for success. Table 1 compares the public sector investment as a share of GDP for Ireland, France and the U.S., illustrating how infrastructural investment has only recovered to the level in other countries in the late 1990s. While the problems with the public finances in the 1980s and the early 1990s constrained investment in public infrastructure, this is no longer the case today.

Even though investment in public physical infrastructure grew quite rapidly over the course of the 1990s it was not sufficient to reduce the serious shortages that existed. If anything, the backlog of projects has increased and the congestion problems today are greater than at any time in the past.

This congestion is manifested in a number of different ways. The most obvious is a shortage of housing. While housing is generally produced and owned by the private sector (Ireland has very high levels of home-ownership, by European standards), constraints due to underinvestment in sanitary services, urban public transport, roads and social and cultural infrastructure have all contributed to a serious shortage of accommodation today. The result is that the price of accommodation in Ireland is very high by the standards of the European Union.

The one exception to the lack of vision, and consequential underinvestment in public infrastructure, has been human capital. In spite of major cutbacks in public expenditure in the 1980s, the state continued to invest in education, bringing about a massive increase in educational attainment over the last 20 years. This can be seen in the change in the educational attainment of the population aged 20–24 today compared to those now aged over 40 who left the educational system before 1980 (Fig. 5).[2]

Demograhphic Trends

While the post-war baby boom petered out in most of the rest of Europe by 1960, Ireland continued to have a very high birth rate until 1980. Since then

Population by Age, 1997

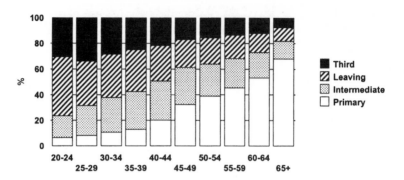

Fig. 5. Educational Attainment of the Population.

Source: Labour Force Survey micro data.

it has fallen fairly steadily (Fig. 6). This delayed fall in fertility has meant that the supply of young people coming onto the labour market has, until now, continued to rise rapidly, long after it had fallen off elsewhere in the EU. It is only in the next five years that the inevitable consequence of the post-1980 decline in the birth rate will impact on the labour market.

Per Thousand Population

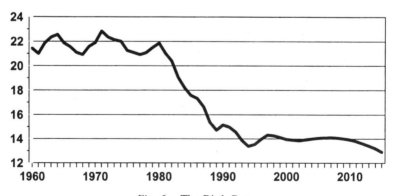

Fig. 6. The Birth Rate.

Source: Duffy, Fitz Gerald, Kearney and Smyth, 1999.

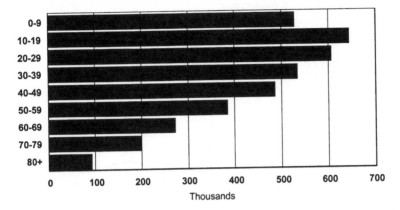

Fig. 7. Structure of the Population, 1999.

Source: CSO: Population and Migration Estimates.

The combination of this delayed pattern of fertility decline, and the lasting effects of the high emigration in the pre-1960 period, makes the Irish population structure very unusual by the standards of the EU. Figure 7 shows the age structure of the population in 1999.

The effects of the "baby boom" of the 1970s can be seen in today's cohort of teenagers that is larger than any cohort that went before, and also larger than the cohort of children aged under ten. The size of this cohort relative to all others will continue to influence the Irish population profile for decades to come. The very rapid fall off in the population aged over 60 reflects the continuing effects of the very high level of emigration in the 1950s. This means that the number of people in the retired age groups will remain relatively low for another 20 years.

Figure 8 shows the movement in the economic dependency ratio for Ireland relative to that of the EU. This ratio measures the proportion of the population not working relative to those working. A combination of many children and low labour force participation meant that Ireland had a much higher dependency ratio than the rest of the EU in the 1960s and the 1970s. In the 1980s rising unemployment further aggravated this situation. However, the changing demographic structure and the improving economic circumstances have been reinforcing one another since the late 1980s, so that Ireland is facing an exceptionally favourable demographic structure in the current period. It is only in the twenty years after 2015 that the rate of old-age dependency will begin to rise rapidly, as it is currently doing in EU countries, such as Germany.

Dependents per Person Employed

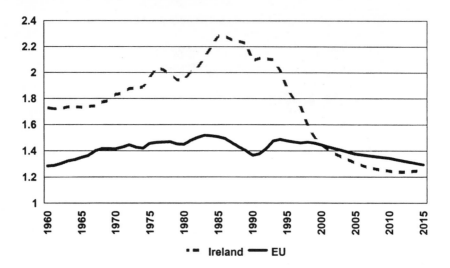

Fig. 8. Economic Dependency.

Housing

The very high proportion of the population between the ages of 15 and 30 is putting huge presure on the housing market. With very few people over 70, the number of existing dwellings being released for new entrants is low. In addition, partly because of low incomes and high unemployment, Irish people in the past tended to remain living with their parents longer than was the norm elsehwere. The result is that the number of adults per dwelling in Ireland is high by EU standards (Fig. 9).

Thus Ireland begins the new century with a low stock of dwellings relative to its population. The combination of rising living standards, and cultural changes driving increased headship (the proportion of a cohort who are "head of household"), and rapidly increasing numbers in their 20s means that the demand for new dwellings is exceptional. Returning emigrants and new immigrants are adding further to the demand for new dwellings (Fig. 10).

As a result of this exceptional set of demographic factors Ireland has to devote a very large amount of resources to investing in new dwellings. As shown in Fig. 11 the rate of house building in Ireland is exceptional by European standards. In recent years Ireland has built one eighth of the number

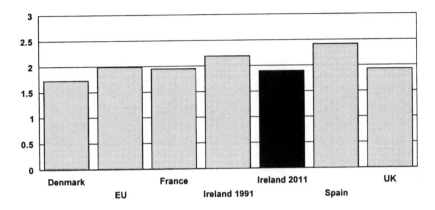

Fig. 9. Adults per Household.

Source: Eurostat, Basic Economic Statistics.

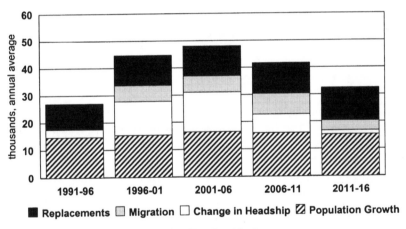

Fig. 10. Housing Needs.

Source: Duffy, Fitz Gerald, Kearney and Smyth, 1999.

of dwellings built in Germany while having under a twentieth of the German population.

The huge expansion in the number of dwellings, in turn, places great pressure on other forms of physical infrastructure: sanitary services, urban transport, roads, energy and telecommunications and social and cultural infrastructure.

Per 1000 Inhabitants, 1994, (Ireland, 1997)

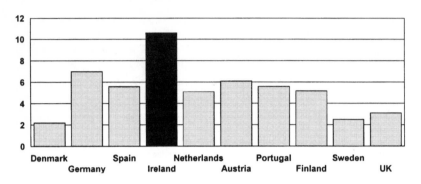

Fig. 11.   Dwellings Built.

Source: Eurostat: Basic Economic Statistics.

While in the latter case the market can and is responding, the capacity of the economy to deliver on all of these needs simultaneously is a problem issue for government.

3. OBJECTIVES OF ECONOMIC POLICY

In the past the combination of high unemployment and the continuing attrition of emigration meant that there was a clear imperative to devote major resources to maximising the growth of employment. This has been a central objective of economic policy in Ireland over a very long period. However, with the success of the economy in recent years, which has led to the current rapid rate of economic growth and full employment, the focus of economic policy objectives generally, and investment priorities in particular, has changed.

What should be the objectives for investment policy over the current decade? The traditional measures of economic well being, such as GNP, take account of the factors that contribute to our welfare and are traded in the marketplace. However, there are other factors, such as the distribution of resources across the population, the quality of the environment, broadly defined, and the health of the population which are all of major importance, even if they are not easily quantified in monetary terms.

The changing economic environment, with the major reduction in unemployment, has benefited the bulk of the population, especially those who have moved from unemployment to employment. However, there remain a significant minority who, by the nature of their educational and employment experience, have difficulty in sharing in the improved economic prospects.

Rapid economic growth is also putting pressure on our environment in a range of different ways. For example, the rise in economic activity will, on unchanged policies, result in a big increase in emissions of greenhouse gases. If the limits on emissions, agreed as part of the Kyoto protocol, are to be achieved, this will constrain future economic growth.

Protection of the environment as a resource for the population as a whole will need to play a more important role in policy making in the future. This will give rise to new demands for investment and will also affect the character of the investment that will take place in all sectors. One aspect of what we broadly define as the environment is the cost of congestion, including the loss of time by commuters and other travellers. While in the past this cost to society has been heavily discounted in assessing investment priorities, in the future it should be given a higher weighting in decision making.

Unfortunately there is no unique way of ordering this range of differing objectives. They cannot be turned into a "GNP like" measure which policy makers can then seek to maximise.

A final issue concerning the objectives of policy is whose welfare are we trying to maximise? While the answer may seem obvious (and was relatively obvious in the past), there are new dimensions to be considered in the context of a changing labour market with high inflows of returning emigrants and immigrants from other countries.

In the past the return of emigrants and the influx of quite a number of people not born in Ireland (who are primarily skilled) has had a beneficial social and economic impact on a very homogenous society (Barrett & O'Connell, 2000). It has added signiifcantly to the growth potential of the economy and has helped reduce unskilled unemployment (Fitz Gerald & Kearney, 2000). Under current circumstances this influx of labour is putting further pressure on the existing infrastructure. The resulting rise in the cost of accommodation and increasing congestion is, in turn, making Ireland a less attractive place to live. This is already impacting on the potential growth rate of the economy. The solution lies in remedying the infrastructural constraints.

4. EXISTING INFRASTRUCTURE

In most comparisons of Ireland's physical infrastructure, human capital and R&D with the rest of the EU, Ireland fares badly. However such comparisons are fraught with measurement and comparability difficulties. In addition, it is arguably more relevant to assess the existing stock of infrastructure relative to the needs of the *domestic* household and commercial sectors. Planning for Ireland's future infrastructural requirements must not only take account of existing pressures, but also allow for future demographic and economic changes which will impact on the demand for infrastructure.

The ongoing demographic and social changes in Ireland are also driving the strong growth in the demand for housing, and the rise in net household formation, in recent years. The strong increase in the level of economic activity has also increased the demand for infrastructure in the commercial sector. These two interrelated factors have placed enormous demands on the existing physical infrastructure.

While Ireland's income per head is converging towards the EU average, the relatively recent nature of the convergence means that the accumulated wealth of the country, represented by physical infrastructure and accumulated human capital, is significantly inferior to countries which have enjoyed a similar standard of living for many years. The other EU member states, with the exception of the cohesion countries (Portugal, Spain and Greece), have been investing in physical infrastructure for many years and have built up a much bigger stock than is the case in Ireland. Many of them also undertook major investment in education in the immediate post-war years. As a result, the standard of living in Ireland, broadly defined, is still somewhat below that of our European neighbours. The gaps in endowment occur not only in obvious areas such as transport and sanitary services, but also in housing and in the average human capital endowment of the labour force.

To achieve a European standard of living, Ireland will need to invest considerable resources over many years to develop a European style infrastructure. However, deciding what constitutes a European standard of infrastructure in an Irish context is difficult. Infrastructure needs reflect the unique features of a country's population density, urban hierarchy, climate, as well as the demographic and industrial structure.

Most attempts at cross-country comparisons rely on some method of ranking countries, for example data from business surveys. Such "soft" data are inevitably highly subjective. While Ireland emerges reasonably well from comparisons of overall competitiveness, it fares much worse in terms of infrastructural provision. The *World Competitiveness Yearbook* (1997) ranked Ireland only 22nd out of 48 countries in terms of infrastructure. Most studies identify a number of deficiencies, particularly in environmental services and transport. In addition, as indicated below, there are serious gaps in the areas of housing and in Ireland's endowment of human capital.

Most importantly, though, we cannot just compare the current state of infra-structural provision – we must look at its likely evolution, both domestically and abroad. In particular, the rapid increase in the number of households will result in increased demand for electricity, sanitation and transport requirements (both public and private) with consequential implications for future investment needs. Increased consumption and higher employment levels also place their own demands on infrastructure. Altogether this means that whatever infra-structural deficits exist at present, they are likely to be significantly exacerbated unless there is considerable further investment, whether it be through public provision, through the actions of the private sector or, by a combination of both.

The costs of congestion may not be obvious but they are nonetheless real. The rise in house prices throughout the country, but especially in Dublin, is making Ireland a less attractive location for returning emigrants. They will seek higher wages than heretofore to return. Similarly, where young people are making their initial choice about where they will work, they, too, will be affected in their decision by the cost of accommodation. Through this indirect mechanism the high and rising cost of accommodation will translate into higher labour costs and a loss of competitiveness.

The growth in congestion on our roads has a direct effect on the competi-tiveness of the tradable sector through increasing transport costs. However, business is only a minor user of most road-space and a very large part of the cost of traffic jams, caused by motorists, is borne by commuters using private and/or public transport. The absence of a satisfactory urban transport system in Dublin (and other major cities) aggravates the problem there. The result of the deterioration in the quality of life will be rather similar to the possible impact of rising housing prices – people will not wish to live in congested surroundings and this will tend to reduce labour supply locally. In turn, this will raise labour costs as firms have to pay more to attract labour to their locality.

In summary, and in direct contrast to the experience in the 1980s, the potential growth rate of the Irish economy is more likely to face input constraints in the coming decade (labour supply, especially of skilled labour, and physical infra-structure) than demand constraints (low demand for Irish output, low demand for labour).

In broad terms it is considered that the principal risks to continuing sustainable growth in Ireland relate to supply side constraints, namely with respect to both infrastructure and certain categories of labour. Moreover, it is argued that the competitiveness of some aspects of Ireland's social and economic infrastructure services needs to be improved significantly if Ireland is to continue to enjoy sustainable growth and development. Ultimately, if the current infrastructural constraints are not addressed, they could undermine the sustainability of growth in the medium term.

5. ROLE OF PUBLIC INFRASTRUCTURE

In the analysis of economic welfare the rationale for public investment spending involves issues of both *efficiency* and *equity/distribution*. Where the economy fails to function efficiently because of what is termed "market failure" or "distortions," then there is a basis for justifying public intervention (Honohan, 1997). In choosing areas where state intervention to provide public infrastructure is needed, it is necessary to establish that market failure exists or may exist. The rationale for public intervention can be classified under three headings, specifically:

* Spending to provide services that are considered to have *public good* characteristics, which would inhibit their optimal provision in the private sector (e.g. education, roads, defence).
* A *corrective tax or subsidy*, aimed at altering the relative prices facing firms and individuals in order to correct for some general persistent externality. They can also be designed to alter behaviour where private agents are thought to be inadequately informed, or where a specific externality exists.
* *Redistributional tax or subsidy*, designed to alter the distribution of personal or household income in favour of specified groups (e.g. agricultural payments, investment in social housing).

In effect, these interventions are aimed at reducing or eliminating distortions that would otherwise impair the economy from performing optimally, both in terms of efficiency criteria and distributional consequences.

When considering the effectiveness of these kinds of interventions in overcoming various distortions, the true economic cost and benefits of these interventions must be assessed (Honohan, 1998).

6. THE NATIONAL DEVELOPMENT PLAN AND INVESTMENT PRIORITIES

The reform of the EU structural funds[3] in 1989 ushered in a series of changes in the domestic administration of public projects which were part funded under the EU Community Support Framework (CSF) (Fitz Gerald, 1998). These changes centred around the need for the Irish government to agree a coherent plan with the EU Commission for the investment to be funded under the CSF. The process by which this agreed plan was prepared was new to the sphere of public investment. It has now become a central part of public planning for infrastructural investment. It involves a number of stages.

The first stage is the establishment by the Irish government of its own investment priorities. The timing of the reform of the structural funds process meant that the preparation of the first plan to be funded under the CSF actually took place after the planning period had begun – in 1989 itself. As a result, the preparation of the plan had to be undertaken with limited background analysis. However, the preparation of the plan for the last planning period (1994–1999) and for the current planning period (2000–2006) has involved a much more structured process of consultation.

The process of preparing the National Development Plan has involved extensive consultation by the Department of Finance, which has responsibility for the planning process. In addition, in 1992 and 1999 the Department of Finance also commissioned an independent study of Ireland's investment priorities from outside experts as an input into the consultation process (Fitz Gerald & Keegan, 1993; Fitz Gerald, Kearney, Morgenroth & Smyth, 1999).[4]

These independent studies provided a macro-economic framework within which the investment priorities were determined. The need for this macro-economic framework reflects the major economic role played by the investment funded as part of the plan. This represents an additional layer in the planning process that is not relevant where cost-benefit analyses are carried out on individual projects, which are generally small in the context of a national economy. As part of the process of preparing the National Development Plan (NDP) the Department of Finance consulted with the Social Partners and the Regional Authorities.

Following on this consultative process, the Department then prepared its *National Development Plan* which was agreed by the government. The plans for the first and second CSFs were published in 1989 and 1993 respectively, and the current plan was published in 1999. These plans each represented the Irish government's view of what should be the priority areas for investment.

The next stage in the CSF process involves negotiations with the EU Commission on the basis of the government's plan. The result of this negotiation process is the *Community Support Framework* which embodies the agreed programme of investment to be funded from the structural funds over the course of the planning period. Because the range of projects which could potentially be funded under the CSF has generally been much greater than the funds available from the EU, this process involves negotiations as to which projects would be funded under the CSF and which would be funded purely by the Irish government. In the case of the first CSF in 1989, however, because of the tight public finance constraints, the negotiations on the CSF did actually influence which projects were actually undertaken and which were postponed – there was genuine "additionality."

While in the first CSF the EU funding was a substantial part of the total expenditure under the NDP, in the current plan the vast bulk of the funding will come from Irish taxpayers (see Table 2).

The revised structural fund process also ushered in important changes in how the CSF is actually implemented. As part of the CSF process independent evaluations must be carried out of the effectiveness of the expenditure financed by the structural funds. This evaluation is formalised in terms of an *ex ante* evaluation before the Plans begin, mid-term evaluations undertaken roughly half way through the planning period and *ex post* evaluation when the CSF is completed. In addition, individual measures and projects are evaluated over the course of the CSF (see Hegarty & Fitz Gerald, 2000). This evaluation process has proved to be quite influential, resulting in some redirection of investment over the course of the CSF.

The objective of a NDP is to make a *lasting* difference to the economy and the country generally. This depends crucially on investing directly and undertaking activities that will promote investment. Ongoing subsidies that do not bring about a permanent change in behaviour will not be sustainable.

Old style plans of the 1960s in France or Ireland included statements of the behaviour expected from the private sector – how much they needed to invest etc. However, without effective policies to persuade the private sector to deliver the objectives, public sector wish lists were meaningless. In addition, the governments were not necessarily good judges of what was good for the private sector.

A modern NDP must concentrate on what the government itself can deliver. To influence the growth in private sector output it must create a suitable environment to encourage private investment. This can involve the provision

Table 2.   Share of National Plans Funded by EU.

Plan	Percent
1989–1993	44
1994–1999	40
2000–2006	7

Source: Government of Ireland: National Development Plans.

of public infrastructure – for example, building roads to get exports from factories to ports. The definition of investment can be construed quite widely – including investment in training and education. Anything that makes a lasting difference is, in principle, included.

In preparing the plans for how Ireland would spend the structural funds, successive governments stressed the importance of allocating the money to investment to ensure that the EU funds make a lasting difference to the productive capacity of the economy. With some limited exceptions this precept has been followed in practice.[5]

In Ireland the resources for investment under the current NDP have been allocated over three broad categories as shown in Fig. 12. In both the first and second CSFs (1989–1999) the Irish government attached a high priority in its plans to investment in education and training and, with the agreement of the EU Commission, it has allocated very substantial resources to these areas. Successive independent reviews of the Irish CSF have reinforced that strategy. A mid-term review of the first CSF, published in 1992, recommended, in particular, that the problem of early school leavers be tackled by enhanced investment in the educational system (Bradley, Fitz Gerald & Kearney, 1992). It went on to say that "while EC policy has emphasised training, more emphasis should in future be given to education in building up the long-term human capital of the workforce." This view was further reinforced by another study which made recommendations on priorities for the current CSF (Fitz Gerald & Keegan,

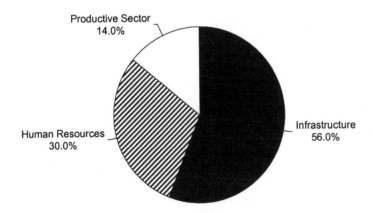

Fig. 12. Allocation of Resources in the National Development Plan.

Source: Government of Ireland: Ireland – National Development Plan, 1994–1999.

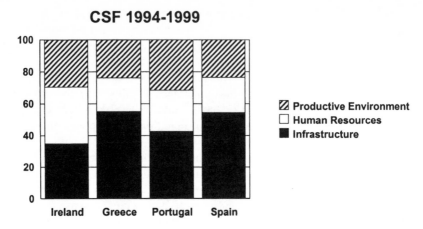

Fig. 13. Comparison of Investment Policies.

Source: European Commission: First Report on Economics and Social Cohesion, 1996.

1993) and the result can be seen in the overall allocation of funds within the programme period 1994–1999.

This contrasts with the choices made in the other cohesion countries where investment in physical infrastructure has received a higher priority (Fig. 13). In Ireland over a third of total funds under both the last two CSFs went on investment in human resources whereas under a quarter was allocated to this role in the other cohesion countries.

In the period 2000 to 2006, the National Development Plan has attached the highest priority for public investment in the broad area of public physical infrastructure. This area of investment has a strong public good element, i.e. it would not be undertaken by the market if left to its own devices.

The most obvious and direct evidence of a constraint on growth arises in the sphere of housing but, in a sense, this is just the tip of the iceberg. The rapid rise in house prices in recent years probably owes more to infrastructural constraints than to any shortage of capacity in the building industry: in particular the restrictions on water supply and sanitary services and the problems of urban transport.[6] As discussed above, some of the constraints in the labour market are also partly attributable to problems of physical infrastructure. While many of these infrastructural services are unpriced (roads and water supply), there is no direct measure of the shortage of capacity and we have to rely on indirect evidence.

Priorities in the area of public physical infrastructure arise under a number of headings. The major areas of public physical investment on which the NDP concentrates are transport and environmental services. There is also a need to increase investment in social and recreational infrastructure. In sectors such as electricity, gas, telecommunications, broadcasting, ports and airports, commercial companies can and will provide the services. While most of these utilities are currently state-owned, the capital programmes of these concerns are funded on a commercial basis, and there has generally not been major EU or Exchequer finance in the recent past. These commercial sectors, and the priorities for investment in them, are treated as part of private (or market sector) capital infrastructure.

Urban public transport is a major priority for investment. Due to delay in the completion of public transport projects in Dublin under the previous NDP and to the rapid growth in traffic, the situation in the city is increasingly critical. Public transport investment, on a scale not hitherto contemplated, is now unavoidable in Dublin. Similar problems are also emerging in provincial cities.

While public investment in social and recreational infrastructure has attracted less attention in the past, in the future it will need to receive greater attention. An important dimension in labour supply in the future will be what determines where people want to live. The most obvious aspect of physical infrastructure that will play such a role is housing but a wide range of other facilities, some of them publicly provided, contributes to location decisions. While some of the necessary social and recreational infrastructure will be provided on a purely commercial basis, there may be a need for increased state provision in areas where the commercial sector is unable or unwilling to provide it.

The second priority area for investment is in education and training. The upgrading of the educational attainment of the adult population has raised the productivity (and earnings) of the labour force. Fitz Gerald and Kearney (2000) estimate that one percentage point a year of the growth over the 1990s was atributable to past investment in human capital. This investment has directly reduced the incidence of unemployment by moving an increasing proportion of the population into the category of skilled labour where there are good employment opportunities in Ireland (and abroad). It has helped increase labour supply by contributing to the rise in female labour force participation.

However, compared with the situation in the 1990s, the ranking in the current NDP represents a somewhat reduced prioritisation for human-capital investment. This change does not mean that this area of activity is not important as it has played a vital role in the rapid growth in the economy. However, changing demographic circumstances in the next decade mean that the pressures facing this sector are likely to ease and there will not be a need for a major increase in resources devoted to it in the next planning period. The evolving structure of the economy will also require a refocusing of the state interventions in this area, in particular in the field of training. The likely success of measures, already in place, in reducing the level of long-term unemployment, should allow a reallocation of resources to target the most disadvantaged.

A third type of investment, which is of considerable importance, is investment in what may be referred to as Research & Development (R&D). However, the resources that can be effectively employed in this kind of activity are small compared to the other major areas of investment.

The fourth major area of public investment is support for private sector physical investment. These interventions comprise targeted interventions and corrective subsidies of a general nature. These would include industrial grants, tourism grants, and some agricultural subsidies, all designed to encourage private sector investment. While Fitz Gerald et al., 1999 argued that the market failures which justified major intervention in the past are greatly reduced and that, as a result, public investment support should be phased out, the current NDP actually provides for some increase. This seems likely to lead to some waste of public resources with serious problems of deadweight.[7]

In the case of income distribution, the appropriate policies for achieving national objectives will be the tax and benefit systems. The National Development Plan, covering investment, has a more strategic role in promoting permanent and sustainable change in the economy's productive capacity.

7. ENVIRONMENTAL CONSTRAINTS

The rapid growth in the economy is also posing new environmental problems. These new problems add to a number of pre-existing environmental problems and, together, they pose a challenge to Irish society. Probably the most serious environmental problem arises from the pollution of watercourses by agricultural activity. Overuse of fertiliser and problems in disposing of farm effluent have contributed to increasing eutrophication in rivers and lakes. This problem is not due to the major increase in output in the economy but rather to specific problems in the agricultural sector.

Pricing measures are not being used to their full potential in Ireland to deal with overuse of the environment. In most cases to do with environmental services, prices are not used to charge for environmental side effects. In others, the price charged does not even reflect the direct cost of the service. This is particularly the case with water and solid waste services. The pressure to use pricing measures is likely to intensify in the future, in order to pay for some of the investment requirements, and as a result of EU pressure to implement the "Polluter Pays Principle" (Scott & Lawlor, 1997). Commercialisation is one way of ensuring that full costs are charged to users of these services. This would include privatisation, but may also include changes in status where public sector bodies are moved to a purely commercial basis with all costs funded by user charges.

The second major environmental challenge Ireland is facing is the rapid growth in greenhouse gas emissions. This is a problem that Ireland shares with the rest of the world, especially the United States. The rapid increase in living standards has made, and is making, a major contribution to growth in this form of pollution. While greenhouse gas emissions tend to rise more slowly than the overall level of economic activity, they are, nonetheless, correlated with economic activity. As part of the programme of implementation of the Kyoto protocol, limits on national emissions have been established for each EU member. In Ireland's case the emissions in the period 2008 to 2012 are required to be no greater than 13% above their 1990 level. The allowance of an increase on 1990 was in recognition of Ireland's low level of output in that year. However, even with this increased headroom, Ireland has already exceeded its limit for the end of this decade.

If Ireland is serious about adhering to the Kyoto protocol major policy changes will be required. As in the case of water usage, it seems unlikely that pleas from successive governments will result in a major change in behaviour. As a result, policy changes will be required which will, either directly or indirectly, raise the cost of emitting greenhouse gases in the future.

Any policy that is adopted to implement the Kyoto protocol should aim to treat all sectors in an even-handed fashion.[8] The marginal cost of reducing a tonne of emissions of greenhouse gases paid by each sector of the economy should be identical. It is clear that whatever regime is adopted, households will have to carry a significant part of the burden of adjustment, directly or indirectly. However, attempts to exclude particular industrial sectors or agriculture could substantially increase the cost to society of compliance. If industry, including the energy utilities, do not face the same costs of compliance as other sectors they will not have the incentive to make the most cost-efficient changes which are needed.

Currently the agriculture sector accounts for over a third of emissions, primarily from livestock production. For Ireland an important part of the solution may involve changing the incentives for farmers to encourage a shift from livestock production to forestry in some form. As returns to farmers are very low from livestock production, and likely to remain low, it is possible that a significant shift in production could take place while leaving farmers no worse off and possibly even better off. Unfortunately lack of co-ordination within the EU Commission in dealing with this issue may prove a major obstacle to finding an efficient solution to Ireland's problems.

The best way of implementing the Kyoto protocol in Ireland would be to impose a suitable tax on consumption of fossil fuels. An alternative, which would not be too inefficient from an economic point of view, would be to require all producers or importers of primary energy to buy permits from the government in an auction. As with a tax, the revenue from the auction should be used to reduce other taxes, leaving the government budget balance unchanged. Under such a regime it is essential that the permits are not given away (referred to as "grandfathering" or, more properly, "grandparenting"), as the revenue from sales plays a vital role in reducing the economic cost of control through lowering the levels of other taxes.

The final serious environmental problem is that of traffic congestion. This is seriously impacting on living standards and it is directly related to past under-investment, especially to under-investment in public transport infrastructure.

8. SUPPLEMENTARY MEASURES

It is desirable that future infrastructure requirements are met in the most timely and efficient manner possible and that policies are applied to ensure that scarce infrastructure resources are used in an economically efficient way. It is considered that improvements can be made to resource allocation in the future through two initiatives:

The first relates to the need to plan the physical development of the country and of the major urban areas. In addition, the physical planning process[9] itself, which controls the implementation of public and private decisions on investment in physical infrastructure, is unduly laborious and inefficient, at present. Clearly this is an area needing much improvement.

The second relates to developing pricing policies for infrastructure services, which reflect the true social cost of their provision. The current practice of widespread under pricing of certain types of infrastructure should be ended, e.g. in the areas of road usage, water abstraction and use of environmental goods. While the investment of public funds is necessary in order to address transport bottlenecks, supplementary measures are also important. The most essential of these is a programme for the management of transport demand. In particular, taxation and pricing measures, especially in cities, will be necessary. Such measures can help restrain demand as well as raising some of the revenue required for investment.

9. CONCLUSIONS

To date there has been a surprising degree of agreement on the key priorities for investment under the National Development Plan. This involves widespread acceptance of the need to greatly increase investment in urban public transport, inter-urban roads, and sanitary services. There may be less agreement on the role of social and cultural infrastructure in development but it is also important. Now that investment in training and education is bearing fruit, there is a need to follow up on the successful formula of the recent past. With declining numbers of young people, an improvement in services will not require as big an increase in funding as occurred under the current plan. Finally, direct aid to investment in the business sector – industry, agriculture and tourism – can be phased down in coming years, reflecting the success of the economy in creating jobs. Increasingly businesses should be able to survive without grant aid. However, the NDP provides for substantial continuing expenditure in this area, expenditure that may well prove wasteful.

Given the strength of the economy, the next planning period should see more than adequate funding available to the government from its own resources to fund its future investment needs.

While the growing bottlenecks in the economy provide evidence of the very pressing needs for major public investment over the next decade, and the funding is likely to be available to undertake the investment, the success of the planning process faces a number of obstacles:

Firstly, in planning for the huge changes which current demographic pressures entail, the NDP may not show sufficient vision or imagination. The very large number of teenagers and young adults today means that over the next decade we will see the number of households in Ireland rise by 30%. After 2010 the rate of growth in household formation will fall off very rapidly. This is both a huge challenge and also a major opportunity. Whereas urban areas elsewhere in Europe are already literally cast in concrete, Ireland will have an opportunity to plan comprehensively for the development of our urban areas. For example, putting in place new urban public transport infrastructure in an existing city is expensive and not terribly efficient. By contrast, if Ireland moves rapidly to implement good public transport systems in its major cities, it can actually influence the pattern of development to enhance the return from the investment. This opportunity will be over after 2010.

A second danger is that even if the plan is suitably ambitious and the funding is available to implement it, sclerosis of the planning process, a painful condition, will result in failure! Unless there is greater efficiency in the future in implementing plans for major infrastructural investment than in the past, economic and social life in Ireland could suffer severely from increasing congestion. It would be a pity if such congestion were to occur, not through lack of resources, but rather through administrative failure.

The *ex ante* evaluation of the plan (CSF Evaluation Unit, 2000) argued that achievement of the ambitious targets set out in the Plan would hinge on the ability to overcome emerging capacity constraints in the construction sector and in the physical planning process generally. Since the plan was published these constraints have proved even more serious than expected. The failure to take appropriate action to free up resources in the building sector to undertake the necessary investment is threatening the NDP's success.

Finally, the need for a huge expansion in the number of households, with all their needs in terms of housing, sanitary services, urban transport etc., will put serious pressure on our environment, especially in the vicinity of urban areas. Ensuring that the essential massive physical development is undertaken in a sustainable way will prove difficult. The growing affluence, with its ever-increasing need for energy, will also pose major problems to Ireland meeting its obligations to reduce greenhouse gas emissions.

NOTES

1. See Fitz Gerald (2000) for a detailed account of the reasons for Ireland's failure and current success.

2. The junior certificate is a state qualification awarded as a result of a national examination taken at around the age of 16. The leaving certificate is awarded as a result of a national examination at high school graduation, generally at around the age of 18.

3. The EU structural funds are paid by richer EU members to poorer members to be used for investment purposes. This investment is designed to promote sustainable convergence in living standards in the EU in the long run.

4. This study was commissioned through an open tendering process where outside groups were invited to bid for the contract to undertake the study according to the terms of reference specified by the Department. In both cases the contract was awarded to consortia led by the Economic and Social Research Institute in Dublin, which included experts from the universities and other consultancy firms.

5. A notable exception was the significant allocation to fund agricultural payments, though that was criticised by successive external evaluations (Fitz Gerald & Keegan, 1993; Honohan, 1997).

6. However, today there are also capacity problems in the building industry itself that make it difficult for the government to fully implement its plans for infrastructural investment.

7. Paying the private sector to do something it would have done without the public support.

8. Ideally at an EU level a similar policy should be adopted to ensure that the "pain" of compliance is equal across countries. This can be achieved through an appropriate

scheme of emissions trading or, preferably, through a common tax rate on emissions across countries.

9. The granting of permits to build, etc.

REFERENCES

Barrett, A., & O'Connell, P. (2000). Is there a wage premium for returning Irish emigrants? ESRI Working Paper No. 125.

Bradley, J., Fitz Gerald, J., & Kearney, I. (1992). *The role of the structural funds: analysis of consequences for Ireland in the context of 1992.* ESRI Policy Research Series No. 13.

CSF Evaluation Unit (1999). *Ex ante evaluation of the national development plan, 2000–2006* (November). Dublin: The Stationery Office (full report can be downloaded at www.eustructuralfunds.ie).

Duffy, D., Fitz Gerald, J., Kearney, I., & Smyth, D. (1999). *Medium-Term Review: 1999–2005.* Dublin: The Economic and Social Research Institute.

Fitz Gerald, J. (2000). The story of Ireland's failure and belated success. In: B. Nolan & P. O'Connell (Eds), *From Bust to Boom.* Dublin: The Institute of Public Administration.

Fitz Gerald, J. (1998). An Irish perspective on the structural funds. *European Planning Studies,* 6(December), 677–695.

Fitz Gerald, J., Kearney, I., Morgenroth E., & Smyth, D. (1999). *National Investment Priorities.* ESRI Policy Research No. 33.

Fitz Gerald, J., & Kearney, I. (2000). Convergence in living standards in Ireland: the role of the new economy? ESRI Working Paper No. 134.

Fitz Gerald, J., & Keegan, O. (1993). *EC Structural Funds. The community support framework: evaluation and recommendations.* Report to Department of Finance, Dublin: Government Publications.

Geary, P. (1978). *How Fianna Fail's Economic Policies Cannot Get This Country Moving Again.* Macgill (April).

Hegarty D., & Fitz Gerald, J. (2000). Ex ante evaluation process for the 2000–2006 period in Ireland, paper given at conference on Evaluation in the EU, Edinburgh (September).

Honohan, P. (Ed.) (1997). *EU structural funds in Ireland: a mid-term evaluation of the CSF 1994–1999.* Policy Research Series, No. 31, Dublin: The Economic and Social Research Institute.

Honohan, P. (1998). *Key issues of cost-benefit methodology for Irish industrial policy.* General Research Series, 172. Dublin: The Economic and Social Research Institute.

Scott, S., & Lawlor, J. (1997). Environmental services. In: A. Barrett, J. Lawlor & S. Scott (Eds), *The Fiscal System and the Polluter-Pays Principle.* Guildford: Ashgate.

World Competitiveness Yearbook (1997). *International Institute for Management Development,* International Thompson Business Press, Lausanne, Switzerland (June).

9. IRELAND IN THE 1990s: THE PROBLEM OF UNBALANCED REGIONAL DEVELOPMENT

Michael J. Keane

1. INTRODUCTION

Beyond the question of economic growth, the question of real convergence has, since the end of the 1980s, captured the attention of policy makers and researchers (European Economy, 2000). Critical questions within the European Union or individual member states are whether the spatial dispersion of per capita incomes tends to decline over time, and whether poor economies tend to grow faster than rich ones and thus converge to the same levels of income per capita. For the EU, regional issues have increasingly been regarded as an essential part of the integration and cohesion process. The objective of economic and social cohesion aimed at reducing disparities between member states, regions and individuals is laid down in article 158 of the Treaty. Indeed, each step towards integration since 1972 has been accompanied by a strengthening of policy aimed at reducing "spatial disparities" and increasing cohesion (Cheshire et al., 1991).

The first response of the EU to the disadvantages from which the less developed regions suffer was the channeling of European Investment Bank lending to the less favored regions. This was followed by the establishment of the European Regional Development Fund (ERDF) in 1975 and by the development of the Structural Funds – the ERDF, European Social Fund (ESF)

The Irish Economy in Transition: Successes, Problems, and Prospects, Volume 85, pages 205–223.
© 2002 Published by Elsevier Science Ltd.
ISBN: 0-7623-0979-2

and the guidance section of the Agricultural Guarantee and Guidance Fund (EAGGF) – after the incorporation of cohesion objectives in the Single European Act of 1986. The ERDF was required, for example, to "help redress the principal regional imbalances in the Community through participating in the development and structural adjustment of economies lagging behind and in the conversion of declining industrial regions" (Article 130C of the Single European Act) as well as rural development. The other funds were expected to contribute to these objectives and to combat long-term and youth unemployment and aid agricultural adjustment.

Regions for which the European Commission has set development objectives include:

- Regions whose development is lagging behind (Objective 1), i.e. regions where per capita GDP is less than 75% of the Community average, or where there are special reasons for their inclusion under this objective;
- Areas in industrial decline (Objective 2). These are mainly areas where the rates of unemployment and industrial employment are higher than the Community average and where industrial jobs are in structural decline;
- Vulnerable rural areas with a low level of socio-economic development which also meet two of the following three criteria: a high proportion of employment in agriculture, a low level of agricultural incomes and a low population density or a high degree of out-migration (Objective 5b); and
- Areas with an extremely low population density (Objective 6), i.e. those with fewer than eight people per sq. km.

For the period 1994–1999 approximately 170 billion euro has been made available from the Community budget for structural and cohesion policies. This represents about a third of total Community spending and around 0.4% of Community GDP. Over the decade 1989–1999, spending amounted cumulatively to 6.5% of annual Community GDP. A historical comparison helps to put the significance of this spending in perspective. Marshall Aid from the U.S. to post-war Europe was equivalent to 1% of U.S. GDP per year and amounted cumulatively (1948–1951) to 4% of U.S. GDP (European Commission, 1996).

This chapter discusses convergence issues in two spatial contexts – international and interregional convergence. At the EU level the former focuses on convergence of Ireland, as a less developed member state, with the rest of the Union (national convergence towards the EU average). The second context is convergence of the regions within Ireland to the national average. Any analysis of convergence issues will face some conceptual and measurement difficulties. Different regional definitions can mask interregional unevenness, there can be a variety of variables used to measures disparities, and there can be a choice of statistical indices applied to these variables. Some standard variables and indices are used in this chapter to measure disparities. The discussion briefly deals with Ireland's economic convergence to the EU average. Then it looks at disparities within Ireland in detail. These differences are shown to be significant. Finally, some of the policy and planning challenges that the problem presents are briefly outlined.

2. IRELAND AND THE EU

The EU has pursued its policy of promoting regional convergence with vigour in the 1990s. The instruments used by the EU have been incorporated into the Community Support Frameworks (CSFs), in the case of Ireland, or Single Programming Documents (SPDs) in other Objective 1 regions. These frameworks are implemented through the formal planning and programming arrangements worked out between the Commission and the member state (Keane, 1999).

The four countries whose per capita incomes were significantly below the EU average during the 1990s – Greece, Spain, Ireland and Portugal – are also referred to as "cohesion countries." The label arises from one of the main objectives defined in the EC Treaty, economic and social cohesion, and from one of the instruments used to achieve this objective, the Cohesion Fund, for which only these four countries are eligible.

Compared to their starting levels in 1960, all four countries can be said to have succeeded in catching-up, at least to some extent, to the EU-15 average. See Fig. 1.

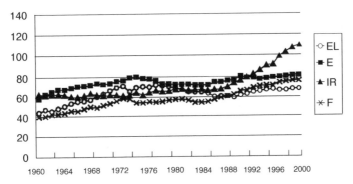

Fig. 1. GDP Per Capita in Cohesion Countries (PPS, EU-15 = 100).

Source: Commission services.
Note: EU-15 average 1960–1990 excluding GDR, 1991–2000 including East Germany 1999 and 2000 estimations and forecasts.

However, the experiences of the four countries in this period have been very different. The rapid rates of growth experienced by the Irish economy, since the end of the 1980s, have improved our relative position dramatically. To obtain from growth rates the number of years it takes for incomes to double, one simply divides these numbers into 69 (the log of 2 times 100). Thus with average 7% rates of growth, Irish incomes will be doubling every 10 years. What all of this means is that Ireland, which in 1990 had a GDP per head of around 64% of the EU average, already well exceeds the European average.

Macroeconomic stability, the functioning of markets and endowments of physical and human capital are generally considered to be among the most important determinants of catching-up. The contribution of Structural Funds per se in promoting economic convergence has been limited (Fitz Gerald, 2000). Factors like the processes and planning in relation to the Structural Funds, in so far as they have positively affected the way the domestic administration and politicians approach public expenditure decision-making, have also been important.

We can understand some of the factors responsible for this improvement by decomposing output per capita into its key components. If Y stands for production, P for population, W for employment, L for the labour force, P_{15-64} for the population aged 15 to 64 years, then per capita output can be decomposed into four components (Raynauld, 1988): worker productivity (Y/W), the employment rate ($W/L = 1$ minus the unemployment rate), the participation rate (L/P_{15-64}) and the dependency ratio [which here is measured as the inverse of P_{15-65} to the total population, that is,

$$\frac{1}{1 + \dfrac{P_{<15+65>}}{P_{15-65}}}$$

where $P_{<15+65>}$ is the dependent population (aged under 15 and over 65), to give the following equation:

$$\frac{Y}{P} = \frac{Y}{W} \cdot \frac{W}{L} \cdot \frac{L}{P_{15-64}} \cdot \frac{1}{1 + \dfrac{P_{<15+65>}}{P_{15-65}}}$$

$$= \text{Productivity} \times \text{Employment Rates}$$
$$\times \text{Participation Rate} \times \text{Dependency Ratio}$$

In terms of output per worker the Irish economy has been converging towards EU standards of productivity fairly steadily since the 1970s. There is some acceleration in the rate of convergence but at a fairly steady pace over the past 30 years. The component that has worked most to accelerate the speed of convergence in GNP per capita has been our falling dependency ratio, measured as the proportion of the population not working to those working. Ireland had a much higher dependency ratio than the rest of the EU in the 1960s and 1970s because of our large families and low rate of labour force participation. The position was accentuated in the 1980s by rising unemployment. However, the changing demographic structure and the improving economic circumstances have had a reinforcing effect on each other since the late 1980s. As a result Ireland is now enjoying an exceptionally favourable demographic structure.

3. THE TRADE-OFF BETWEEN NATIONAL AND REGIONAL CONVERGENCE[1]

It is often the case that catching-up countries, enjoying a high national growth rate, will also see a widening of interregional disparities in terms of per capita income (Williamson, 1965). What happens is that national growth tends to be driven by growth-pole effects which emerge in capital cities and other major agglomerations. Although regional convergence may increase as development proceeds, the early stages of the catching-up process tend to be characterized by a potential trade-off between national and regional convergence. The cohesion countries show some evidence of such a trade-off, as those countries experiencing higher aggregate growth rates have also seen a widening of regional disparities, while regional convergence seems to be associated with low national growth (European Economy, 2000).

One hypothesis is that regional disparities in catching-up countries follow the shape of an inverted U curve over the national growth path. This is known as the Williamson hypothesis. What it suggests in the present context is that the same forces which drive the high growth are also, in the initial phase, generating a widening and subsequently a narrowing of regional disparities in per capita income levels. The higher growth in catching-up economies tends be located in a limited number of growth poles, which see the emergence of agglomeration economies, in the form of knowledge spill-overs and economies of scale. Private capital and skilled workers are attracted by the new opportunities widely available in the growth pole region, leading to cumulative increases in productivity and growth. So, the rapid growth in these growth pole regions leads to a widening of disparities.

However, it is likely that with time diseconomies in the form of congestion and higher factor costs will emerge in the growth pole regions. "Capital is therefore likely to move to other regions where marginal returns are higher, assuming that their factor costs are lower. Similarly, the spatial concentration of knowledge spill-overs may fall due to technological diffusion, particularly if there are improvements in country-wide communications" (European Economy, 2000). In addition, while the early period of the catching-up process may be characterised by strong disparities between urban and rural areas, the reallocation of productive factors across sectors over time, and in particular the decline in agriculture, will help to reduce the disparities between urban and rural areas. The cohesion countries do show mixed support for the Williamson inverted U hypothesis. There is some evidence of a trade-off between national and regional convergence. See Figs 2 and 3. In Fig. 2 disparities are measured on the vertical axis by a population-weighted coefficient of variation. This statistic provides a convenient single index of the degree of dispersion or differences around the mean in the income levels of the given set of regions in a particular country. Despite differences in the evolution of national growth paths and interregional disparities in the 1980s and 1990s, there appears, in general, to be a correlation between high growth rates and a rise in regional disparities. Ireland and Spain have seen higher growth rates and a widening of regional disparities, while Greece has experienced a low growth rate and a fall in regional disparities" (European Economy, 2000, p. 200). Ireland provides a good example of the growth pole effects as the strong national growth in the 1990s was driven by the particularly rapid growth of the East and Southern regions, in particular Dublin and its surrounding area (see Fig. 4, Regions in Ireland) which have accounted for a growing share of national gross

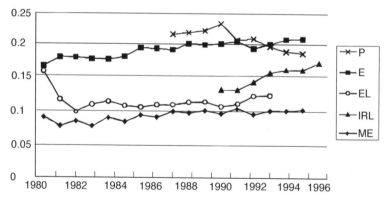

Fig. 2.   Regional Dispersion in the Cohesion Countries and Southern Italy.

Source: Eurostat and Istat data, own calculations. ME = Mezzogiorno.

(Vertical Axis – population weighted coefficient of Variation. *Source:* European Economy, 2000).

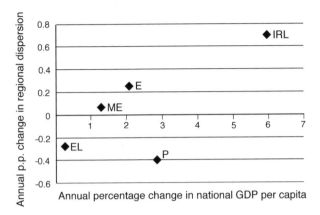

Fig. 3. National GDP Per Capita Growth and Regional Dispersion of GDP Per Capita in the Cohesion Countries and Southern Italy.

Source: Commission services, Istat and Central Statistics Office, Dublin, own calculations.
Note: Data are for 1980–1996 except Ireland (1991–1997) and Portugal (1988–1996).
ME = Mezzogiomo.

value-added or GVA. See Table 1. Gross Value Added (GVA) is a measure of the value of the goods and services produced in a region priced at the value which the producer receives minus any taxes payable and plus any subsidies receivable as a consequence of their production or sale (Government of Ireland, 1999). Although the higher growth rates of these regions have led to a widening of regional disparities within Ireland, all regions did converge towards the EU-15 average level of GVA per capita in 1991–1997.

4. A CLOSER LOOK AT INTERREGIONAL DISPARITIES

In this section we look at a decomposition of the variance in per capita income differences between the Irish regions. This exercise will help to highlight certain features and help us to understand better the problems posed by the existence of significant regional disparities in Ireland. The regions used in the analysis are the Planning Authorities as defined in 1995. See Fig. 4. It should be pointed out that now, as a result of Ireland's spectacular economic performance vis-à-vis the rest of Europe in recent years, only the Border, Midlands and West regions (know collectively as the BMW region) qualify for Objective 1 status.

As shown earlier in this chapter, the regional variation in GVA per capita at a point in time can be decomposed into four terms – productivity (GVA per

Table 1. Gross Value Added (GVA) Per Capita in Irish Regions 1991–1997.

Region		Indices of GVA per person						
		1991	1992	1993	1994	1995	1996	1997
Border	IRL = 100	83.2	83.2	81.1	79.9	77.4	76.6	76.5
	EU = 100	63.3	65.7	66.5	72.7	74.3	74.3	79.6
Midlands	IRL = 100	73.5	76.2	72.9	69.4	67.3	67.1	64.5
	EU = 100	55.9	60.2	59.8	63.2	64.6	65.1	67.1
West	IRL = 100	76.5	75.1	73.6	70.4	72.2	73.5	69.6
	EU = 100	58.1	59.3	60.4	64.1	69.4	71.3	72.4
BMW	IRL = 100	78.7	78.8	76.7	74.2	73.4	73.4	71.4
	EU = 100	59.8	62.2	62.9	67.5	70.4	71.2	74.3
Dublin	IRL = 100	132.4	130.9	131.1	133.8	131.9	133.0	135.3
	EU = 100	100.6	103.4	107.5	121.7	126.6	129.0	140.8
Mid-East	IRL = 100	69.8	89.1	87.3	74.7	88.0	83.5	87.0
	EU = 100	53.0	54.6	55.2	68.0	84.5	81.0	90.5
Mid-West	IRL = 100	93.7	94.3	92.4	94.9	92.0	94.0	90.5
	EU = 100	71.2	74.5	75.8	86.3	88.3	91.2	94.2
South-East	IRL = 100	90.6	91.3	93.3	91.2	87.3	88.9	84.1
	EU = 100	69.0	72.1	76.5	83.0	83.8	86.3	87.4
South-West	IRL = 100	104.3	106.7	111.2	106.2	107.1	105.0	106.8
	EU = 100	79.3	84.3	91.2	96.6	102.8	101.8	111.1
East & South	IRL = 100	107.8	107.8	108.5	109.4	109.7	109.6	110.3
	EU = 100	82.0	85.2	89.0	99.6	105.3	106.3	114.7
σ Convergence	Employment weighted CV	27.3	25.9	28.5	29.5	28.0	28.6	31.7

Source: CSO Regional Accounts 1991–1997.

Fig. 4. Regions in Ireland.

worker), the employment rate, the participation rate and the dependency ratio. While the four components of per capita production are interlinked, we can explain the change in any of them by specific economic or institutional factors within each of the regions (Coulombe, 1997). For example, the dynamic process of neoclassical convergence assumes the gradual elimination of disparities in worker productivity through the interaction of the phenomenon of accumulation of physical capital and the law of diminishing returns. If major differences persist in worker productivity between the regions of the country they might be attributed to delayed development or to some barriers to capital accumulation in regions where it is relatively scarce. As for major inter-regional differences in the employment rate (unemployment rate) or the participation rate, they will be explained by considerations relating to labour market functioning and adjustments, the balance between work and leisure and households' choice of geographic location. We can also write

$$Y_{in} = Prod_{in} \cdot ER_{in} \cdot Pr_{in} \cdot DR_{in}$$

where; i = region; n = the state; and the subscript in denotes a regional value relative to that of the state.

For example

$$Y_{in} = \left(\frac{Prod_i}{Prod_n}\right) \cdot \left(\frac{ER_i}{ER_n}\right) \cdot \left(\frac{PR_i}{PR_n}\right) \cdot \left(\frac{DR_i}{DR_n}\right)$$

in logs, $\log Y_{in} = \log Prod_{in} + \log Er_{in} + \log Pr_{in} + \log DR_{in}$

This decomposition has been estimated by Boyle et al. (2000) and the results are presented in Table 2 with respect to GVA per capita measured at basic prices for 1991 and 1996.

The results clearly point to productivity differentials as the dominant explanation for the inter-regional variation in per capita GVA. Over the two years under examination the variation in the other components, the employment rate, the participation rate and the dependency ratio, only ranges from 0 to about 6%.

The substantial variation that is observed for productivity can be examined further in terms of "within" and " between" sector effects. The "within" sector effect suggests that specific sectors may experience different conditions in different regions (which are conducive to productivity) while the "between" sectors effect is suggesting that certain high productivity sectors may be strongly concentrated (localised) in some locations thereby giving these locations a high productivity reading.

The results of this analysis (Boyle et al., 2000) are presented in Table 3. The data show that the variation in sectoral employment shares is of minimal importance in accounting for inter-regional differences in productivity and that the productivity differences are primarily due to "within" sector effects. What this suggests is that there are features in the regions that give rise to the differences in productivity. The conclusion that is drawn is that these significant productivity differences are closely related to the presence (or absence) of urban

Table 1. Decomposition of Regional Variation in GVA Per Capita
[log y_{in}], 1991 and 1996.

Region	GVA per capita	Employment rate	Participation rate	Dependency rate[a]	Productivity
1991					
Border	−18.09	−2.56	0.86	−4.82	−12.81
Dublin	28.06	−2.01	1.62	6.37	22.69
Mid-East	−36.13	0.70	−2.93	0.00	−35.76
Midlands	−31.03	1.91	−3.01	−3.64	−22.51
Mid-West	−6.80	1.87	−1.96	−1.23	−5.24
South-East	−9.56	−0.39	−1.17	−1.83	−7.15
South-West	4.23	1.84	−1.38	−0.62	4.92
West	−26.70	3.60	0.76	−5.41	−27.93
1996					
Border	−26.16	−3.87	−0.15	−4.45	−21.04
Dublin	28.70	−1.12	3.17	4.65	23.65
Mid-West	−18.57	3.05	1.63	0.65	−16.47
Midlands	−40.14	2.88	0.49	−3.82	−30.00
Mid-West	−10.86	3.08	−4.71	−1.29	−7.92
South-East	−11.26	−0.73	−1.63	−1.93	−11.26
South-West	6.44	0.41	−2.66	−0.65	9.20
West	−30.70	0.56	−1.15	−4.45	−34.02

Source: Boyle et al. (2000).

growth poles where there would appear to be opportunities to enjoy increasing returns and where multinational corporations (MNCs) seem to prefer to locate their facilities. The observation by NESC (1997) that "almost 71% of the net increase in manufacturing and internationally traded services employment between 1986 and 1996 took place in the East region and the four counties containing the main urban centres" is clear evidence of the importance of the urban factor in explaining the concentration of employment. However, other than knowing that economic agents have strong preferences to agglomerate geographically, little is known about the exact dynamics of these urban growth poles. An additional difficulty for Ireland is that the urban system is weak, and consequently it does not offer too many possibilities outside of the larger urban centres like Dublin, Cork, Limerick and Galway.

Table 1. Decomposition of Regional Variation in GVA Per Worker (Productivity) (Log Prodin × 100) into "Within" and "Between" Sector Effects 1991 and 1995.

Region	"Within" sector effect	"Between" sector effect	Productivity
1991			
Border	−11.84	−0.94	−12.81
Dublin	19.23	−0.40	22.69
Mid-East	−37.38	1.64	−35.76
Midlands	−20.50	−2.10	−22.51
Mid-West	−0.66	−4.49	−5.24
South-East	−6.49	−0.58	−7.15
South-West	4.64	0.27	4.92
West	−20.80	−7.16	−27.93
1995			
Border	−23.15	2.12	−21.04
Dublin	29.67	−4.41	23.65
Mid-East	−19.27	2.50	−16.47
Midlands	−27.12	−1.82	−30.00
Mid-West	−11.05	2.58	−7.92
South-East	−10.87	−0.82	−11.26
South-West	10.81	0.39	9.20
West	−24.10	−7.77	−34.02

Source: Boyle et al. (2000).

5. REGIONAL EMPLOYMENT GROWTH

The trend in the regions' shares in national employment provides a summary measure of regional fortunes with regard to employment. Regional performance 1990–2000 is illustrated in Fig. 5 which shows the cumulative percentage change in each region's employment share over the past five years. This is calculated as

$$\sum_{t}^{n} \Delta(\ln E_{it} - \ln E_{t})$$

where E_{it} is employment in the ith region in year t and E_{t} is national employment in year t.

The trends in the employment shares of the BMW regions are shown in Fig. 5a. These regions' share of national employment has declined. The most dramatic decline is in the Midlands (−11.4%) and the Border region (−8.2%).

A: BMW Region

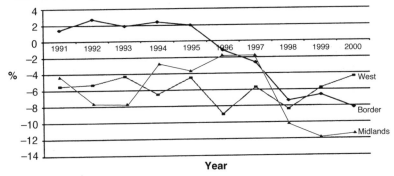

B: Dublin, Mid-East & South-East

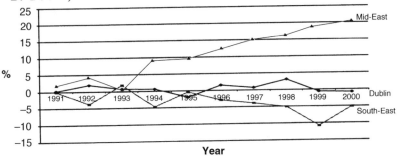

C: Mid-West & South-West

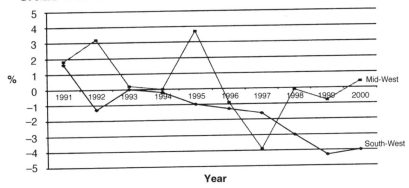

Fig. 5. Regional Share of National Employment.

Recent trends in the Dublin, Mid-East and South East regions are presented in Fig. 5b. The Mid-East shows very impressive gains over the time period, rising by more than twenty percent.

Dublin just about keeps its share, while the share of the South-East has declined. The trends for the Mid-West and South-West regions are presented in Fig. 5c. The South-West region has seen its employment share decline over the ten year period, but not so dramatically. The behaviour of the Mid-West is quite erratic but with very little overall change in employment share over the entire period.

The picture that emerges from this analysis is one of significant redistribution of employment in favour of the Mid-East region. The shares of the Midlands, the Border and, interestingly enough, the South-East have declined significantly.

The polarisation tendencies present in employment patterns in the economy can be detected right across the spectrum of economic activities. Tourism is one example. Ireland has experienced rapid tourism growth during the 1990s but again this business growth has not been evenly spread. The cities and Dublin, in particular, have made the most gains from tourism. The success of Dublin in establishing itself as a city tourism destination has been helped by improved access coupled with more competitive air fares and by the increase in global trends towards short holiday breaks. In contrast, the traditional holiday regions in the West have not kept pace.

6. POLICY AND PLANNING ISSUES

The National Development Plan 2000–2006 contains a commitment to a better regional distribution of public and private investment in Ireland. This commitment is a political commitment, but it may also be about efficiency in the sense that the government feels that national policy must turn to strategies of spatial evolution to further the general development objectives of the economy. The policy challenge is to continue giving priority to the objective of maximising national growth by seeking to manage the diseconomies of agglomeration in the original growth pole regions while also seeking to provide the conditions needed to attract private investment to the other regions.

The policy issues must eventually come down to the specific operational questions of obviously managing what is already there but also of the priority and location of new activities. In this context the government has been preparing a National Spatial Strategy (Department of the Environment and Local Government). This strategy should, in theory, provide a platform for managing spatial development and for negotiating the spatial allocation of resources across the national territory. The fact that this Spatial Strategy will kick in two years into the National Plan is, in my view, symptomatic of the fragmented and largely aspirational approach to strategic spatial planning adopted over the years by successive governments. A good case in point at present is the growth problems manifesting themselves in the Dublin/East region.

The spatial expression of the increased level of economic activity/prosperity in the East region has been the dispersal of both population, housing and employment functions from the Dublin Metropolitan Area to an expanding commuter belt [90km +, see Fig. 4]. Williams and Shiel (2000, pp. 39–40) describe the emerging development of this region:

> As a result of infrastructure-led speculative development with a notable absence of intra-suburban transport links and essential infrastructure, it is clear that the current planning and development control systems are inadequate. This is reflected in terms of the absence of procedures for implementation of strategic planning at a regional level, delayed processes for the delivery of essential infrastructure and the failure to address the full economic and environmental cost of individual developments in terms of congestion, pollution and other external impacts. The functional urban area of Dublin defined by where people work and travel to spend their daytime is now developing without structures, systems or processes of control for their integrated transportation and land use development.

What is equally worrying, perhaps, is that while Strategic Planning Guidelines have been developed for this region they are being widely disregarded. For example, high levels of activity have occurred in the hinterland wedge areas where development was not desired and the implementation of the main transportation requirements have been delayed. This failure in implementation has, as Williams and Shiel (2000) point out, caused a loss of trust in the planning and development system. The classic pattern that has occurred in the Dublin metropolitan area, and to a lesser extent at other growth poles around the country, is that the momentum of development has evolved rather rapidly, be it of new residential communities without adequate infrastructure or facilities or increased car usage without adequate roads. The scale and suddenness of these events have caught administrations napping and have caused many communities throughout the country to adopt defensive and negative responses to all development proposals. A reaction of widespread coordinated opposition to all development proposals has become a feature of Irish life. Localised development impacts are feared and positive attitudes to development are rare.

The policy issues we are talking about here do involve decisions about the priority and location of investment and activities. Therefore, it is inevitable that there will always be strong political considerations seeking to match, if not override, economic considerations. For example, the balance sheet for a given piece of investment may show the largest national gains at one location A, but political considerations may favour another location B. In any democracy there will always be pressures to favour some places at the expense of others; and conflicts are inevitable. It is important that we avoid overselling such place-based policies, endeavoring instead to calculate their true costs more accurately and focus on curbing their worst excesses (Bolton, 1992).

It is not easy to escape the influence that politics can have on decision making. Elected officials will always seek to maximise opportunities for their own local areas. Place oriented programmes and policies are a continuous feature of the Irish policy landscape. Some examples of the kinds of polices involved are illustrated in Fig. 6. These are different tax incentive schemes introduced by various governments during the late 1980s and 1990s. These schemes are aimed at promoting property development and re-development in areas that are deemed to be experiencing some degree of economic difficulty.

Significant resources have been expended on these schemes. Not surprisingly, the advocates of these type of schemes usually seek to link capital projects and investment to meritorious goals like inner-city revitalisation and local economic redistribution. The few programmes that have been evaluated have been shown to give bad value – the net cost to the Exchequer of the urban renewal schemes has been estimated at between £367–461 million, while the estimate of net employment created for the country as a whole over the lifetime of the schemes is only around 1,600 jobs. Moreover, in those designated areas that had adjacent indigenous communities, the evaluation showed that urban renewal did not address the issues that were central to the regeneration and sustainability of the community – public facilities, education, training and youth development (KPMG, 1996). It should be said that the more recent schemes, the Integrated Area Plans, do redress some of these local socio-economic deficiencies (Molloy, 1999). These lessons and the economist's principle of indifference should warn us about designing policies and programmes around locations, land or sites. These policies will not be socially beneficial because the benefits end up in the pockets of the owners (who are probably not needy) of these fixed resources. Based on this principle one can argue that the kind of tax-based measures spawned by political pressures and illustrated in Fig. 6 are invariably bad policies for regional and local development.

7. CONCLUSIONS

The regional development challenges for the National Spatial Strategy and the National Development Plan, are essentially twofold: (a) managing the dynamic within the existing growth poles; and (b) seeking to foster wealth creation in the slower growing regions. The first challenge has already been discussed in the context of the greater Dublin region. Here we will briefly focus on the second

U Designated in 1986 – Cork, Dublin, Galway, Limerick and Waterford

S Designated in 1988 – Athlone, Castlebar, Dindalk, Kilkenny, Letterkenny, Sligo, Tralee, Tullamore and Wexford

T Designated in 1990 – Balina, Bray, Carlow, Glonmel, Droghada Ennis, Longford and Port Laoise

W Designated in 1994 – Ballinasloe, Dungarvan, Enriscorthay, Killarney, Mallow, Mullingar, Navan, Nenagh,
                 Roscommon and Wicklow

\# Designated in 1995 – Cobh   IAP – Integrated Area Plan

▨ Rural Tax Designation   S – Seaside Town Renewal

Fig. 6. Tax-Based Schemes.

of these challenges and first state that it is a difficult task. There is no blueprint that can tell us how to do this. There is a viewpoint that supports the significance of increasing returns, given the appropriate conditions and capabilities, in regional development. However, much of this is based on theoretical argument that is fuzzy in the concepts used, often tautological in its explanations, e.g. "growth regions can be identified by their success in development," and quite insulated from policy decision making (Markusen, 1999). There are few specific insights into what it is that matters for economic success that can be of assistance to regional planners who wish to repeat this success so as to improve the economic performance and quality of life in their regions. The short-run response from the National Spatial Strategy is likely to be a strategy to support the large cities that already possess some of the capabilities for success – be they institutions, skills, organisations or key actors. The task of working out more nuanced plans that will be sensitive to local conditions, to smaller places, and to specific local development dynamics will unfortunately, in all likelihood, be left to a later stage.

NOTE

1. This section of the paper draws heavily on Commission of the European Union, *European Economy* (2000).

REFERENCES

Bolton, R. (1992). "Place prosperity vs. people prosperity" revisited: an old issue with a new angle. *Urban Economics, 29*, 185–203.

Boyle, G., McCarthy, T., & Walsh, J. (1999). Regional income differentials and the issue of regional equalisation in Ireland. Paper read to the Statistical and Social Inquiry Society of Ireland at University College Cork (April 15th).

Cheshire, P. C., Camagni, R. P., Gaudemar, J.-P., & Cuadrado, J. R. (1991). 1957 to 1992: moving towards a Europe of regions and regional policy. In: L. Rodwin & H. Sazanami (Eds), *Industrial Change and Regional Economic Transformation: The Experience of Western Europe*. London: Harper Collins.

Coulombe, S. (1997). Regional disparities in Canada: characterization, trends and lessons for economic policy. Working Paper No. 18. Ottawa: Industry Canada.

Commission of the European Communities (2000). *European Economy*, No. 71. Luxembourg: Office for Official Publications of the EC.

Duffy, D., Fitz Gerald, J., Kearney, I., & Smyth, D. (1999). *Medium-Term review: 1999–2005*, No. 7. Dublin: Economic and Social Research Institute.

Commission of the European Union (2000). *European Economy. Economic and Financial Affairs*, No. 70. Luxembourg: Office for Official Publications of the EC.

Fitz Gerald, J. (2000). The story of Ireland's failure – and belated success. In: B. Nolan, P. O'Connell & C. T. Whelan (Eds), *Bust to Boom? The Irish Experience of Growth and Inequality* (Ch. 3). Dublin: Institute of Public Administration.

Government of Ireland (1999). *Regional Accounts*. Dublin: Central Statistics Office.

Government of Ireland (2000). *The National Spatial Strategy. Indications for the Way Ahead.* Dublin: Department of the Environment and Local Government.

Keane, M. J. (1999). European regions: performance and measurement. In: E. O'Shea & M. J. Keane (Eds), *Core Issues in European Integration* (Ch. 4). Dublin: Oak Tree Press.

KPMG (1996). *Study on the Urban Renewal Scheme*. Dublin: Department of the Environment.

Lucas, R. E., Jr. (1988). On the mechanics of economic development. *Journal of Monetary Economics, 22*, 3–42.

Markusen, A. (1999). Fuzzy concepts, scanty evidence, policy distance: the case for rigour and policy relevance in critical regional studies. *Regional Studies, 33*, 869–884.

Molloy, R. (1999). *Molloy announces new urban renewal designations*. Dublin: Department of the Environment and Local Government.

National Economic and Social Council (NESC) (1997). *Population distribution and economic development: trends and policy implications*. Report No. 102. Dublin: NESC.

Raynauld, A. (1988). Regional development in a federal state. In: B. Higgins & D. J. Savoie (Eds), *Regional Economic Development Essays in Honour of Francois Perroux*. Boston: Unwin Hyman.

Walsh, B. M. (1999). Labour market adjustment in the Irish regions. Department of Economics UCD, Working Paper WP99/6.

Williams, D., & Shiel, P. (2000). Acceleration into sprawl: causes and potential policy responses. *Quarterly Economic Commentary*, (June). Dublin: Economic and Social Research Institute.

10. IRELAND'S SOCIAL SAFETY NET

Eithne Fitzgerald

1. OUTLINE OF CHAPTER

This chapter examines Ireland's social safety net of income maintenance and health services. It sketches some of the historical influences which have shaped the Irish welfare state. It looks at Ireland's income maintenance system including pensions, lone parent support and unemployment payments, and policies designed to bring people from welfare and into work. It examines the effectiveness of the social safety net in preventing poverty, and considers Ireland's National Anti-Poverty Strategy. It outlines key features of the Irish healthcare system. Finally, it examines some choices for better social protection which can now be afforded in a more prosperous Ireland.

2. INFLUENCES ON IRELAND'S WELFARE STATE

For much of Ireland's recent history, social policy has been shaped by two key influences – the Catholic church and British social policy (Burke, 1999).

Influence of Catholic Church

The Catholic Church has been a key provider of education and health services, and up to recent times a powerful voice in Irish social policy. Ireland has a strong tradition of provision of social services such as health and education

The Irish Economy in Transition: Successes, Problems, and Prospects, Volume 85, pages 225–247.
Copyright © 2002 by Elsevier Science Ltd.
All rights of reproduction in any form reserved.
ISBN: 0-7623-0979-2

through voluntary, mainly Church bodies. Today these are virtually all publicly funded but remain in Church ownership and management. Traditional Catholic social teaching was strongly suspicious of social services run or controlled by Government. This ethos has contributed to the slow development of a comprehensive welfare state in Ireland. The Catholic Church in 1951 played a pivotal role alongside the medical profession in blocking proposals for a free health service, initially for mothers and children, in a controversy which brought down the government of the day (Whyte, 1980; Barrington, 1987). While the Church in the post-Vatican-Two era has moved to the left on social policy, emphasising social rights and social justice, this has coincided with a sharp decline in its political influence in a modern secular Irish society, and a loss of moral authority as Church scandals unfolded.

U.K. Legacy

Whereas the political success of Left parties and post-war reconstruction were major influences on the development of modern European welfare states, Ireland, a late developer, does not fall easily into this model (O'Connell & Rottman, 1992). Ireland's welfare state in many ways is rooted strongly in the British tradition. There was a common government until 1922, but even after independence, the Irish state tended to look to its nearest neighbour Britain for models of policy and legislation. The state's income maintenance system, known in Ireland as the social welfare system, is closely modelled on the Beveridge (1942) proposals for the U.K. Ireland, as the poorer neighbour, however, was much slower to develop a more comprehensive welfare state. Ireland's copy of the British system was at the outset a pale shadow of the original – social security mainly confined to manual workers until 1974, no free education at second level until 1967, and no national health service.

Expansion of Social Protection from 1970s

From the early 1970s on, as Ireland modernised, policy horizons widened away from the U.K. and towards mainland Europe. The next quarter of a century saw a steady expansion in Ireland's social protection, as new schemes of weekly payments were introduced, payments were raised, coverage of social insurance was widened, and entitlement to health services improved. Expansion of the welfare state in Ireland, given a new impetus by the Report of the Commission on Social Welfare (1986), continued in the 1980s in contrast to the Thatcher years of retrenchment in the U.K. The result today is a social safety net in Ireland which is recognisably derived from a U.K. model, but which has developed its own distinctive features and in some areas is considerably more generous than its U.K. counterpart.[1]

3. INCOME SUPPORT

Income maintenance means income support from public or private sources which offers protection during interruption or loss of earnings. Social welfare, as Ireland's state system of income maintenance is called, includes both social security and means-tested welfare payments. Occupational welfare includes occupational pensions, occupational sick pay and redundancy (unemployment) compensation. Under purely private arrangements, individuals may go to the private market to buy pension plans or insurance against income loss through illness.

Income maintenance fulfils a number of different functions in any society. The first is protection against poverty and destitution. The second is the replacement of income, the maintenance of customary living standards during income interruption or absence. The third is to smooth income over the life cycle. Other aims of Ireland's social welfare system are to promote social solidarity (Department of Social Welfare, 1996) and redistribute income (Commission on Social Welfare, 1986).

Ireland's social welfare system is designed to protect against poverty rather than to maintain previous living standards up the income scale. Social insurance payments, both short-term and pensions, are flat-rate rather than earnings-related as in most other EU countries and in the U.S. In terms of Korpi and Palme's (1998) typology, Ireland, alongside the U.S., the U.K. and Canada offers a "basic security" model of welfare state, unlike Continental European "corporatist" models or the Scandinavian "encompassing" welfare state.

As in the U.K. system, originally designed on male breadwinner lines, Ireland's payment structure provides additions for dependent spouses and children. There is also a universal monthly Child Benefit.[2] This contrasts with the main Continental European model. Countries like France and Germany pay purely earnings-related social security payments with no family additions. Children of benefit recipients are supported through the generous child benefits payable to all families.

4. DESCRIPTION OF IRISH SOCIAL WELFARE SYSTEM

In Irish society, the social welfare system is the most important vehicle for redistribution. The poorest 30% of Irish households have virtually no income from economic activity. Welfare payments bring their share of pre-tax incomes up from under 1% to about 8%.[3] Although countries with more generous earnings-related systems distribute their transfers farther up the income ladder, they also achieve greater redistribution since the scale of transfers is much larger (Korpi & Palme, 1998). Countries whose welfare systems are better targeted on the poor tend also to be less generous ones, and thus redistribute less of total income. Ireland's welfare system is among the most targeted of OECD countries (Förster & Pellizzari, 2000), but also among the less generous in the European Union in its level of spending (ILO, 1999).

In Ireland, both social security (social insurance) and means-tested income support (social assistance) are administered by the same government department.[4] Unlike the U.S., there is no sharp difference between social security and means-tested welfare in terms of administration or of popular culture. For every social security payment, there is a means-tested equivalent. In popular discussion, no distinction is made between pensioners on an old age contributory pension or a non-contributory pension, between unemployed people on unemployment benefit or unemployment assistance. Insurance benefits where there is no means test and means-tested assistance are both fairly well targeted on poor households;[5] indeed a high share of those on non-means-tested payments are below the poverty line.[6] Child Benefit is more evenly spread across income groups.

Structure of the Welfare System

Ireland's social welfare system comprises five separate elements:

- social insurance;
- social assistance;
- universal child benefit;
- in-work benefits;
- secondary benefits.

Social Insurance

The social insurance system gives replacement income as of right, based on the record of social insurance contributions, to people whose income loss or interruption comes into one of the categories covered. Social insurance in Ireland covers all the standard international categories – old age and retirement, widowhood, unemployment, illness, disability and work injury, maternity.[7] There is also a carer's benefit for up to a year for those who leave a job to care full-time for a disabled relative.

Beveridge's vision of social insurance was built around assumptions of full employment, stable families, and the breadwinner male. Women in the Beveridge schema were to be protected through the cover earned by their husbands. With comprehensive cover of the working population, Beveridge argued, means-tested payments would play only a minor residual role. However, in a world of long-term unemployment and changing family structures, means-testing did not wither away, either in the U.K. or in Ireland. Overall, about 45% of Irish social welfare recipients were on means-tested payments in 2000.[8]

Long years of limited coverage of social insurance have added to reliance on means-tested benefits in Ireland with about a third of pensioners in 2000 receiving means-tested payments. Coverage of Ireland's social insurance at its outset in 1953 was limited to manual workers and poorer private sector white collar workers. Most of the middle class and the self-employed including Ireland's large farming sector were excluded from this obligation of social solidarity (Cousins, 1997). The slow extension of social insurance coverage saw private sector white collar workers included from 1974, the self-employed from 1988, part-time workers from 1991 and newly recruited public servants from 1995. Since 1994, parents who opt to stay at home with their young children can earn social insurance credits.

Social Assistance

Means-tested social assistance provides a parallel system of income support to social insurance. Social assistance covers the same contingencies as social insurance (unemployment, disability, widowhood, pensions, full-time care of the elderly or infirm). In addition, there is the One Parent Family Payment, the main income support measure for single parents, which has no direct social insurance parallel. There is also a generic scheme of weekly payments, Supplementary Welfare Allowance, for those without an income who do not come into any of the listed categories. Social assistance provides both for people with no social insurance cover (e.g. people without a recent work record) and for those who have reached the time limit on entitlement to insurance benefits.

Supplementary Welfare Allowance, the assistance scheme of last resort, is the linear descendant of the Poor Law. When the Irish Famine of the 1840s overwhelmed the capacity of the Poor Law's workhouse system, a new discretionary and locally administered income measure named Outdoor Relief (later retitled Home Assistance) was introduced in 1847. Basic national rates of payment of the scheme, now renamed Supplementary Welfare Allowance, were finally standardised in 1977, but the scheme retains a discretionary element to provide for exceptional needs. The officials who administer it are still known colloquially as Relieving Officers. Rent allowances for private sector tenants living on a welfare payment also come under Supplementary Welfare.

Child Benefit

Monthly children's allowances, payable for all qualified children without a means test, were first introduced in 1944 for families with three or more children. Later extended to second children and then to all children, children's allowances were merged with income tax allowances for children into a single monthly cash payment renamed Child Benefit. Child Benefit is seen as an effective way of targeting resources on poor families and of tackling child poverty (Nolan, 2000). All families benefit, so that unlike child additions to weekly welfare payments, Child Benefit is neutral as to the work status of parents. Monthly values for Child Benefit are given in Table A2 of the Appendix.

After an extended public debate about how best to help working parents with childcare costs, Child Benefit was chosen in 2001 as the vehicle to give extra help towards these costs. A three year programme of significant increases in Child Benefit was therefore put in place, whose effect has been to raise Child Benefit towards mainland European levels. Child Benefit, although it is not differentiated by the age of the child, was favoured as it would be neutral as between working families and stay-at-home parents, between parents on high earnings and those in full-time education or low-paid work. The individualisation of the tax code which favoured two-income families had earlier provoked a major public outcry when introduced in 2000.

In-work Benefits

The earnings of low paid workers with families can be topped up through Family Income Supplement, although proposals are to be examined to replace this with an Earned Income Tax Credit as in the U.S. Under the Back-to-Work Allowance scheme, people who have been long-term unemployed may retain a proportion of their previous welfare payment on a sliding scale to ease the transition back into work or self-employment. For those moving into employment, it is spread over three years (75%, 50%, 25% of previous entitlements) and for those moving to self-employment it is spread over four years (100%, 75%, 50%, 25% of previous entitlements). There is a high drop-out rate back into unemployment, however (Fitzgerald, Ingoldsby & Daly, 2000, p. 51).

Secondary Benefits

This is the term given to a range of ancillary, primarily non-cash additions, funded from the welfare system. Every person aged 66 or over is entitled to free travel on state-owned buses and trains. Elderly people may also qualify for free electricity units, free telephone rental, and a free TV licence. The average weekly cost of these benefits is just over €10 a week per person. Social welfare recipients also get specific funding towards seasonal expenses – an extra weekly payment over the winter months towards fuel costs, a double week's benefit before Christmas, and back to school grants in August to help with new shoes and school uniforms. Whereas the U.S. welfare system gives earmarked help with food costs under the food stamps programme, the Irish system singles out fuel bills for extra help.

A particularly prized benefit is the medical card, conferring entitlement to free family doctor care, free prescription medicines and free hospital in-patient care. There is a strict means test which effectively confines medical cards predominantly to welfare recipients. Since July 2001, those aged 70 or over irrespective of income are entitled to a medical card. To help smooth the path from welfare back into work, people who have been long-term unemployed and who get a job can retain their secondary benefits including the medical card for up to three years.

Funding the Social Welfare System

Social assistance and universal benefits (just over half of total welfare spending) are paid for out of general taxation while today the social insurance system is paid for entirely by social security contributions via earnings-related payroll deductions.

In 2000, almost a quarter of the population received a weekly welfare payment and social welfare accounted for about a quarter of current government spending and 7.8% of GNP. While the share of recipients in the population has risen slightly in the last decade, social welfare's share of both government spending and of GNP has fallen sharply over the period. As the Irish economy and earnings grew rapidly in the 1990s, social welfare payments, while outperforming inflation, have not kept pace with real earnings growth. Sharply falling unemployment (from 18% down to 4%) has also kept welfare spending in check.

Ireland has at present a pay-as-you-go system where current outgoings are financed by current income and today's pensions are being paid by today's working generation. However, anticipating the ageing of the population into the current century, since 1999 it has been government policy to set aside 1% of GNP into a National Pensions Reserve Fund to partially fund future obligations for social welfare pensions and the pensions of Government employees.[9]

Although traditionally social insurance was funded on a tripartite basis with contributions from employers, insured workers and the government, there has been no subvention from general taxation since the mid-1990s. As taxes on corporate profits in Ireland are low, a quid pro quo is that employers pay the lion's share of social insurance contributions, and indeed employer social insurance contributions bring in over two thirds the revenue earned from Corporation Tax.[10]

Social security contributions are low by international standards. Specific reasons include:

- flat-rate rather than income-related benefits;
- a favourable demographic balance with a low ratio of elderly people compared to the working generation, in contrast to rapidly ageing societies elsewhere (OECD, 2000);
- about a third of pensioners being on means-tested payments (as a result of past gaps in social security coverage) which are funded from general taxation rather than social insurance contributions;
- unlike most European countries, the funding of health care from general taxation rather than financed under social security.

During the 1990s, social security contributions, especially by the low paid, were reduced as part of a strategy to improve disposable incomes without excessive wage increases.

5. COMMISSION ON SOCIAL WELFARE

Having developed in a piecemeal manner from the 1950s, the first overall strategic review of the social welfare system was undertaken by the Commission on Social Welfare (1986). The Commission set out five key principles – adequacy, comprehensiveness, consistency, simplicity and redistribution. It recommended reforming and simplifying the existing system rather than its replacement by an alternative model. The Commission's central focus was on raising welfare benefits to an adequate level, a suggested £50–£60 a week in 1986 terms. The lower bound of this adequacy target was finally reached in 1999. The Commission also recommended harmonising the multiplicity of welfare benefits and extending the reach of social insurance to cover all workers. The Commission's report served as a blueprint for change into the mid-1990s. Benefit payments were increased significantly faster than inflation with the lowest benefits increasing fastest in order to harmonise rates and social insurance cover was gradually extended. Then as concerns about the transition from welfare to work took centre stage, the process of simplification went into reverse with the introduction of transitional measures, in-work benefits, and higher benefit increases for pensioners no longer in the labour market.

Irish society has changed radically in the fifteen years since the Commission's last review. Unemployment has fallen to reach 3.7% of the workforce by mid-2001 and inward migration has replaced a century and a half of heavy emigration. Women's participation in the workforce has increased dramatically, with two thirds of women under 50 in a job. Family life has changed, and a third of all babies are now born outside marriage. Real incomes have risen by 70% in the last decade of the twentieth century, but social services have not kept pace with rising expectations. There are new strategic challenges for the welfare system. Is the Beveridge model now outdated? Should we move from preventing poverty to income replacement? How should benefits be upgraded in future? Should individualisation replace dependency?

6. SOME POLICY ISSUES

Income-Related Pensions?

About 90% of those aged 66 or over receive a state social welfare pension or have a spouse payment made on their behalf (Pensions Board, 1998, p. 4). Social welfare pensions are of particular importance because of the poor coverage of occupational pensions – a little under half the workforce (half of employees and a quarter of the self-employed) are covered by occupational pensions, and only a third of the currently retired are receiving a pension from a former job (Hughes & Whelan, 1996).

Ireland is highly unusual among OECD countries in neither having income-related social security pensions, as in the U.S. and most of Western Europe, or widespread or compulsory occupational pension cover. While the flat-rate state pension addresses the poverty objective, for a sizeable proportion of the population the present system fails to meet the objective of maintaining pre-retirement income. Although proposals for a state earnings-related pension scheme were floated in a government Green Paper (Department of Social Welfare, 1976), they were not a priority at a time when welfare payments for other categories had a long way to go to meet basic adequacy targets (Commission on Social Welfare, 1986, p. 328). Instead, a Pensions Board was set up to monitor and regulate occupational pension schemes and advise on general pensions policy.

Following a major review of pensions policy, the National Pensions Policy Initiative, which it conducted, the Pensions Board (1998) recommended as a target that post-retirement income from all sources should achieve fifty percent of gross pre-retirement income. The Board recommended that the personal rate of social welfare pension should be set at a level of a third of average earnings. Such a state pension, the Pension Board estimated, would deliver the target pre-retirement income for the poorest third of the population. However, supplementary pension coverage would be needed by the remainder of the population in order to reach half of pre-retirement income.

The Pensions Board recommended a portable personal pension savings arrangement, similar to U.S. Individual Retirement Accounts, would be available through employers, and the Pensions Act of 2002 gave effect to this strategy. It is not compulsory for employers to ensure employees have pension coverage or to contribute to a pension scheme, merely to make a voluntary facility available for pension saving. Take-up is optional for employees. It is unlikely that this purely voluntary strategy will make any significant increase in the proportion of employees who have supplementary pension coverage, particularly given that those who lack pension coverage at present are predominantly the poorest-paid and least unionised workers, working for small companies. Unless it is obligatory, it is difficult to see how the proportion of workers with additional pension cover would increase through a voluntary savings scheme.[11]

Lone Parents

Irish society has changed, and there is now a much wider diversity of family types. Almost a third of all births are now outside of marriage, marriage breakdown has increased and divorce is legal since 1996. In the 1970s a series of welfare schemes, modelled on provision for widows, were introduced for different categories of lone parents, those labelled as deserted wives, unmarried mothers, or prisoner's wives. All such lone parent payments are now grouped together in the means-tested One-Parent Family Payment. While this payment can be paid to male or female lone parents, in practice the overwhelming majority of claimants are mothers.

Unlike Temporary Assistance to Needy Families which replaced Aid to Families with Dependent Children in the U.S., support for lone parents in Ireland is not time-bound. A lone parent who satisfies other conditions (means-test, cohabitation rule) can receive payment until her youngest child leaves the education system (up to age 22). A survey of claimants in 1998 (Swinburne, 1999, quoted in Department of Social Community and Family Affairs, 2000) showed that about half of those who started out on a lone parent payment ten years earlier were still in receipt of a lone parent welfare payment. Lone parents are encouraged to earn, through generous treatment of any earnings in the means test, but there is no obligation to get a job unlike, for example, the Wisconsin Works programme. A review of the one-parent family payment (Department of Social Community and Family Affairs, 2000) concluded that in the absence of well-developed child care, that a younger age limit on children or a work requirement would not be a practical change at this time.

Lone parents may earn up to € 7,600 without loss of benefit, a much more generous disregard of earned income than offered to other categories of welfare recipients. Over half of all lone parents hold a job, with a majority of them working part-time, mainly by choice (QNHS, 2001)

The fundamental premise of the widows' pension schemes on which the lone parent payment was modelled was that the social protection offered was for being alone, financially unsupported by a partner, rather than for carrying out a parenting role. As currently structured, Ireland's welfare system creates strong disincentives to unmarried parents to live together and share in the upbringing of their children. One option for reform would be to recognise the care of young children as a contingency affecting welfare support, rather than lone-parent status per se. (NESC, 1999) The Carer's Allowance and Carer's Benefit schemes already provide income support in the case of full-time care of an adult with a disability.

The Irish welfare system is based on a breadwinner male model that has become increasingly outdated as society changes. Women's groups have argued that the concept of dependency should be replaced by personal entitlement to benefits for all adults. Agreement in principle has been reached on the concept of administrative individualisation of welfare payments where each of a couple would personally receive their share of the "couple" payment. (Programme for Prosperity and Fairness, 2000).

Unemployment

Unemployment payments under social insurance may last for up to fifteen months (compared with six months in the U.S.), after which if still out of work, a person may switch to the means-tested unemployment assistance at the same rate.

Until the 1980s, Ireland's difficulties in providing enough jobs appeared more as heavy emigration than domestic unemployment, but the economic difficulties of the 1980s resulted in sharply increased unemployment. There was a rapid expansion of labour market programmes for the unemployed, the largest of which, Community Employment, offers work experience on community and public sector projects, on a half-time basis. When the Commission on Social Welfare (1986) recommended a minimum adequacy target, the weekly payment received by the long-term unemployed represented only two thirds of the Commission's lower target.[12] As unemployment payments were the farthest below the Commission's adequacy target, they were raised substantially in the years following the Commission's report, at a pace which exceeded the growth in earnings, and also significantly faster than pension rates. When payments to the unemployed had improved relative to these other incomes, concerns about high replacement rates and disincentives to work then came to the fore. Because Irish welfare rates, unlike wages, include additions for partners and children, replacement rates are highest for unemployed recipients with a family. In fact, some 60% of recipients of unemployment payments have no dependents.[13]

The solution adopted to address the disincentive problem took more of the carrot than the stick approach. Rather than cutting welfare payments to the unemployed, as some countries have done, in Ireland unemployed people who take up a job are allowed to retain a proportion on a sliding scale of their previous payments for a period, as well as their secondary benefits. This has made the system more complex, cutting across the efforts made following the Commission to simplify the social welfare system and harmonise benefits across schemes. Policing of the benefits system has also effectively been tightened through systematic interviewing of people claiming unemployment payments as they reach a threshold period out of work. Employment Guidelines agreed at the European Community's Luxembourg Employment Summit in 1997 call on member governments to intervene when young unemployed (under 25) reach six months out of work with other unemployed after twelve months, to try and prevent them drifting into long-term unemployment.

The surging growth in the Irish economy and the demand for labour has led to a very significant fall in the numbers out of work over the decade of the 1990s, including a drop in long-term unemployment. The proportion of the labour force out of work for over a year has come down from a peak of 10.4% in 1988 to 1.4% by the autumn of 2000.[14] Those who remain as unemployed in the jobs boom are disproportionately drawn from those with poor education and low skills, and are often significantly detached from the mainstream labour market (Fitzgerald, Ingoldsby & Daly, 2000). Social programmes which address problems of poor education or literacy, which build up skills and confidence and which provide a bridge for the marginalised unemployed back into the world of work are just as important as economic success in reducing unemployment even further.

Relief of Poverty

How effective is the Irish social welfare system in its aim of poverty relief? Callan and Nolan (2000, pp. 186–192) use the measures of efficiency and effectiveness devised by Beckerman (1979) to measure this. We can calculate a poverty gap by aggregating the shortfall in income below a chosen poverty line of those people below the poverty line. The Beckerman measure of effectiveness looks at the proportion of the pre-transfer poverty gap which is eliminated after social welfare transfers. The efficiency measure calculates the percentage of social security spending which goes towards reducing the pre-transfer poverty gap. Taking as a poverty line 50% of average income, Callan and Nolan's results show poverty reduction effectiveness in 1997 was almost 90%, while efficiency was 65%. International results on these lines show Ireland's welfare system scoring better on efficiency and effectiveness in reducing poverty than the U.K., Sweden or France.[15]

Uprating Welfare Payments

Irish welfare payments have over time increased faster than inflation. Even in the difficult economic times of the 1980s, real increases in welfare benefits were given. But even if welfare payments are improving in real terms, unless they keep pace with incomes generally in society, the relative position of those who remain on welfare will deteriorate. While social welfare rates grew faster than prices over the 1980s and 1990s, they failed to keep up with disposable incomes generally. Old age pensions fell from 1984 to 1997 in relation to average incomes, forming a lower proportion at the turn of the century than they did twenty years earlier. Payment rates to the unemployed grew throughout the 1980s but from the early 1990s onward began to fall relative to earnings as concerns about work incentives moved more into the foreground.

The official target (Pensions Board, 1998) for social welfare pensions is that they reach 34% of average earnings. Using the argument that existing relativities between pensions and other welfare payments should at least be maintained, the group which reviewed benchmarking of social welfare payments (2001) recommended that welfare payments should be targeted at 27% of gross average industrial earnings.

7. TAX AND WELFARE STRATEGY – AND SOCIAL PARTNERSHIP

Both income taxes and social security contributions are low in Ireland by international standards, with a higher-than-average share of revenue from expenditure taxation (OECD Revenue Statistics). Ireland is a fairly low tax, low spending economy, and partly this reflects a more modest welfare state than most European countries; Ireland's flat-rate welfare benefits absorb a lower share of GDP than would pay-related benefits. Latest published figures, those for 1998/9 (Revenue Commissioners 2000), show an effective income tax rate of 21.2%.[16]

Social Partnership

Ireland's modern social partnership is widely seen as an important ingredient in the recovery of the Irish economy from the depths it reached in the 1980s, and of Ireland's modern economic miracle. Falling unemployment and rising real incomes have been significant factors in reducing poverty and the demands on social welfare services. Social partnership has also been a significant ingredient in the move to a lower tax climate.

There had been previous tripartite agreements on pay throughout the 1970s, but they collapsed in 1981 when employers withdrew from the process. The background to Ireland's modern social partnership was a crisis in the public finances. The economic slump that hit Europe in the wake of the oil price crises of the 1970s ended the post-war period of steady economic progress and full employment. Ireland's problems of adjusting to the economic downturn of the 1980s were particularly difficult, as previous economic policies had left an over-hang of national debt. This debt problem was compounded by high interest rates, leading to a crisis in the public finances that forced further contraction in the economy. In 1986, unions, business and farm leaders prepared a shared analysis of these deep economic problems – A Strategy for Recovery (NESC, 1986). Based on this shared view, these social partners concluded a formal agreement, the Programme for National Recovery in 1987 (Hardiman, 2000).

Modern social partnership in Ireland has evolved in a unique way that has been highly influential in terms of the both the broad thrust of public policy and its detail. It has enjoyed strong cross-party support, although criticised by Ó Cinnéide (1998) for undermining the elected parliament (the Dáil) in assigning such influence to unelected groups. Ireland is a small society. Key actors in the social partnership process have built up shared understandings, good working relationships with each other, and enjoy easy access to government. In 1996 social partnership was broadened out to include a social pillar representing groups such as the unemployed, women, and disadvantaged communities.

The 1987 social partnership deal, the Programme for National Recovery, focused mainly on taxation, pay, and the public finances. At the heart of this deal, and each of the four subsequent detailed three-year social partnership agreements, has been a trade-off between lower nominal pay increases and reductions in personal taxation. Workers were prepared to accept lower pay rises and maintain competitiveness, relying mainly on lower taxes to deliver improved disposable incomes. Any process that has tax reduction at its heart is likely to give less weight to spending commitments that might compete with tax cuts for available resources.

While some significant new commitments around welfare improvements and other social programmes have been written in to certain partnership agreements, social partnership has helped shift the emphasis of public policy more towards tax reduction than to service improvements. So on the big picture, it has signalled relatively lower emphasis on social spending compared to cuts in personal and business taxation.

On the smaller picture, however, the involvement of voluntary sector representatives has helped accelerate a reform agenda within individual social services, most notably social welfare. A myriad of working groups involving the traditional social partners and those social partner groups who directly represent social welfare recipients have tackled issues like how to benchmark welfare payments and administrative individualisation in the welfare code.

From 1987 to 1997, the size of the Budget Day income tax packages ranged from once to twice the scale of the welfare packages. In 1998 the tax package was almost three times the welfare package, in 1999 and 2000 around five times the welfare package. Callan, Keeney and Walsh (2001, p. 46) make the point that that the relative size of the tax and welfare packages within a given budget envelope has a significant impact on whether the poorest income groups (dominated by welfare recipients) lose out in relative terms.[17]

While social partnership has helped the thrust towards tax cuts, in practice the scale of tax cuts under social partnership has significantly exceeded those promised under the partnership agreements. For example, the money spent on cuts in taxes over 1987–1990 were almost three times the level promised by government in the Programme for National Recovery. Tax cuts beyond those agreed under partnership must be attributed to the explicit political choices made by the governments concerned. The government which took office in 1997 was wedded to tax reduction and used the fruits of the economic boom to make income tax cuts on a much deeper scale than those committed under social partnership. (Fitzgerald, 2001).

8. NATIONAL ANTI-POVERTY STRATEGY

Following the commitments given at the UN World Summit on Social Development in Copenhagen in 1995, Ireland became the first European Union country to adopt a national anti-poverty strategy (Department of Social Welfare, 1997). The strategy dealt with five key themes – income adequacy, education, unemployment, urban disadvantage and rural poverty. The official definition of poverty adopted was framed in terms of current social norms:

> People are living in poverty if their income and resources (material cultural and social) are so inadequate as to preclude them having a standard of living which is regarded as acceptable in Irish society generally.

Sharing in Progress – National Anti-Poverty Strategy, p. 3.

The official poverty line measure in the U.S. based on the work of Orshansky (1965) is a simple one, multiplying the cost of a standard food basket by three. The official measure used to set the global target in Ireland's national anti-poverty strategy is more complex, and is expressed as a range not as a single figure. It derives from what ESRI researchers (Nolan & Whelan, 1996) term consistent poverty, following Ringen (1988) in defining poverty both in terms of low income relative to the average and in terms of consumption. These researchers call someone consistently poor if income is below a proportion of average income (conventionally 50% or 60% of average income) and the person is forcibly deprived through low income of any one of some very basic items such as a main meal or a winter coat.

The strategy's global target of a specified reduction by 2004 in the numbers of consistently poor from their 1994 level had in fact been reached in 1997. Likewise, the long-range targets set for reductions in unemployment and in long-term unemployment have now already been exceeded. Following the achievement of the original targets, new targets for reduced poverty for children, women and older people, and targets on health and housing were published in 2002. There has been little progress to date, however, on the targets set for reduction in early school leaving. In terms of long-term impact on the underlying causes of poverty, this failure to meet the targets for retaining more children in school is ultimately a serious one.

9. HEALTH SERVICES

Ireland's health services are of a high quality, but are under increasing strain as demand for healthcare rises and as staff are attracted to work elsewhere in the booming economy.

Family Doctor Care

The poorest third of the population, mainly welfare recipients and the elderly, get family doctor care and prescription drugs free of charge on their medical card. The rest of the population pay for family doctor care, their prescription costs are capped at about $50 a month, and unreimbursed medical expenses above a threshold of about $230 a year can be deducted from taxable income.

Hospital Care

Hospital services are run on a mixed public/private system. Most specialists see both public and private patients. This is facilitated by designating about 20% of beds in public state-funded hospitals as private care beds, and by sister private hospitals built on the campus of some of the major hospitals. Everyone, irrespective of income, is entitled to care as a public patient in a public hospital. For all but the poorest third of the population, who hold medical cards, there is a nominal daily charge.[18] Public patients are assigned to the medical team, private patients choose their consultant. The Commission on Health Funding (1989, p. viii) rejected arguments for separating private care from the public domain, arguing that the best skill, care and technology are available to the full population including the lower income group through the mixed care system.

About 40% of the population have private health insurance to cover hospital care, and there is tax relief on the premiums. Private patients in public hospitals get a double subsidy, as it is estimated the charge represents about half the economic cost. The principal reason for buying insurance is the perception of quicker access to diagnosis and treatment (Nolan & Wiley, 2000). Consultants in the public health care system are paid a salary to care for public patients, but are also allowed to accept private patients, for whom they charge fees.[19]

In spite of official commitments to switch resources into community-based care, the Irish health care system remains dominated by institutional and hospital care which absorb about half of all public health spending. With the voracious appetite of established institutions for limited funds, services such as community-based home support for the elderly remain underdeveloped, although this is contrary to official policy (Fitzgerald, 2000).

10. USING PROSPERITY TO IMPROVE SOCIAL PROTECTION

In the decade of the 1990s, average real income per head in Ireland has grown by about 70%. There are important choices to be made as to what share of growth should be set aside for public and private investment, what share for personal consumption, and what share for improved social protection. Ireland's welfare state has followed Korpi and Palme's basic security model, but now as a newly prosperous society Ireland can afford to make more generous social provision for its citizens.

Ireland's welfare system succeeds reasonably well in providing a basic level of social protection against poverty. It does not succeed, however, in maintaining previous living standards for many people, a problem that will grow more acute if welfare incomes and earnings in the labour market continue to diverge as they have done (Nolan, Maître, O'Neill & Sweetman, 2000). The fact that 54% of workers can expect no earnings-related occupational pension to supplement a basic state pension is a major omission, unlikely to be rectified by employers facilitating deductions for voluntary Personal Retirement Savings Accounts. There are two possible routes – either to make pension provision for employees compulsory for employers, or for the state to develop, as in Sweden, a national income-related pension scheme.

Ireland now has levels of female participation in the workforce on a par with those in other Western European societies, indeed higher in terms of the age groups with young children. But social protection has not kept pace with this change. There is a crisis of child care supply. There is no paid parental leave, available for the first three years of a child's life under social protection systems in Sweden and Germany. The social welfare system, although formally equal as between men and women following a European Union Directive on Equal Treatment which came into force in 1986, is still constructed on male breadwinner lines rather than on individual entitlement. Provisions of the welfare code which treat adult partners as dependents of each other rather than as individuals in their own right are overripe for change (Department of Social Community and Family Affairs, 1999).

Access to health care is a critical element in the quality of life. Ireland's two-tier health care system needs reform to ensure patients on low incomes can get as speedy access to care as currently achieved by those with health insurance. Countries like France and Canada have world-class health systems, free at the point of use, and well-resourced to ensure fair treatment for all.

Prosperity is not an end in itself; its purpose is the well-being of citizens. Ireland can now use some of its new found wealth to build world-class standards of social protection, which form such a key element of the basic quality of life.

NOTES

1. See Appendix Table A1 for a comparison.
2. Child Dependant Allowances payable with welfare payments are €16.80 a week per child in 2002 for most payments. Higher rates (up to €21.60 a week per child) apply for children of widows and other lone parent payments. Table A2 gives monthly rates of child benefit for 2002. In the 1980s, allowances for children under the tax code were abolished and incorporated into higher child benefit payments.
3. Nolan, Maitre, O'Neill and Sweetman (2000), Table 3.12; 1998 figures.

4. The Department of Social and Family Affairs, known until 1997 as the Department of Social Welfare.

5. Callan et al. (1989), Tables 11.4 and 11.5. In 1987, 58% of contributory payments went to the poorest 30% of households (by pre-transfer income) compared with 70% of mean-tested payments. See also Callan et al. (1996) Table 4.4.

6. Callan et al. (1996) Table 4.5.

7. For example, International Labour Office Convention 102 on Social Security addresses the following – medical care, sickness benefit, unemployment benefit, old age benefit, employment injury benefit, family benefit, maternity benefit, invalidity benefit, survivors' benefit.

8. Excluding those on in-work benefits and Child Benefit. *Statistical Information on the Social Welfare Services 2000* Table A10.

9. The Budget Strategy for Ageing Group (1999) predicted that the state's pensions costs would rise from 1999 levels by 3.5% of GNP by 2015, and 7% of GNP by 2050, due to the ageing of the population. See John McHale's paper in this volume for a detailed analysis of the pension funding issue.

10. Employer social insurance contributions pay about three quarters of total social insurance spending. Employer deductions for 2002 are 8.5% of payroll on annual earnings up to €18,512 and 10.75% of payroll thereafter. In 2000, employer social insurance contributions totalled €2,778m and revenue from Corporation Tax €3,887m.

11. John Douglas of shopworkers' trade union MANDATE told a Council for Social Welfare conference in Nov. 2001 that the voluntary pension scheme in one major supermarket chain has a take-up rate of under 20% in comparison to 100% membership of a virtually identical pension scheme in another Irish supermarket chain where the pension scheme is compulsory.

12. See Callan et al. (1996, p. 85).

13. Statistical Information on the Social Welfare Services 1999, Table 10.F4.

14. Quarterly National Household Survey Q3 2000, Table 10.14.

15. Callan and Nolan, Tables 10.3 and 10.5.

16. In the tax year 1998/1999, 42% paid income tax at the (then) higher rate of 44% and the remainder at the lower rate of 22%. By 2002, income tax rates had been reduced to 42% and 20%, and the lower-rate tax band considerably widened for single people and dual-earner couples. See Appendix A3 for further details.

17. *Budget Perspectives 1998*, pp. 33–34.

18. In 2001, the charge was £25 a day, with a ceiling on the charge of £250 a year, equivalent to about $30 a day, with a ceiling of $300 a year.

19. As one commentator put it, if a barman is paid a wage for serving some customers and is paid by the drink by others, who will get quicker treatment?

REFERENCES

Barrington, R. (1987). *Health, Medicine and Politics*. Dublin: IPA.

Beveridge, W. (1942). *Social Insurance and Allied Services* (Cmd. 6404). London: HMSO.

Burke, H. (1999). Foundation stones of Irish social policy: 1831–1951. In: G. Kiely, A. O'Donnell, P. Kennedy & S. Quin (Eds), *Irish Social Policy in Context*. Dublin: UCD.

Callan, T., Nolan, B., Whelan, B. J., Hannan, D., & Creighton, S. (1989). Poverty, income and welfare in Ireland. ESRI paper 146.

Callan, T., Nolan, B., & Whelan, B. J. (1996). A review of the Commission on Social Welfare's minimum adequate income. ESRI Policy research paper 29.

Callan, T. et al. (1996). *Poverty in the 1990s*. Dublin: Oaktree Press.

Callan, T. et al. (1999). *Monitoring poverty trends*. Dublin: ESRI/Combat Poverty/DSCFA.

Callan, T., & Nolan, B. (1992). Income distribution and redistribution: Ireland in comparative perspective. In: J. Goldthorpe & C. T. Whelan (Eds), *The Development of Industrial Society in Ireland*. Oxford: Oxford University Press.

Callan, T., Nolan, B., & Whelan, C. T. (1996). A review of the Commission on Social Welfare's minimum adequate income. Dublin: ESRI Policy Research Paper 29.

Callan, T., & Nolan, B. (1999a). Tax and welfare changes, poverty and work incentives in Ireland 1987–1994. Dublin: ESRI Policy Research Paper 34.

Callan, T., & Nolan, B. (1999b). Income inequality in Ireland in the 1980s and 1990s. In: F. Barry (Ed.), *Understanding Ireland's Economic Growth*. Basingstoke: Macmillan.

Callan, T., Layte, R., Nolan, B., Watson, D., Whelan, C. T., Williams, J., & Ma'tre, B. (1999). *Monitoring poverty trends*. Dublin: ESRI, DSCFA and Combat Poverty.

Callan, T., Nolan, B., Walsh, J., & Nestor, R. (1999). Income tax and social welfare policies. In: *Budget Perspectives*. Dublin: ESRI.

Callan, T., & Nolan, B. (2000). Taxation and social welfare. In: B. Nolan, P. O'Connell & C. T. Whelan (Eds), *Bust to Boom*. Dublin: IPA.

Callan, T., Keeney, M., & Walsh, J. (2001). Income Tax and Welfare Policies: Some Current Issues in Budget Perspectives. T. Callan & D. McCoy (Eds).

Central Statistics Office, Labour Force Surveys (annual) Cork, CSO.

Central Statistics Office, Quarterly National Household Surveys Cork, CSO.

Commission on Social Welfare (1986). *Report of the Commission on Social Welfare*. Dublin: Government Publications.

Cousins, M. (1997). Ireland's place in the worlds of welfare capitalism. *Journal of European Social Policy*, 7(3), 223–235.

Commission on Health Funding (1989). *Report*. Dublin: Government publications.

CSO (2001). *Quarterly National Household Survey, Households and Family Units*. Cork: Central Statistics Office.

Department of Finance (1999). *Report of the Budget Strategy for Ageing Group*.

Department of Finance website: www.irlgov.ie/finance/pubstag

Department of Social Community and Family Affairs (2000). *Review of the One-Parent Family Payment*.

Department of Social Welfare (1976). A national income related pension scheme – a discussion paper. Dublin: Government Publications.

Department of Social Welfare (1996). *Social Insurance in Ireland*. Dublin: Government Publications.

Department of Social Welfare (1997). *Actuarial Review of Social Welfare Pensions*. Dublin: Government Publications.

Department of Social Community and Family Affairs (various years). *Statistical Information on the Social Welfare Services*. Dublin: Government Publications.

Duffy, D., FitzGerald, J., Kearney, Í., & Smyth, D. (2000). *Medium-term Review 1999–2005*. Dublin: ESRI.

European Union (1999b). *Employment Guidelines 1999*. Luxembourg, Commission of the European Communities.

Fitzgerald, E. (2000). Community services for independence in old age – rhetoric and reality. *Adminstration*, 48(3), 75–89.

Fitzgerald, E., Ingoldsby, B., & Daly, F. (2000). *Solving long-term unemployment in Dublin*. Dublin: Dublin Employment Pact.

Fitzgerald, E. (2001). Redistribution through Ireland's welfare and tax systems. In: S. Cantillon, C. Corrigan, P. Kirby & J. O'Flynn (Eds), *Rich and Poor*. Dublin, Oaktree.

Förster, M., & Pellizzari, M. (2000). Trends and driving factors in income distribution and poverty in the OECD Area. Paris, OECD, Labour Market and Social Policy occasional Paper No. 42.

Government of Ireland (1996). *Report of the Expert Working Group on the Integration of the Tax and Social Welfare System*. Dublin: Government Publications.

Government of Ireland (1997). *Sharing in Progress – the National Anti-Poverty Strategy*. Dublin: Government Publications.

Government of Ireland (1999). *Report of Working Group examining the Treatment of Married, Cohabiting and One-parent Families under the Tax and Social Welfare Codes*. Dublin: Government Publications.

Government of Ireland – national agreements:

(1987) Programme for National Recovery

(1991) Partnership for Economic and Social Progress

(1994) Programme for Competitiveness and Work

(1996) Partnership 2000

(2000) Programme for Prosperity and Fairness; Dublin: Government Publications

International Labour Office (ILO) (1999). *Inquiry into the Changing Cost of Social Security 1994–1996*. www.ilo.org/public/english/protection/socsec/publ/css/cssindex.htm

Hardiman, N. (2000). Social partnership, wage bargaining and growth. In: B. Nolan, P. O'Connell & C. T. Whelan (Ed.), *Bust to Boom*. Dublin: IPA.

Korpi, W., & Palme, J. (1998). The Paradox of redistribution and strategies of equality. *American Sociological Review, 63*(October), 661–687.

Layte, R., Fahey, T., & Whelan, C. (2000). *Income, Deprivation and Well-being among Older Irish People*. Dublin: National Council for Ageing and Older People.

Lazar, H., & Stoyko, P. (1998). The future of the welfare state. *Journal of the International Social Security Association*.

National Economic and Social Council (1986). *A Strategy for Recovery*. Dublin: Stationery Office.

National Economic and Social Council (1999). *Opportunities, Challenges and Capacities for Choice*. Dublin: National Economic and Social Council.

National Pensions Board (1998). *Securing Retirement Incomes – Report of the National Pensions Policy Initiative*. Dublin: Government Publications.

Nolan, B. (2000). *Child Poverty in Ireland*. Dublin: Oaktree.

Nolan, B., Callan, T., Whelan, C. T., & Williams, J. (1994). Poverty and time: perspectives on the dynamics of poverty. ESRI General Research Paper, 166.

Nolan B., & Callan, T. (1994). Poverty and health inequalities. In: B. Nolan & T. Callan (Eds), *Poverty and Policy in Ireland*. Dublin: Gill and Macmillan.

Nolan, B., Whelan, C., & Williams, J. (1998). *Where Are Poor Households?* Dublin: Oaktree Press.

Nolan, B., & Whelan, C. T. (1996). *Resources, Deprivation and Poverty*. Oxford: Clarendon.

Nolan, B., Ma'tre, B., O'Neill, D., & Sweetman, O. (2000). *The Distribution of Income in Ireland*. Dublin: Oaktree Press.

Nolan, B., & Wiley, M. (2000). *Private Practice in Irish Public Hospitals*. Dublin: Oaktree Press.

Ó Cinnéide, S. (1998). Democracy and the constitution. *Administration*, 1998/1999.

O'Connell, P., & Rottman, D. (1992). The Irish welfare state in comparative perspective. In: J. Goldthorpe & C. T. Whelan (Eds), *The Development of Industrial Society in Ireland*. Oxford: Oxford University Press.

OECD (1999). *Revenue Statistics 1965–1998*. Paris: OECD.

OECD (2000). *Reforms for an Ageing Society*. Paris: OECD.

Orshansky, M. (1965). Counting the poor: another look at the poverty profile. *Social Security Bulletin, 28*(1), 3–29.

O'Donnell, A. (1999). Comparing welfare states: the case of Ireland. In: Kiely et al. (Eds), *Irish Social Policy in Context*. Dublin: UCD Press.

Revenue Commissioners Statistical Report (1998/9). Dublin: Stationery Office.

Ringen, S. (1988). Direct and indirect measures of poverty. *Journal of Social Policy, 17*, 3.

Shaver, S. (1998). Universality or selectivity in income support to older people? a comparative assessment of the issues. *Journal of Social Policy, 27*(2), 231–234.

U.S. Department of Health and Human Services (1998). *Health, United States 1998*.

Whyte, J. (1980). *Church and State in Modern Ireland: 1923–1979*. Dublin: Gill and Macmillan.

APPENDIX

Table A1. Comparison of Irish and U.K. benefit rates, 2002.

	Ireland €	U.K. £ stg	U.K. € equivalent*	Irish as % of U.K. benefit
Standard adult rate	118.80	53.95	83.13	143%
Old age compensation	147.30	75.50	116.33	127%
Child benefit *(weekly equivalent)*				
1 child	27.14	15.75	24.27	112%
2 children	54.28	26.30	40.52	134%
3 children	88.27	36.85	56.77	155%

*Exchange rate end June 2002,   0.649 = £1 stg.

Table A2. Irish Social Welfare Payments 2002.
Rates of Benefit (Euros).

	Single €	Couple* €	& 2 kids €
A. Weekly			
Old age contributory pension	147.30	261.10	
Old age non-contributory pension	134.00	268.00	
Unemployment/disability	118.80	197.60	231.20
One parent family	118.80		157.40
B. Monthly equivalents			
Old age contributory pension	638.30	1,131.43	
Old age non-contributory pension	580.67	1,161.33	
Unemployment/disability	514.80	856.27	1,001.87
One parent family	514.80		682.07

Table A2. Continued.

C. Child benefit (monthly)	
1 child	117.60
2 children	235.20
3 children	382.50
4 children	529.80
5 children	677.10

* each over pension age.

Table A3. Income Tax Regime in Ireland 2002.

	Personal tax credit	Employee tax credit	Taxed @ 20%	Taxed @ 42%
Single person	€ 1,520	€660	First €28,000	Balance
Married couple, 1 earner	€ 3,040	€660	First €37,000	Balance
Married couple, 2 earners	€ 3,040	€1,320	First €56,000	Balance

11. THE CELTIC TIGER: A VIEW FROM THE TRENCHES OF ACADEMIA

I 21

Michael P. Mortell

1. INTRODUCTION

"It all began in the cold." My wife Pat and I arrived in Bethlehem, Pennsylvania in the snow in November 1967, having driven from sunny California in a Volkswagen Beetle. I was to teach at Lehigh University in the Centre for the Application of Mathematics. Our two daughters were born here. It is nice to be back.

Lehigh University was then, as now, on the hill. The hometown plant of Bethlehem Steel, whose blast furnaces dominated the river valley, is no more; and Lehigh has even captured the highest point of the hill – the old Bethlehem Steel eating facilities!

There may be a moral here: industries come and industries go, but universities go on forever. Why is that? Because, the modern university is essentially in the business of the FUTURE. The researchers in a university are like scouts beyond the horizon bringing back the word to business, government and to society at large about where the future lies. I can recall learning how to write a FORTRAN programme as a student in Cork in the early 1960s, and there wasn't a single computer in Ireland at the time. In today's terms I was a budding "software engineer" – and the term had not even been coined! Nobody could then have foreseen the future; but the university could educate you for that future.

The Irish Economy in Transition: Successes, Problems, and Prospects, Volume 85,
pages 249–257.
Copyright © 2002 by Elsevier Science Ltd.
ISBN: 0-7623-0979-2

2. THEME

Ireland is a huge success story, and we have been exploring that theme at this conference. Education in Ireland is also a huge success story; and now, at last, it is being recognised as the essential component of a modern knowledge-driven economy. However, it will be part of my thesis that this recognition in Ireland, particularly of the contribution of the University sector, was, until recently, merely window dressing to be mouthed by politicians and other public officials, to encourage investment, when on their travels abroad. The conundrum I wish to explore is how on the macro level, and over the long haul, we have achieved such a large measure of success in the field of third level education; and yet for someone like me who was involved in university administration for 20 years – with 10 years as President of University College Cork – it was a daily grind of largely unsuccessfully trying to persuade government Ministers and senior Civil Servants of the long term economic and social necessity of funding properly the university sector under their care for the benefit of the nation.

3. BACKGROUND

The universities in Ireland – all seven of them – are funded by the state – just like the University of California system. Essentially this means they get a recurrent block grant each year to run the university, and also a capital grant for buildings, equipment, etc. This money comes through a body appointed by the government called the Higher Education Authority. The key figures for any university president are the Minister for Education, the Secretary of the Department of Education (a civil servant) and the Chairman of the Higher Education Authority. Because Ireland is very small, you can take it that any university president will also know the Taoiseach (Prime Minister of the Republic of Ireland), the Minister of Finance, and the Secretary of the Department of Finance (a civil servant). There will also be other government departments and public sector bodies where an acquaintance with the Minister and/or chief executive is important for the welfare of your institution.

Senior civil servants are a power to be reckoned with as, retired or otherwise, they are a familiar sight as executives, or on the boards, of public sector and semi-state bodies. For example, the Governor of the Central Bank is appointed by the government and has usually been a former Secretary of the Department of Finance, or the Chairman of the Higher Education Authority would have been a Secretary of the Department of Education. The economist and Nobel Laureate Merton Miller makes an interesting comment, in an essay "Financial Regulation: The Inside Game," on how the Japanese build a sense of solidarity in their Ministry of Finance. They have, he says, a play they call "amakudari," which translates literally as "the descent from heaven." A hard working team player in the Ministry can look forward on his retirement to ending up on the board of a bank or an insurance or brokerage firm. We would seem to have a somewhat similar sense of things in Ireland!

For about the last five years, university education in Ireland is free; no student from within the European Union pays a tuition fee if they choose to pursue their university education in Ireland. This government decision, which simply increased demand for access to universities, failed to provide a single extra place to meet the demand, and the Irish taxpayer pays for all students – rich and poor alike. Entry to any university is by competition based on a national examination (called the Leaving Certificate) which is taken at the end of high school. Every student is awarded an overall "point score" based on subject results. Up until now, not every student who wished to enter university found a place available. In other words, because the cost is low relative to the benefits, there were more students seeking to enter university than there were places available. This situation of quantity rationing has pertained in many subject areas, e.g. Medicine and Engineering, since the 1970s. The point score, set by peer competition and the *numerus clausus*, for entry to such areas was always high. Thus, there was a competitive cut-off to the ability range entering the universities.

4. DEVELOPMENT IN EDUCATION

To give an idea of how vast is the improvement in the educational standard of the Irish population over the past 40 years, I give you the following indices:

- In 1965, about 12,000 students sat the Leaving Certificate examination at the end of high school (and about one third of those who obtained this certificate went on to university);
- In 2000, this number was 64,000;
- In 1965, there were 21,000 students in 3rd level (with 13,000 in the universities);
- In 1998, there were 116,000.
- When I was a university student in Cork in 1960, there were about 1,500 students; today there are 12,000.
- There are three new university institutions (University of Limerick, Dublin City University, National University of Ireland, Maynooth) and about 15 institutes of technology, all created over a 30-year time span.

- Today, about 45% of the age cohort go on to 3rd level (however, about 20% of the same age cohort do not complete high school). About 17% of the age cohort attend university.

These figures are a record of tremendous success by any standard. How did it come about?

In my view, there were a *small number of very significant policy initiatives* – coupled with sporadic and intermittent follow-through in the form of resources.

The first half of the 1960s saw three seminal government reports on education – *Investment in Education, The Report of the Commission on Higher Education* and *The Report of the Steering Committee on Technical Education*. These reports set the long-term agenda and the policy directions for education from the primary school level up through university.

In 1967 the Minister for Education, apparently without consulting the cabinet, announced that high school education would henceforth be free, i.e. no tuition. Up to that time, while the state (or religious community) provided the school building and paid the teachers, the students had to pay a tuition fee. (Unlike the U.S., education in Ireland is run on a national basis and is not explicitly resourced by local taxation.)

The introduction of a no-fee regime at second level had a profound and enduring effect. Now the numbers came pouring in. By 1980, more than 36,000 sat the Leaving Certificate, and five years later this had increased to over 45,000. We had gone from 12,000 to 45,000 in 20 years. Over the next 15 years we were to increase this number to 64,000.

The other major policy initiative was the decision to create two new Higher Education Institutes, which evolved to become universities – one in Limerick and one on the north side of Dublin; and the decision to create a system of Regional Technical Colleges throughout the State. These latter were to supply a cohort of people with sub-degree level training, as well as training in the various trades.

The early part of the 1970s saw a rapid expansion of the universities in response to the increasing numbers coming out of second level. There was now a state-run third level grant system to financially support those who were less well off in continuing to a university education.

These two policy initiatives, at the high school level and at third level, which enabled a growing flood of young people to complete high school and pursue a university education, had major resource consequences. The funding to implement these seminal initiatives caused ongoing difficulties for us in the university sector.

The concept of *mass third level education*, where more than 50% of the age cohort would proceed to the third level, had not entered the European mind in the early 1970s. So nobody could, or did, accurately predict what the long-term number of third-level students might be; and consequently what the long-term investment might have to be. The problems arising from this were exacerbated by the centralised nature of the Irish educational system. In the U.S., where you have state universities, land grant universities, private universities, community colleges, etc, the decision making is dispersed. The total system is not dependent on a single entity making the right decision. In Ireland, however, the Department of Finance has a stranglehold on the resources, and it is my experience that the vision coming from that source is quite limited. This, indeed, may be unavoidable because of the nature of its role. The Department of Finance has a *financial control role*; but this role, with time, and particularly after bad times, has enabled it to implicitly determine policy where theoretically it has no role. It has the further consequence of tending to squeeze the vision in other departments of the government. The Department of Finance seemed to have a policy of underestimating future growth in the third level sector, and hence have a rationale for constraining resource requests from that source; or they simply insisted that resources could not be provided, and thus the provision of places had to be tailored to meet their constraints. Thus, the universities were continually under-funded, as they chose to respond to demands to increase the number of students to meet the social needs of the nation.

The Government White Paper of 1980 envisaged 51,000 full time students in higher education by 1990. Within three years it was clear that this projection was much too conservative. In 1982, just two years later, the Chairman of the Higher Education Authority was signalling "serious curtailment of expectations for the years immediately ahead." This was the context in which Irish universities worked over the next 15 years: a continuous rapidly growing demand for university education, coupled with a continuous underestimate of numbers. In 1992 a government Green Paper predicted 100,000 third-level students for 2001; a 1995 projection for 2001 was 111,500. The actual number for 1998/1999 was 116,000. Even these conservative predictions were under-funded.

It is worth noting that the cost of educating an Irish graduate, whose quality was accepted internationally, was consistently among the lowest figures for the OECD. For every $1 we spent in the South of Ireland, our sister universities in the North spent more than $1.5. We were, and are, very efficient and produce a high quality product. So we were not wasting taxpayers' money.

The successive governments took the view, and it is not for me to argue with it, that the top priority was to get the economy under control and boost the level of inward investment to reduce the unemployment. We must remember that in the early 1980s, inflation and unemployment in the Republic of Ireland were both approaching 20%. In this scheme of things the universities were not central to the thinking in government. Indeed, it was quite clear that they were largely viewed as a form of social welfare – keeping the young people off the unemployment rolls ("bums on seats" was a phrase we heard) – and not as an investment in the future. This was forcibly brought home to me in a conversation in the middle 1990s with a junior minister who assured me that neither he nor the people around the Cabinet table perceived the funding of universities as an investment in any way comparable to funding the Industrial Development Authority (IDA) to put up advance factory buildings. Another clear indication was the disbursement of the billions of dollars of structural funds coming from Europe – less than 1% found its way into the universities. The necessity for physical infrastructure was clearly understood, and everyone can understand the pork-barrel nature of this spending; the necessity for an intellectual infrastructure, even with the rapidly approaching knowledge-based world, was not understood at the political level until very late in the 1990s.

The critical role that research plays in promoting economic growth was even less well understood. Ireland had one of the lowest proportionate expenditures in the OECD for Research and Development in the early 1990s. An influential report on *Industrial Policy for the 1990s* (the Culliton Report – 1992) had a significant bias against what it called "high tech" areas and propounded the view that Ireland could not expect to develop world class research in many modern technologies. It wanted a focus on the practical needs of indigenous industry. This attitude pervaded the thinking of policy makers throughout the 1990s, where the accepted wisdom was that Ireland could thrive by importing the results of research done elsewhere. Fortunately, that attitude is now jettisoned – but I notice the same policy makers still in situ!

In the somewhat depressing context I have just given, how did the universities expand to try to meet student demand and maintain an international standard? My own university in Cork had fewer than 5,000 students in 1980; by 1990 there were over 7,000; and now, a decade later, there are 12,000 students. How did this come about?

The 1980s, when Ireland was struggling with high inflation and high unemployment, were very difficult times for universities. During that decade, the unit of resource in the universities, i.e. the resource per student, fell by about 25%. We took in extra students without extra staff, equipment, etc. In 1987, the university budget was cut overnight as part of an overall effort to bring public expenditure under control, and every staff member in my university who was over 65 years was retired – that would be illegal in the U.S.! The opening chink of light emerged in 1990 when the Minister for

Education was coming under severe public pressure, and therefore political pressure, about the lack of access to the universities. All the universities now had a *numerus clausus* on every area of study and jointly refused to increase the intake of students. The Taoiseach of the day, Mr. C. J. Haughey, met with the presidents of the universities and agreed to provide extra funding to try to meet student demand. He did this without any civil servant present; the minister was present but did not take part in the discussion, which was based on a short paper prepared by the presidents. Subsequently, there was an "agreed" sum per extra student plus some capital monies, which were worked out at civil service level. This allowed the universities to expand student numbers faster, and the system took off from there. At that meeting, the Taoiseach also approved a scheme of "new-blood" appointments for certain areas of technology, which was duly implemented. I believe this was a significant and timely intervention by the Taoiseach.

Over the next several years, some of the European Structural Funds money began to flow to the universities for capital projects, and the Department of Education, through its Secretary, was very energetic in pursuing these monies. With expanding numbers we could begin to hire new staff and develop new areas, which had been impossible during the 1980s. The university Presidents now actively sought out support from the private sector at home and abroad. In Cork, for example, more than half of the $100 million of capital projects over the decade of the 1990s came from non-governmental sources; and, remember, this is a public university.

At this time the European Union (EU) put in place its Framework Programme for Research. Irish scientists competed extremely well for this pool of money and began to build up research teams of international class. As we expanded we were able to attract back to Ireland many Irish scientists who had trained in the U.S. and Europe. With research funding available from Europe, they could now have a full international career based in Ireland. The system began to snow ball.

The dedication of the people within the university, who had laboured in the vineyard throughout the heat of the day, was now paying off for the Irish people. There was a new air of confidence. But even as late as 1997, the Taoiseach of the time deemed it unnecessary to meet with the presidents of the universities to hear proposals for dealing with a looming high-tech skills shortage, and the Department of Finance was still adamant there was no need for further investment in the universities. There had been a marked decline in the birth rate during the decade of the 1980s; and the view from there was that the forthcoming downward demographic trend would solve the problem of resources. Their mantra apparently had not changed from that of the previous 20 years.

But something had snapped in the official mind. In 1998 the new Minister for Education (a graduate of my own university!) now talked about investment in education as an investment in the future economic welfare of the country. The Chairman of the IDA, as a result of a Pauline conversion of the first order, declared that "there is a need to recognise education as our single most important substantial competitive advantage and allocate resources accordingly." The Taoiseach, in a new government, launched a $250 million research programme (this is a huge sum in Irish terms) aimed mainly at the universities, saying "The continuing development of our economy requires us to be a centre for innovation, and our universities and colleges are critical for this. This unprecedented investment will make sure we deliver on this strategic necessity." This massive investment came about because the Minister for Education and the Chairman of the Higher Education Authority seized the opportunity made for them by the contacts the Conference of Heads of Irish Universities had made in the international arena.

We had crossed the Rubicon! The nation's finances were under control. The supply of graduates which had emerged from the universities in the 1980s and 1990s, many of them emigrating to gain invaluable new skills and experience, turned out to be the seed corn for the economic recovery of the middle-to-late 1990s. A new conventional wisdom prevails – fully thirty years after the first seminal policy initiatives – the universities and education are central to economic well-being. In the "new" Ireland we are making an investment of 2.5 billion euro on research under the National Development Plan 2000–2006, and, of this, 700 million euro will be spent on the Programme for Research in Third Level Institutions.

So what conclusions do I draw from this story?

Individuals with a vision do make a difference. They are ahead of their time, and so the vision is only slowly and imperfectly implemented – but the Great Wheel is set in motion and it will not be stopped.

In the public policy arena, as in most human affairs, rationality does not prevail; politics prevails. Politics may not be the most efficient means of achieving an end, but in a democracy, to which we all subscribe, it may be the only possible means. We must it seems, like Shakespeare, "By indirection, find direction out."

The initial vision of providing education accessible to all the people was proved correct. Ireland's future in the third millennium is essentially dependent on its educated population, especially as knowledge is now the fundamental resource. We should explicitly recognise the value of that long-term vision and investment. It is yielding, and will continue to yield, massive returns thirty years after the initial investment was made. Investment in the fundamentals will always pay – but we must have the focus, and the steady determination, to stay with it.

I believe that the steady focus of the universities over the last three decades on the long-term fundamentals of teaching and research, on maintaining standards and the refusal to respond like a weather vane to every passing whim is also a major contribution to Ireland's success story.